THE LOST BOOK OF ADVENTURE

WARNING

This book contains a number of dangerous activities which should be done under the supervision of an adult. The Publisher expressly disclaims liability for any injury or damages resulting from engaging in the activities contained in this book.

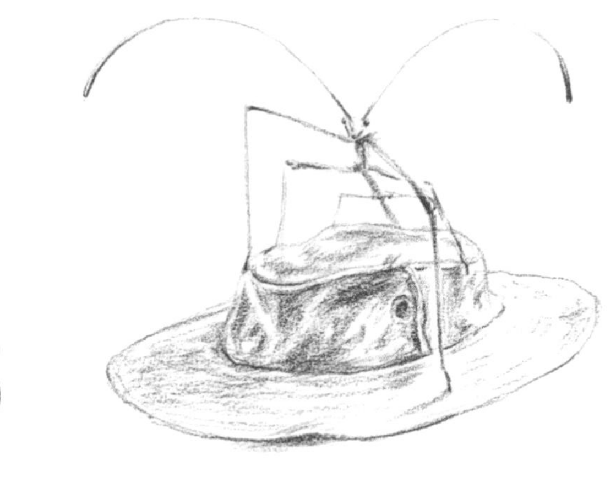

Frances Lincoln
Children's Books

When you next feel the wind brush by, think about where it has come from and where it goes.

Some of it has touched the tops of mountains deep within the Sahara. Some carries the fragrant pine scent from the vast Siberian Taiga forests. Or perhaps it has come from the yawning jaws of a lion on the African grasslands. Every breeze brings a story of its journey.

If you listen hard enough, you can hear its whisper. It is the quiet call to adventure, asking you to step into the wild.

A photograph of the found notebooks on the day they were discovered.

A NOTE FROM THE EDITOR...

Four years ago whilst trekking with friends through a remote part of the Amazon, we stumbled across an old hut. In the corner of the dwelling buried under some fallen palms we found a metal case, sealed shut by years of rust. Intrigued, we carefully opened it. Inside was a collection of notebooks, journals and various sketchbooks — all incredibly well preserved given the environment.
We didn't realise it then, but we had stumbled across the lifetime's work of an unknown artist and adventurer.

As we carefully leafed through the delicate pages we discovered a treasure trove of adventuring knowledge, as well as many sketches and coloured illustrations depicting adventures from around the world. The case and its contents were duly shipped back home where it has been painstakingly restored and edited together over the past 2 years to create this: *The Lost Book Of Adventure*.

The identity of the adventurer remains unknown, but alongside the writings and drawings was a letter which appears to have been written for the benefit of two young family members. Its message is clear — be good and be adventurous.

Hopefully it will inspire us all to step into the wild and live a life of adventure, too.

Teddy Keen
Compiler and Editor

A copy of the letter that accompanied the notebooks.

Dear A and L,

If you are reading this it means my notebooks have been found. I am leaving them here at camp for safekeeping along with a few other belongings that I won't be taking with me. The notebooks are a lifetime's worth of knowledge, which I'm passing on to you. In them, you will find detailed instructions – from how to build shelters, to raft building, wild camping and much more – along with a few tales of my own adventures.

Read them carefully. You will need them, should you choose to set out on your own journey of discovery.

REMEMBER: be good, be adventurous....

and look after your parents.

Yours always,

The Unknown Adventurer

CONTENTS

CAMP WILD
8 – 59

RAFTS
60 – 83

SHELTERS, DENS AND TREEHOUSES
84 – 121

EXPLORATION
122 - 169

USEFUL KNOWLEDGE
170 - 191

The universe belongs to the adventurous.

CAMP WILD

If you can, sleep out in the wild.

Most adventures happen in daylight, but to really experience the wild, you need to inhabit it. When the sun dips beneath the horizon something magical happens. Your senses become highly tuned, and every sight and sound is amplified. The universe unveils itself, just as the glinting eyes of our nocturnal neighbours come out to play.

This is when we feel just how small we are in the scheme of things. We come together around the campfire to warm our socks and souls, as we have done for thousands of years. It's like we've been given the key to the universe, and here under the stars, we glimpse its secrets.

Head deeper into the wild to unlock incredible habitats, from quiet riverbanks to open beaches, and mountains to ancient forests.

There is no better way to see wildlife than to respectfully share its habitat.

THE MAKINGS OF A WILD CAMP ADVENTURE

Camping in the wild is often just part of a bigger adventure, but with so many things to experience, it is really an adventure in itself.

Whether you head deep into the wilderness on foot, or spend time finding a wild campsite before you leave home, be prepared for an experience away from noise and people, where nature sets the rules.

SEVEN THINGS THAT MAKE A WILD CAMP:

* Setting up away from roads, busy paths and built-up areas;
* Avoiding lots of people;
* A place where you can hear birds sing and trees creak;
* Somewhere that smells distinctly wild;
* A place where you can see the Milky Way on a clear night;
* A spot where the only light at night comes from a torch, fire or the night sky;
* A location where your only neighbours are wild animals.

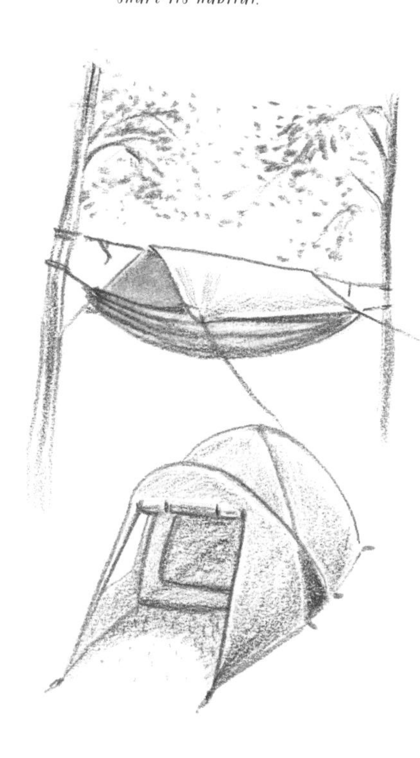

Tents are great, but there are many different ways to make a shelter.

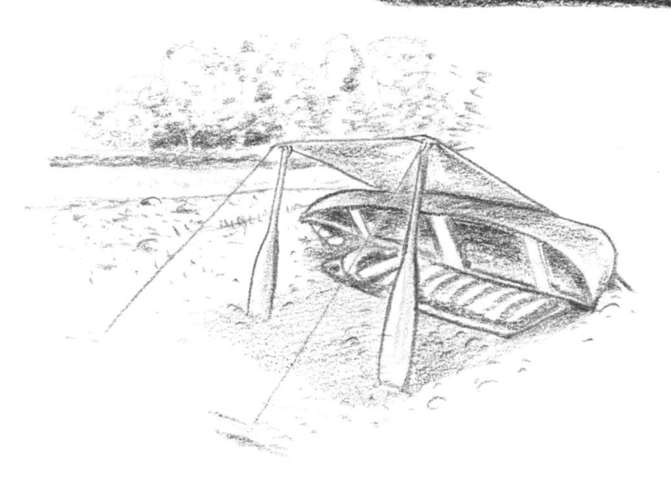

Camp life often requires knives and other tools – and the safety skills to use them.

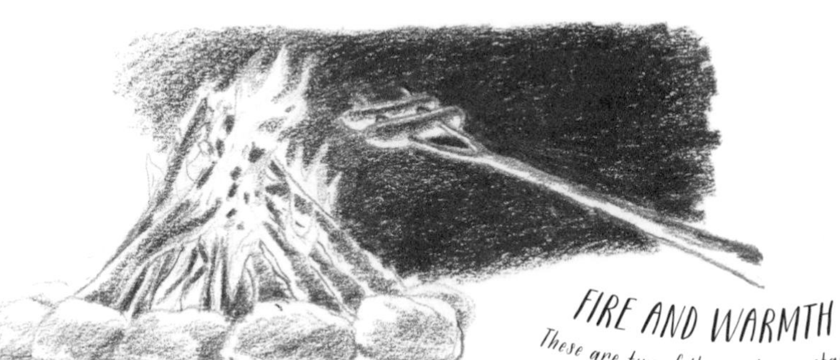

FIRE AND WARMTH

These are two of the most important elements of wild camping.

You'll need to pack some essential kit to get started.

Locating a source of drinking water is often key when finding a spot to base your camp.

Planning your adventure is exciting. Explore maps to find your dream wild location.

Are you ready to explore the universe for real?

A FEW MEMORABLE EXPERIENCES

A sketch from my time beneath the Aurora Borealis or Northern Lights – the greatest light show on Earth.

A large meteor lights up the Namib Desert as it passes overhead. The sound was like thunder.

A large brown bear silhouetted by the moonlight. We could hear its breathing a few centimetres from the side of the tent.

Here, a column of soldier ants tried to eat into our tent. My flip flops were a valiant but doomed method of defence.

Falling snow on a hot summer's night in Eastern Europe that turned out to be clouds of ash from a huge forest fire. A lesson in how unforgiving the forest is to careless travellers.

Once I was woken by an intrepid and clearly talented emperor penguin in Antarctica. One of many memorable encounters with wildlife.

WALKING AMONG GIANTS

This is the spot where I headed deep into The Redwoods. Ancient giants looked down at us through the mist as the tracks of wild deer crossed our snowy path.

The forest was silent, except for the occasional thump of snow falling from laden branches.

FOREST CAMP

Of the many different camping environments, the forest is the most magical. Here, in the wilds of Canada, we entered an untouched kingdom. Sheltered from the elements, I felt a quiet calm that befitted this ancient family of trees. Birds and mammals went about their day under the protection of the canopy. Our senses became sensitive to every sight and sound. The forest was whispering to us, calling us deeper into its midst.

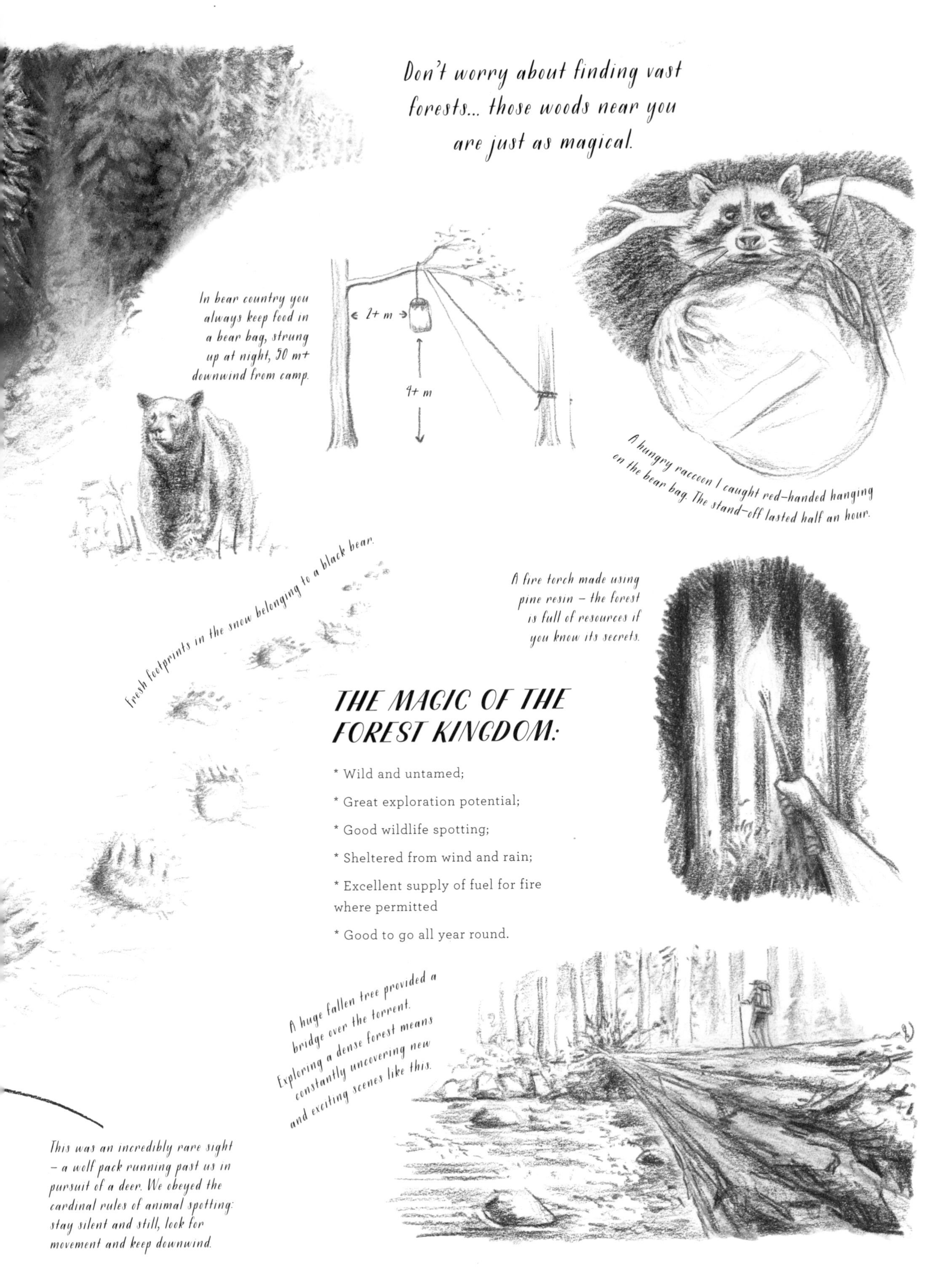

Don't worry about finding vast forests... those woods near you are just as magical.

In bear country you always keep food in a bear bag, strung up at night, 50 m+ downwind from camp.

A hungry raccoon I caught red-handed hanging on the bear bag. The stand-off lasted half an hour.

Fresh footprints in the snow belonging to a black bear.

A fire torch made using pine resin – the forest is full of resources if you know its secrets.

THE MAGIC OF THE FOREST KINGDOM:

* Wild and untamed;
* Great exploration potential;
* Good wildlife spotting;
* Sheltered from wind and rain;
* Excellent supply of fuel for fire where permitted
* Good to go all year round.

A huge fallen tree provided a bridge over the torrent. Exploring a dense forest means constantly uncovering new and exciting scenes like this.

This was an incredibly rare sight – a wolf pack running past us in pursuit of a deer. We obeyed the cardinal rules of animal spotting: stay silent and still, look for movement and keep downwind.

AFTER DARK

SPOTTING NOCTURNAL ANIMALS

At dusk, many animals come out from their hiding places. From deer and raccoons to bats and scorpions, you can often spot the local fauna in the camp vicinity with a good torch.

NIGHT-TIME EXPLORATION

When safe to do so, exploring around camp in the dark is exciting. Always know your bearings - it's easy to get lost, especially in wooded areas. Take a head torch, stick together and keep camp in sight.

NIGHT VISION

It takes ten minutes for your eyes' night vision to start working. After 30-45 minutes, your ability to see in the darkness is at its peak. Note how your hearing and sense of smell is amplified. This is your inner hunter surfacing.

LISTEN

Before you head off on your adventure, take note of the wild animals in the forest and learn their sounds. After dark, try and identify the owners of the noises.

You may not see jaguars - yet - but trust me: spotting any nocturnal animal gets your heart going.

A pair of eyes shone out from the jungle undergrowth. As I turned on the torch, there appeared the unmistakable form of a jaguar. It paused – its eyes transfixed by the light – then it was gone, deep into the darkness.

A tide pool is a great place to have a bath. Dig a deep hole on the edge of the high water mark. Lay down a waterproof tarp and bury the top edge beneath sand. Wait for the sea to fill up your pool.

COASTS

This was one of my favourite camp sites — a deserted beach on a remote island in Micronesia. A simple tarp tent was all I needed for cover. By day, I explored beneath the waves and caught my dinner. At dusk, I sat by the fire and watched the sun set. When the moon showed its face I lay down and explored the stars.

When the weather is good, get to the coast and find a remote beach or dune on which to make camp. It doesn't have to have swaying palm trees or coral reefs — you'll have an adventure wherever you go. Take a tent or a tarp — or just a sleeping bag if it's warm. Be sure to set up camp above the high tide mark.

There is nothing better to wake up to than the sound of rolling waves.

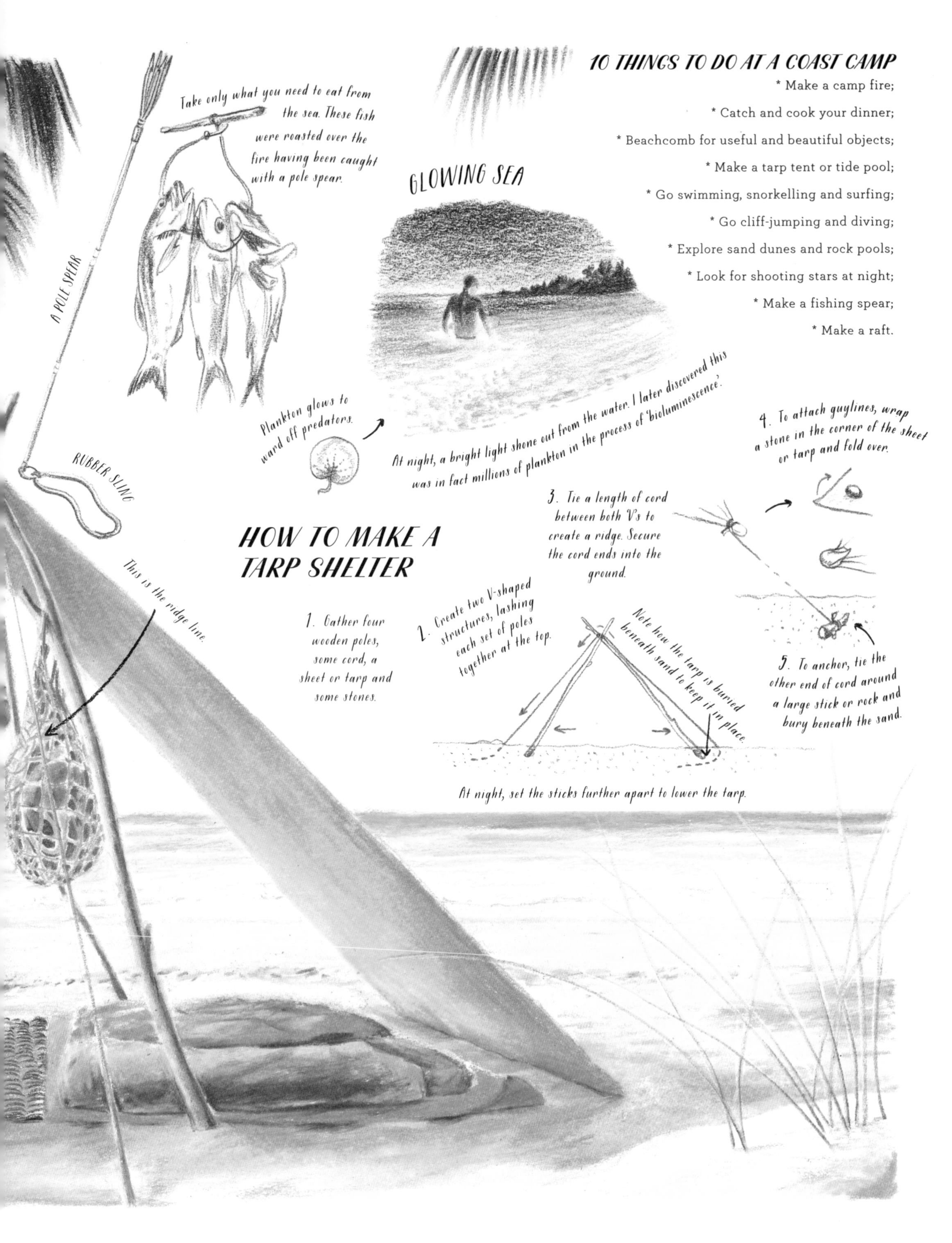

10 THINGS TO DO AT A COAST CAMP

* Make a camp fire;
* Catch and cook your dinner;
* Beachcomb for useful and beautiful objects;
* Make a tarp tent or tide pool;
* Go swimming, snorkelling and surfing;
* Go cliff-jumping and diving;
* Explore sand dunes and rock pools;
* Look for shooting stars at night;
* Make a fishing spear;
* Make a raft.

HOW TO MAKE A TARP SHELTER

1. Gather four wooden poles, some cord, a sheet or tarp and some stones.
2. Create two V-shaped structures, lashing each set of poles together at the top.
3. Tie a length of cord between both V's to create a ridge. Secure the cord ends into the ground.
4. To attach guylines, wrap a stone in the corner of the sheet or tarp and fold over.
5. To anchor, tie the other end of cord around a large stick or rock and bury beneath the sand.

EXPLORE THE UNIVERSE

You may have seen the stars at night, but in the wild you'll be given the universe. But the night sky is not just a thing of wonder, it is also a great tool. The stars have been a source of human navigation for thousands of years, guiding explorers on countless epic journeys into the unknown. There's no better place to plan your next adventure than from the comfort of your sleeping bag.

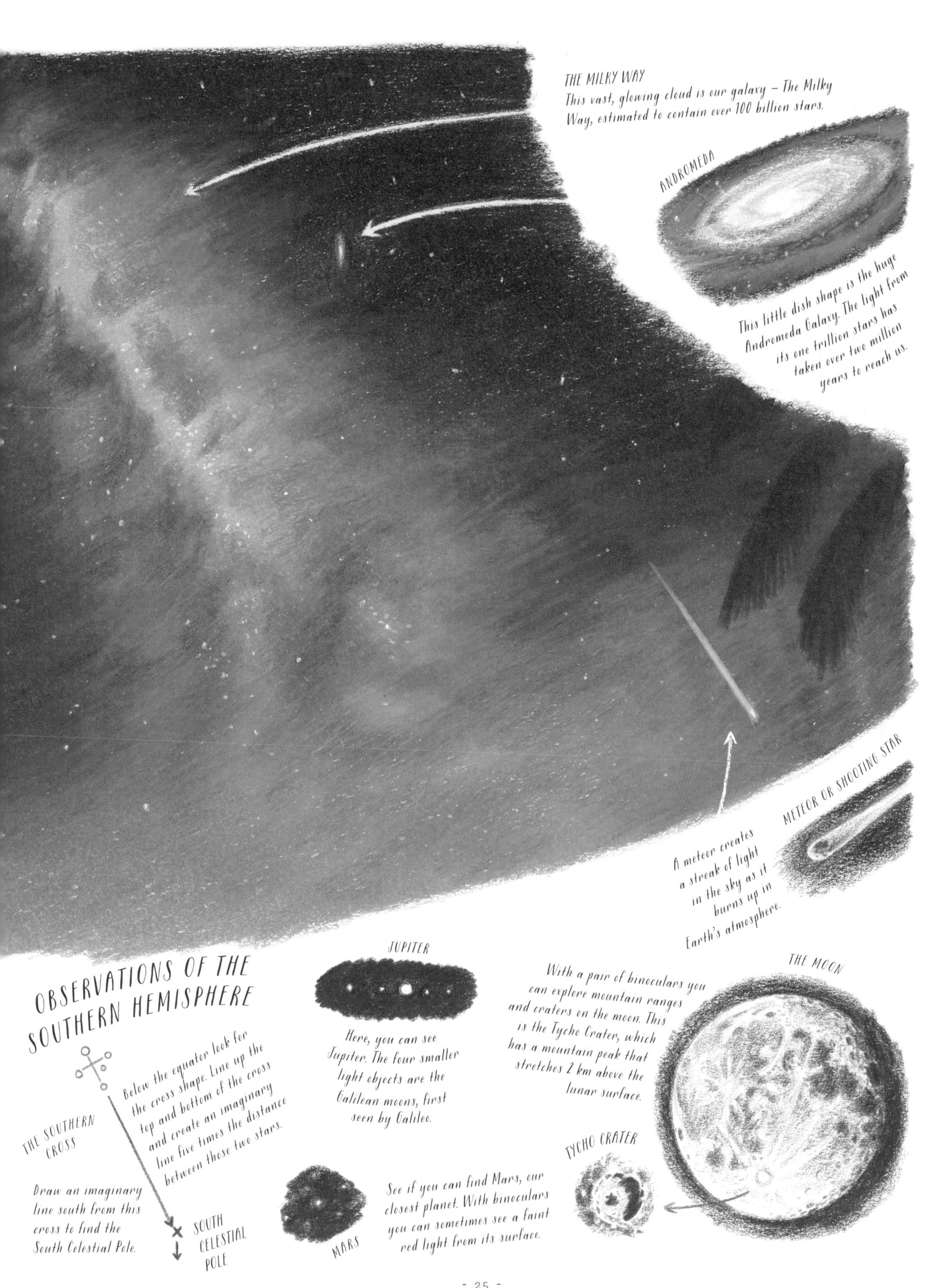
THE MILKY WAY
This vast, glowing cloud is our galaxy – The Milky Way, estimated to contain over 100 billion stars.
ANDROMEDA
This little dish shape is the huge Andromeda Galaxy. The light from its one trillion stars has taken over two million years to reach us.
METEOR OR SHOOTING STAR
A meteor creates a streak of light in the sky as it burns up in Earth's atmosphere.
OBSERVATIONS OF THE SOUTHERN HEMISPHERE
THE SOUTHERN CROSS
Below the equator look for the cross shape. Line up the top and bottom of the cross and create an imaginary line five times the distance between those two stars.
Draw an imaginary line south from this cross to find the South Celestial Pole.
SOUTH CELESTIAL POLE
JUPITER
Here, you can see Jupiter. The four smaller light objects are the Galilean moons, first seen by Galileo.
MARS
See if you can find Mars, our closest planet. With binoculars you can sometimes see a faint red light from its surface.
THE MOON
With a pair of binoculars you can explore mountain ranges and craters on the moon. This is the Tycho Crater, which has a mountain peak that stretches 2 km above the lunar surface.
TYCHO CRATER

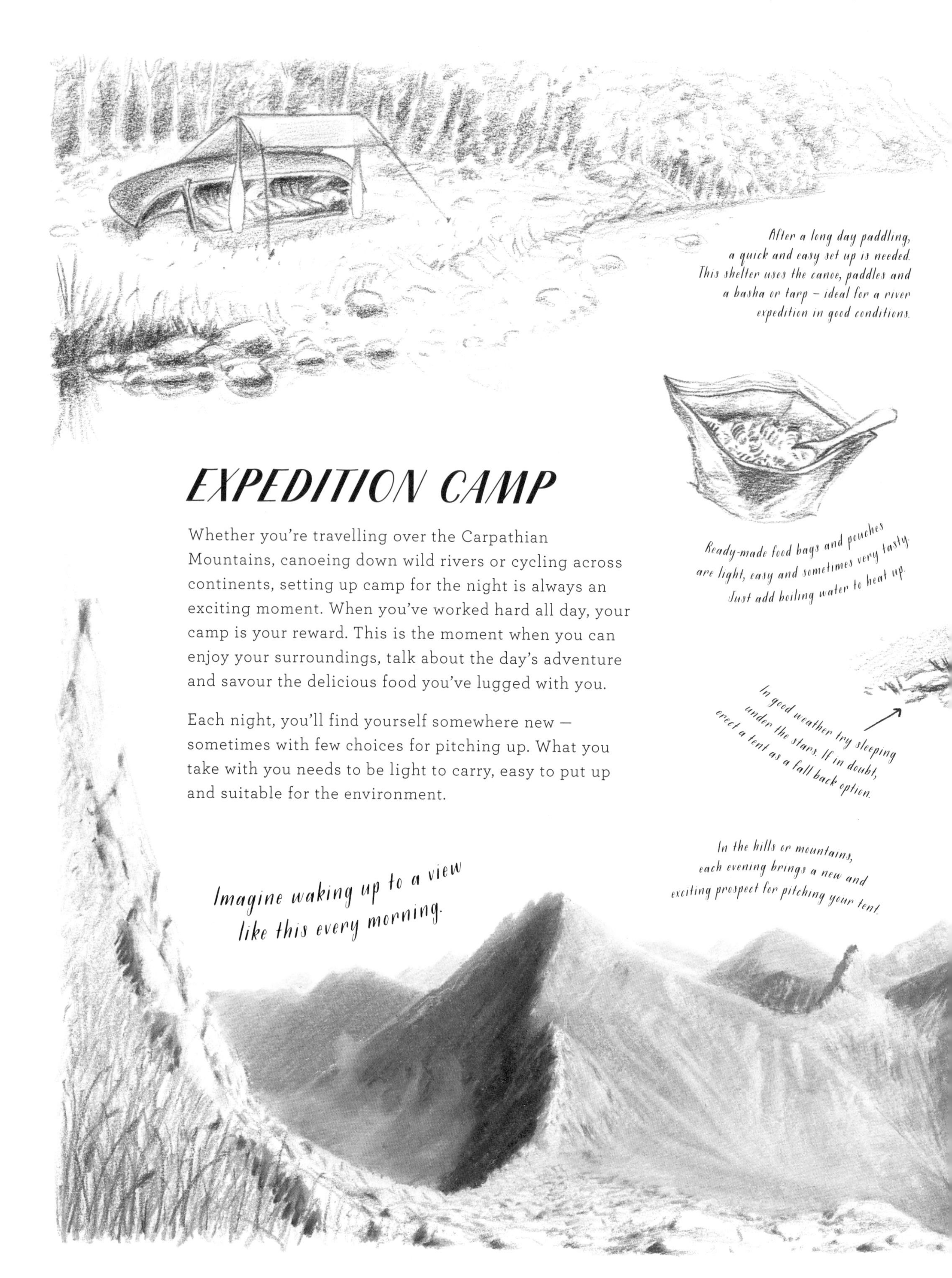

After a long day paddling, a quick and easy set up is needed. This shelter uses the canoe, paddles and a basha or tarp – ideal for a river expedition in good conditions.

Ready-made food bags and pouches are light, easy and sometimes very tasty. Just add boiling water to heat up.

EXPEDITION CAMP

Whether you're travelling over the Carpathian Mountains, canoeing down wild rivers or cycling across continents, setting up camp for the night is always an exciting moment. When you've worked hard all day, your camp is your reward. This is the moment when you can enjoy your surroundings, talk about the day's adventure and savour the delicious food you've lugged with you.

Each night, you'll find yourself somewhere new — sometimes with few choices for pitching up. What you take with you needs to be light to carry, easy to put up and suitable for the environment.

In good weather try sleeping under the stars. If in doubt, erect a tent as a fall back option.

In the hills or mountains, each evening brings a new and exciting prospect for pitching your tent.

Imagine waking up to a view like this every morning.

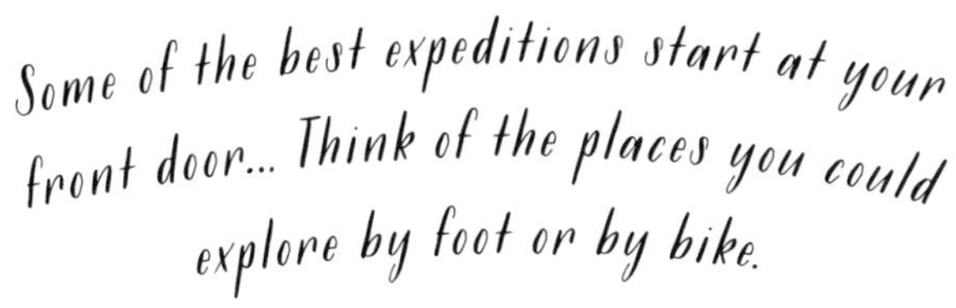

Some of the best expeditions start at your front door... Think of the places you could explore by foot or by bike.

Brazen thievery in action in India.

Memories of a bike expedition in the foothills of the Himalayas. On a bike, your gear needs to be portable, easy to put up and tamper-proof.

TIP: Lifestraws are a marvellous invention that filter water as you drink through a straw.

Running water high above human and livestock habitation is often safe to drink. If in doubt, boil water first.

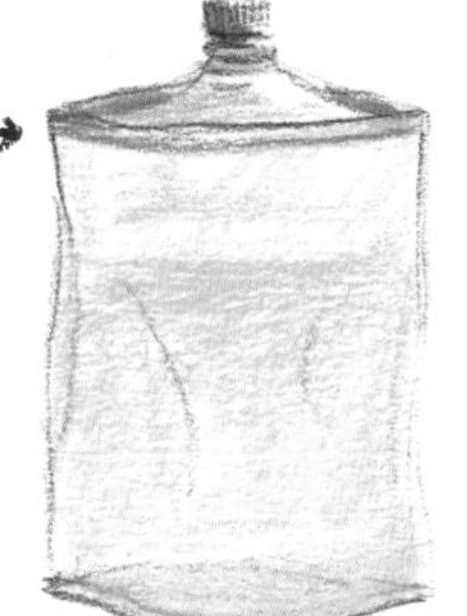

Plastic water carriers like this take up less space.

It may look like wee but it will probably be the best water you have ever drunk.

Water is key on any expedition, if you can, camp near a good source.

WILD WATER SPECTRUM

Don't judge a brook by its colour.

A FEW USEFUL POINTERS:

* Pack as lightly as possible;

* Plan ahead: it's always good to have an idea of where you'll make camp;

* Choose your spot well. A good sleep is invaluable when adventuring all day;

* Set up camp first, then sort food. If in a group, delegate;

* Remember: even rubbish food tastes good after a challenging day.

For all my memories of mountain traverses or river descents, it's the quiet evenings spent tending to blisters around the campfire that I most cherish.

Cooking over a gas stove is the best way to eat when open fires are illegal or impractical.

I'll never forget my first adventure under the Northern Lights. On the first night, a lucid green curtain enveloped the horizon. Mesmerising patterns of purples and blues began a slow dance across the sky. It was as if a celestial chorus had put on a show for an audience of one.

Unimaginable patterns evolved for over three hours.

The neon night sky is the result of radiation from the sun as it hits the polar atmosphere.

I hope one day you too will be here, feeling the hairs stand up on the back of your neck.

In the jungle, the machete is your best friend. I dived to the river bottom to retrieve this, knowing that we'd be in serious trouble without it.

SURVIVAL CAMP

On one adventure, a backpack full of provisions and kit was lost down the rapids when our canoe capsized. All that remained were hammocks, water bottles, a few clothes, a machete and a first aid kit. This was the moment to set up a survival base camp and take stock.

This isn't the sort of wild camping you choose to do, but for those moments when you're without supplies, you can set yourself the goal of providing your own shelter, water, fire and food. In a survival situation these four elements are everything.

SHELTER

We were fortunate to salvage our hammocks and bashas (overhead covering) from the submerged canoe. First on the agenda was getting a camp set up.

Once, a Goliath bird-eating spider fell onto my travel companion one night when he slept without a basha. Both he and the spider were shaken but unhurt.

A hammock is the shelter of choice in the jungle. They are suspended between two trees to protect you from creatures on the ground – and getting swamped by rainwater. A mosquito net completes the set up.

WATER

You can only last a day or two without water. Look for rivers, streams or even puddles. This must be purified or boiled. Generally, only rainwater and some mountain streams are safe to drink.

TIP: Purifying tablets or liquid drops can also be used to make water drinkable.

FIRE

This is essential for boiling water, cooking food and providing heat. Carrying fire-lighting gear in a survival tin will help you avoid a lengthy fire-making process.

FOOD

Here, on the banks of a small lagoon, we hunted caiman by torchlight with a makeshift lasso.

HOW TO MAKE A SURVIVAL TIN

This small survival tin contains nearly everything you need to survive in the wild. You can personalise it, of course — but it should include a number of the essentials listed here.

After our canoe capsized and our gear was swept away down the rapids, this survival tin kept us going for days... it probably saved our lives.

A good survival tin needs to be small enough to keep on you. A sweet or lozenge tin works well.

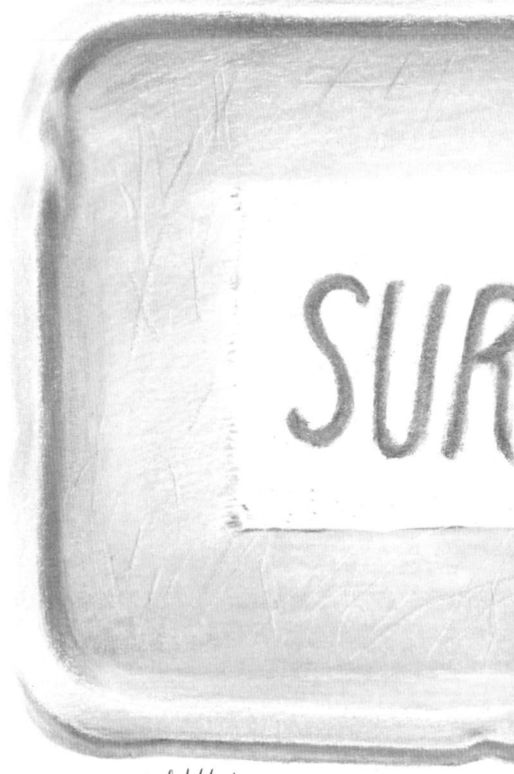

NAVIGATION & COMMUNICATION

BUTTON COMPASS: An essential tool for any adventure.

Actual size

12 mm

TIP: If you get lost, draw a rough map of landmarks while they are still fresh in your memory.

WATERPROOF PAPER: On one side write down all emergency names and numbers.

SMALL PENCIL

THE EMERGENCY CODE: Three blasts every 30 seconds.

SMALL TORCH

EMERGENCY WHISTLE: Use cord to make neck strap.

A torch beam at night or sunlight on a reflective surface can be used to gain attention and help. The morse code below will help you spell out messages.

SMALL MIRROR

Use your fingers to line the mirror up with potential rescuers.

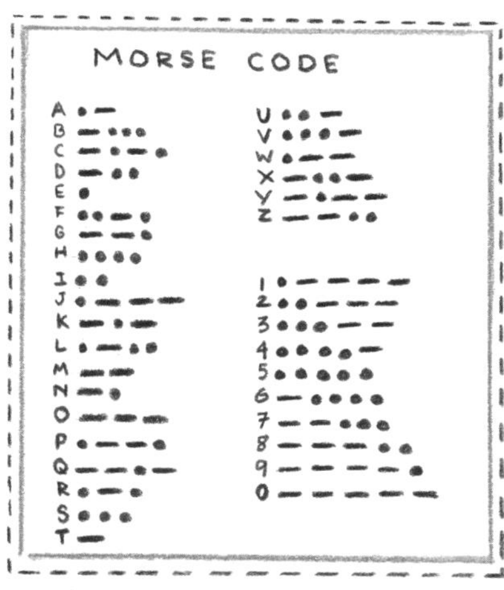

MORSE CODE

A	•—	U	••—
B	—•••	V	•••—
C	—•—•	W	•——
D	—••	X	—••—
E	•	Y	—•——
F	••—•	Z	——••
G	——•		
H	••••		
I	••	1	•————
J	•———	2	••———
K	—•—	3	•••——
L	•—••	4	••••—
M	——	5	•••••
N	—•	6	—••••
O	———	7	——•••
P	•——•	8	———••
Q	——•—	9	————•
R	•—•	0	—————
S	•••		
T	—		

MOSE CODE: A short flash signifies a dot, while a long flash signifies a dash.

FIRE TOOLS

Useful blade

SHARPENER: Pencil shavings can make emergency tinder.

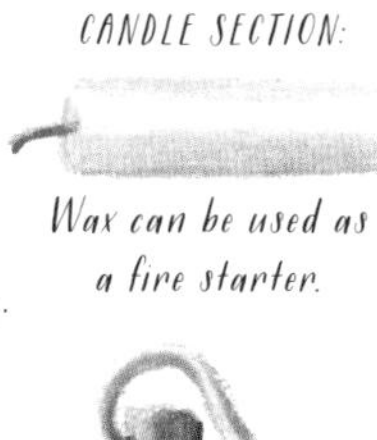

CANDLE SECTION: Wax can be used as a fire starter.

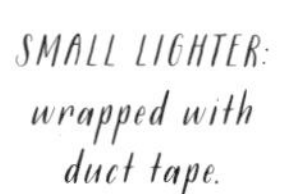

SMALL LIGHTER: wrapped with duct tape.

STORM MATCHES: These can be lit anywhere.

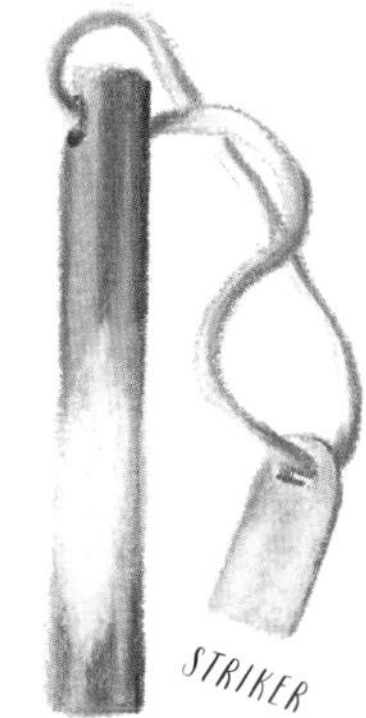

STRIKER

FIRE STEEL

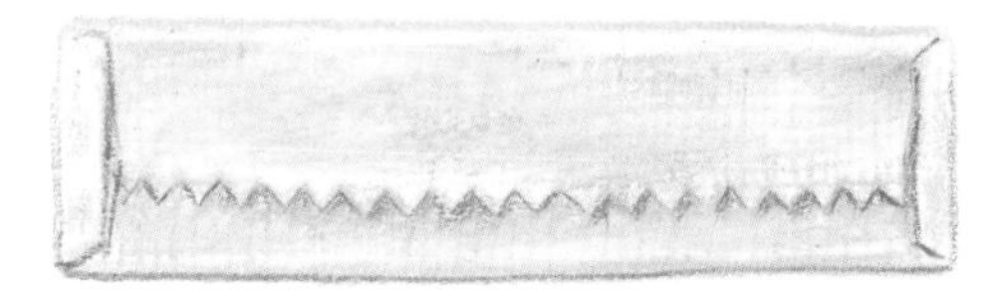

Make the wrapper 2 mm thick at the centre.

THREE REASONS TO CARRY CHEWING GUM:

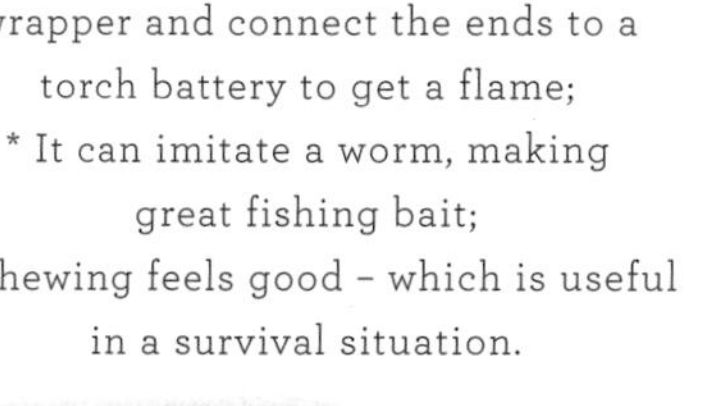

* It can help start a fire. Cut the silver wrapper and connect the ends to a torch battery to get a flame;
* It can imitate a worm, making great fishing bait;
* Chewing feels good – which is useful in a survival situation.

FIRST AID

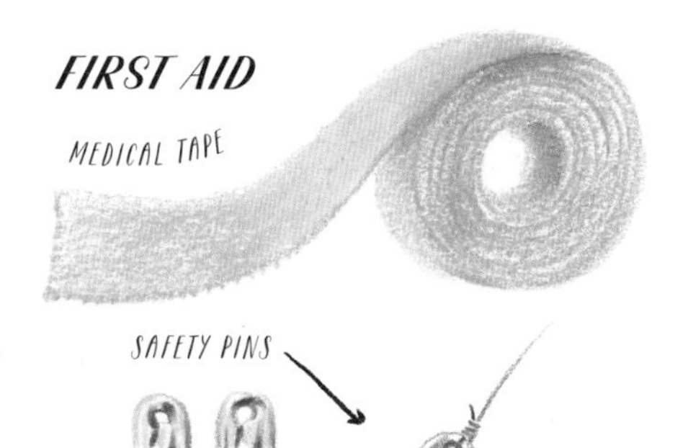

An emergency fish hook made from a safety pin.

TIP: Roll up some money and store it in your tin. You never know when you may need it.

TIP: Seal the lid of your tin with duct tape to keep it waterproof.

FISHING TOOLS

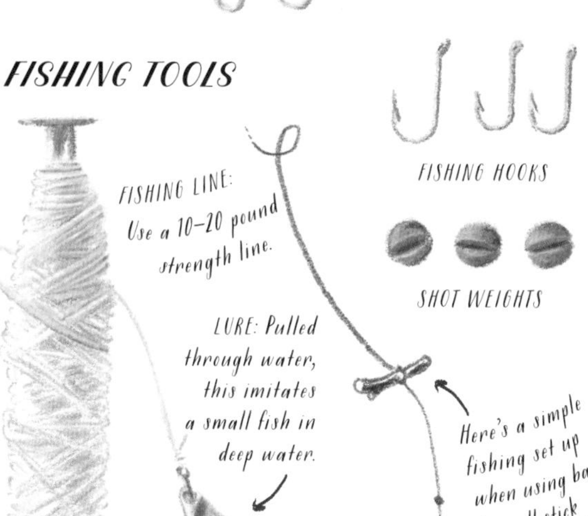

FISHING LINE: Use a 10–20 pound strength line.

FISHING HOOKS

SHOT WEIGHTS

LURE: Pulled through water, this imitates a small fish in deep water.

Here's a simple fishing set up when using bait. A small stick can act as a float.

A nail can also make a hunting spear point.

NAIL: This can be held or secured to a tree.

WATER PURIFYING TABLETS: A great way to make water drinkable.

OTHER USES FOR A LARGER TIN

Boiling water

Digging for worms

Cooking food

OTHER TOOLS

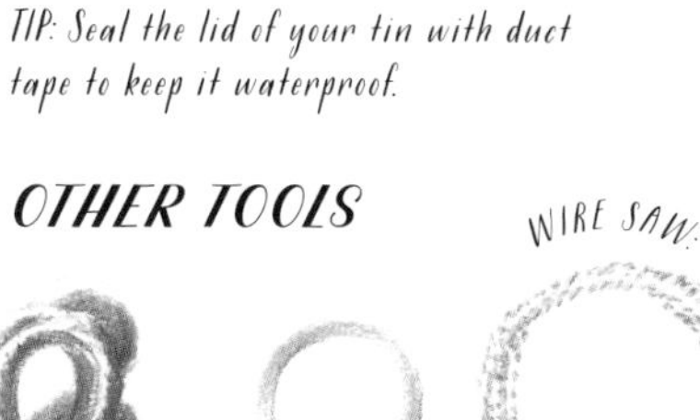

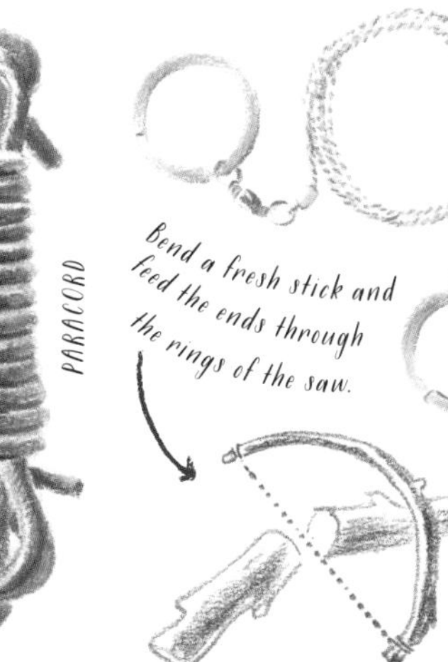

WIRE SAW: Bend a fresh stick and feed the ends through the rings of the saw.

SMALL MULTI-FUNCTION POCKET KNIFE: Ideally with a cutting blade, a saw blade and an opening blade or scissors.

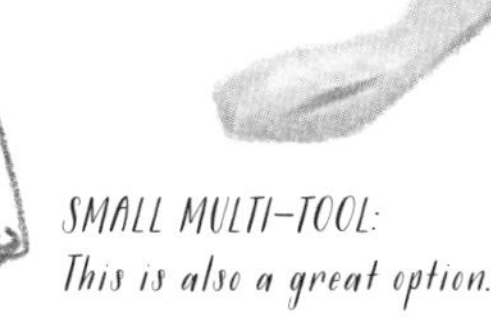

SMALL MULTI-TOOL: This is also a great option.

TIN FOIL: Flatten a sheet into the base of the lid of your tin.

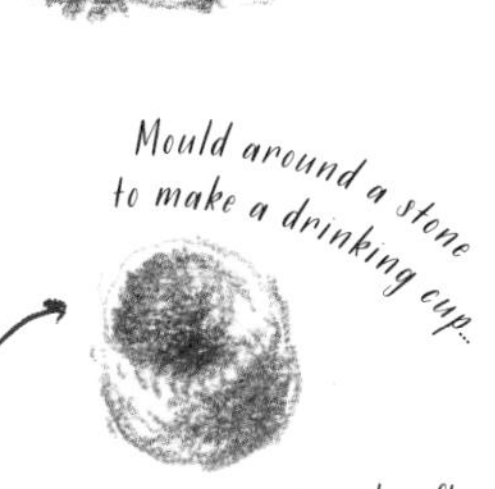

Mould around a stone to make a drinking cup.

Or use as a signal reflector.

KNIVES

Knives are an essential tool, to be used with the upmost care. With a knife you can make tinder, as well as the sparks to light it. You can also make many tools: eating implements like spoons and bowls; and bows, arrows and spears for hunting. On its own, a knife can provide and prepare foraged or hunted foods. It can also cut you free from ropes, and be your saving grace in emergency situations. In the wild, a good knife is the most useful and vital tool you can carry.

KNIFE SAFETY:

* Blunt blades are dangerous as they can slip when cutting or carving; always keep your knife sharpened;

* When passing a knife to someone else, fold it up or put it in its sheath;

* Always know where and when you can carry a knife;

* Keep all knife motions away from the body.

Hold the handle facing outwards and the blade edge facing away from your hand.

THE BLOOD BUBBLE: Always think about your knife safety zone. Hold the knife at arm's length and make an arc around your body. You don't want anyone within this bubble when using your knife.

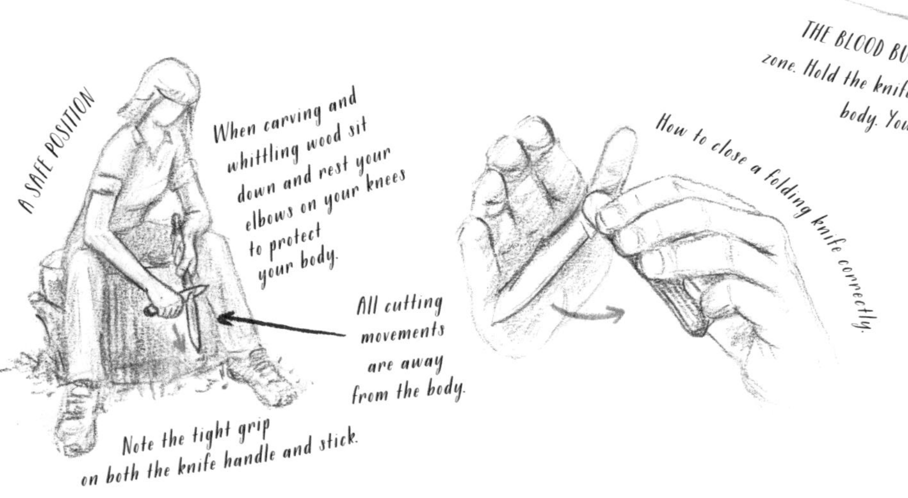

ADVENTURERS:

* Don't show off their knives;

* Never point them at others;

* Never carry them where they are not allowed;

* Never walk with an open or unsheathed blade;

* Always treat their knives with the respect they deserve.

A KNIFE FOR THE WILD

In the wild you'll need a good all-rounder — something not too big and heavy, but strong and multi-purpose. From my experience, a fixed blade bushcraft knife or a folding knife is best.

BUSHKNIFE

A bush knife or bushcraft knife has a fixed blade.

This bushknife comes in a sheath which is worn around the waist. Take great care when putting the knife back in its sheath.

The bushknife is a good all-rounder, ideal for carving, cutting and preparing food.

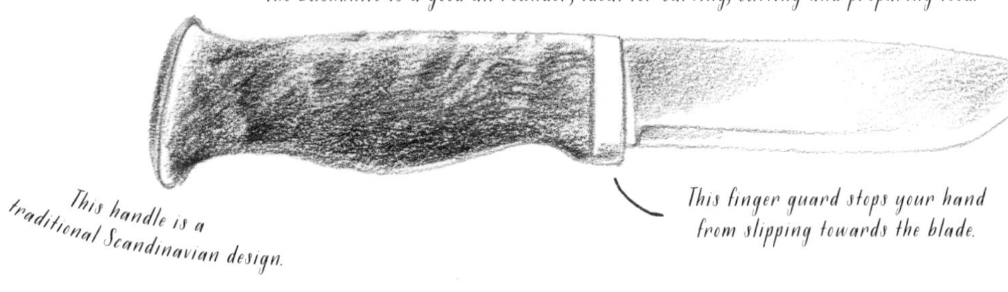

This handle is a traditional Scandinavian design.

This finger guard stops your hand from slipping towards the blade.

FOLDING KNIFE

This strong but lightweight design can be folded up and carried in a pocket.

The single blade folds away into the handle.

The blade locks into place. Pressing here releases the blade.

MULTI-TOOL KNIFE

The pocket knife is also an adventurer's knife of choice. It offers multiple tools for multiple situations. There are many designs but you need just a few good functions.

The main blade can be used for cutting tasks.

Whittling blade

Opening blade

Small detailing blade

Saw blade

This knife folds up compactly and is ideal for your survival tin.

There are so many uses for this vital tool.

This was a makeshift candle holder I once made from a knife. I'm fond of a bit of ambience in the wild.

MAKING FIRE

1. Hit a blade against a flint stone to create a spark.

2. Flammable tinder such as cotton wool will catch light.

Stones such as flint or quartz will produce sparks.

CUTTING

A serrated blade is good for cutting rope and cord – useful in the wild.

Knives can be used to carve an effective wooden spear for fishing.

GUTTING

A knife is needed for gutting and preparing fish and other food.

WILDLIFE

My knife came in handy when needing to pacify this scorpion after it had given me a nasty sting.

'COVERT' means
hidden, secret or disguised.

COVERT CAMP

There have been times when I've made a camp in private or hostile environments. This image shows one such night where I camped with just my bivvy bag (a waterproof outer bag that your sleeping bag goes into) and backpack (all packed and ready for a fast escape). I've documented some useful tips and tricks should you find yourself in a situation where you need to camp by stealth.

As with any camp, never leave a trace — clean up mess before you leave.

COVERT CAMPING TIPS:

* Arrive late; look for a good camp spot, but wait until it's nearly dark to set up;

* Always choose a hidden location away from footpaths;

* Pack up camp, leave at dawn;

* Have breakfast on the move;

* Remember: if you can see people, they can see you.

THINGS THAT WILL GIVE YOU AWAY:

* Torches and headtorches;

* Fire light and smoke;

* Brightly coloured tents and clothes;

* Noise – talking, laughing, snoring;

* Movement – especially if you are silhouetted against the skyline;

* The smell of cooked food.

HOW TO MAKE A BIN LINER BIVVY BAG

1. Collect two extra strong, large bin liner bags or tough sacks.
2. Cut one open at the bottom.
3. Tape the two bags together with duct tape.

4. Cut the top bag leaving a flap to create the head area.
5. Insert your sleeping bag.

TIP: Double up liner bags for more durability.

Here, overhanging ferns disguised my camp. The red light is from my head torch's night vision setting.

Always avoid being silhouetted against the skyline.

It's good to set yourself up in a high position. It's easy to see and harder to be seen.

There's a real thrill to stealth camping... learning to become invisible is an exciting skill to master.

SILENT ALARM CLOCK:
A traditional method of waking up is to drink water before bed. The more you drink, the earlier you will wake up needing to wee.

MAKING A FIRE PIT

If you need a fire this is the stealthiest one to make.

Air

1. Dig a large main hole about 30 cm deep and the flames should remain hidden from view.
2. Dig a connecting hole for air to pass through.

Tip: Harder woods generally create less smoke.

Some hardwood varieties:
- oak
- beech
- birch
- apple
- ash
- maple

USING RED LIGHT

Turn your head torch on to its red light setting if it has one.

Red light is harder for others to see and retains your night vision.

To make your own, cut and stick some transparent red plastic on the torch lens.

PLANNING YOUR ADVENTURE

You may already have a good idea of the sort of camp you want to make, but here are a few things worth thinking about.

Recce* the local countryside if you can, looking for good camping spots.
*(pron. 'recky', short for 'reconnaissance')

* Think about what kind of adventure you want to go on. What do you want to experience? Who do you want to go with?
* Ask people – family, friends, adventurous neighbours – if they know a location that fits your list;
* Explore maps of your area or further afield;
* If camping locally, go and explore the countryside for a good location;
* Get the adults to help with the organising and planning.

Get hold of a local map or draw one and start making a plan.

HEADING INTO THE WILD – THREE WAYS TO DO IT

KEY:
ROUTE
CAMP SPOTS
TREES/WOODS
FOOTPATH
RIVER
BOG
1 KM

THE WILD LINE: Once you cross this line you're in wild territory.

WILD DOMAIN
HUMAN DOMAIN
WOODS
FOOTPATH
COWS
FIELD
ROAD
FARM
FIELD
RIVER
FIELD

You can either keep a low profile (be stealthy) and explore the land for a quiet camp spot out of the way. Or you can ask permission from the landowners.

SETTING OFF FROM HOME

You don't have to travel to the ends of the earth to camp wild. If you're near the open countryside you can often head out from your front door into the woods and the fields. It is exciting and easy to do without huge planning.

Bikes will get you deeper into the wild.

GETTING PERMISSION ON PRIVATE LAND:

* Send local farmers or landowners a letter;
* Go and knock on their door and ask;
* Offer them something in return, like help on the farm or a photo of the sunset. Be imaginative.

A wild campsite is often the best way to start your wild-camping adventures.

Camping among the sand dunes beside the sea – serious exploration potential.

WILD CAMPSITES

There are a number of wild campsites out there. Some are organised campsites with facilities – but a bit quieter. Others are wilder, designated camping areas but often simply bits of open, flat ground found in national parks. Do your research and you'll discover one that fits your adventure.

Wake up with a swim in the sea.

Go for campsites that will let you build a campfire or supply a fire pit.

Out here you're completely self-reliant. And that is what makes it a very real adventure.

INTO THE WILDERNESS

True wild camping is about heading off the beaten track and finding a remote spot to suit you. It could be in the mountains, in the forests or by the sea. The further from civilisation the better. You'll need to be well prepared and take all your needs with you, but the rewards are worth it.

* Do your research. Many places allow responsible wild camping;

* In remote spots there's often no other option;

* By car, by train, by bike, by canoe... there are a few ways to access the wild places;

* Car access will mean you can take more stuff;

* If possible allow two or more nights for a wilderness adventure.

Don't be afraid to ask for permission to camp. Many farmers and landowners love the land and want the younger generation to appreciate it too.

BOOTS
FIRST AID KIT
TORCH
TIP: If you're carrying a backpack, pack the essentials first. If there's still space, then add your extras.
BACKPACK
GLOVES
FORK AND SPOON
TRAINERS
WATERPROOF JACKET
PENKNIFE
WATER BOTTLE
COMPASS
SMALL AXE
WATCH
HIKING BOOTS
HAT
Don't spend lots of money on kit. When you are starting out, beg and borrow what you can.
TENT
GAS STOVE
COLLAPSIBLE WATER CARRIER
BATTERIES
COOKING POT
KNIFE
MAP
NOTEPAD/ SKETCHBOOK
PAINTBRUSHES
TOOTHBRUSH AND TOOTHPASTE
SLEEPING MAT
SLEEPING BAG

FISHING EQUIPMENT

INSECT REPELLENT

A GOOD BOOK

SMALL TOWEL

NEWSPAPER

KINDLING

BIN LINER

DRY BAG

TIP: Take a small amount of dry kindling if conditions are wet. It can get a wet campfire started.

BINOCULARS

CLOTHES

TIP: Take a pillow case. Stuff it with clothes to make a comfy pillow.

PILLOW CASE

THICK JUMPER

PARACORD

HEAD TORCH

WARM HAT

SURVIVAL TIN

LANTERN

SUNGLASSES

LIGHTER

TIP: You won't need all this for your camping adventure. Adapt your pack to suit your needs.

MUG

HAMMOCK/BASHA

A TRUSTY WALKING STICK: Try making one when you are in the wild.

CAMP WILD KIT

Here is some of the wild camping paraphernalia I take on my adventures. Which items you take on yours depends on the environment you're heading into, the weather and temperature, and what you plan to be doing. You can have a successful camping adventure with a fraction of this kit, but always remember to pack the essentials.

CHECKLIST

CORE ITEMS:

* Backpack;
* Tent;
* Sleeping bag;
* Sleeping mat;
* Dry bag or bin liner.

AROUND CAMP:

* Head torch or torch;
* Spare batteries;
* Water bottle/carrier & water;
* Extra water bottle;
* Knife or penknife;
* Toothbrush & toothpaste.

EATING & COOKING:

* Adequate food supplies;
* Tasty snacks;
* Gas cooker/gas canisters if required – adult's responsibility;
* Cooking pot & utensils;
* Lighter & spare matches;
* Materials for a raised fire pit;
* Plastic or metal bowl;
* Plastic or metal mug;
* Fork, spoon, knife.

NAVIGATION ITEMS:

* Compass;
* Good map of the area;
* Map case for wet weather;

CLOTHING & FOOTWEAR:

* Waterproof jacket;
* Insulated fleece, liner or thick jumper (x2 if cold);
* Enough suitable clothes;
* Spare pants and socks;
* Small towel;
* Boots or hiking boots – in wet weather;
* Suitable trainers or sandals;
* Warm hat and gloves – it gets cold at night.
* Sun hat or cap;
* Sunglasses;

SURVIVAL:

* First aid kit;
* Whistle;
* Personal medicines;
* Insect repellant;
* Survival blanket;
* Survival tin;
* Emergency/useful telephone numbers.
* Suncream.

EXTRAS:

* Basha, hammock or bivvy bag;
* Gas or electric lantern;
* Biodegradable soap;
* Paracord;
* Good book;
* Animal identification book;
* Binoculars;
* Fishing equipment;
* Swimwear;
* Notepad and sketchbook;
* Small axe.

Always set up your tent and snug it out before night falls.

TENTS

There are many different types of tent. If you can, go for something simple and lightweight – a two-person tent is ideal as there's space for you and one or two others.

BASHA: A simple waterproof overhead cover

TRADITIONAL RIDGE TENT

DOME TENT

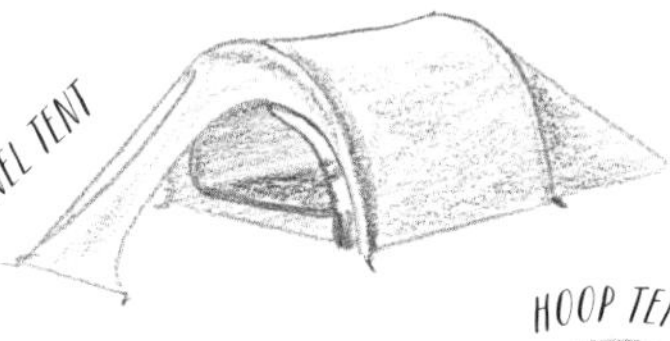

TUNNEL TENT

HOOP TENT

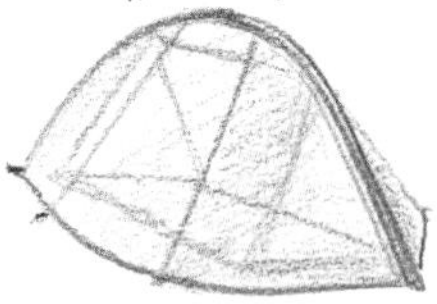

EXPEDITION TENT: Reinforced for extreme weather.

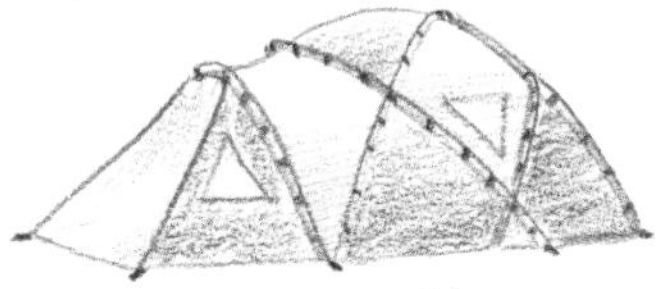

TENT CHECKLIST:

* Lightweight;
* Easy to put up;
* Strong;
* Waterproof groundsheet;
* Has a porch (ideally).

Here, 160 km/h winds battered our position as we hunkered down and cooked dinner. A good tent should be able to withstand all the elements, but positioning is important. Find the most sheltered spot. Face the entrance away from the wind and secure the guylines firmly. On this trip, we had to use rocks to hold the pegs down.

HOW TO PITCH A TWO-PERSON TENT

Every tent comes with its own instructions – follow them closely.

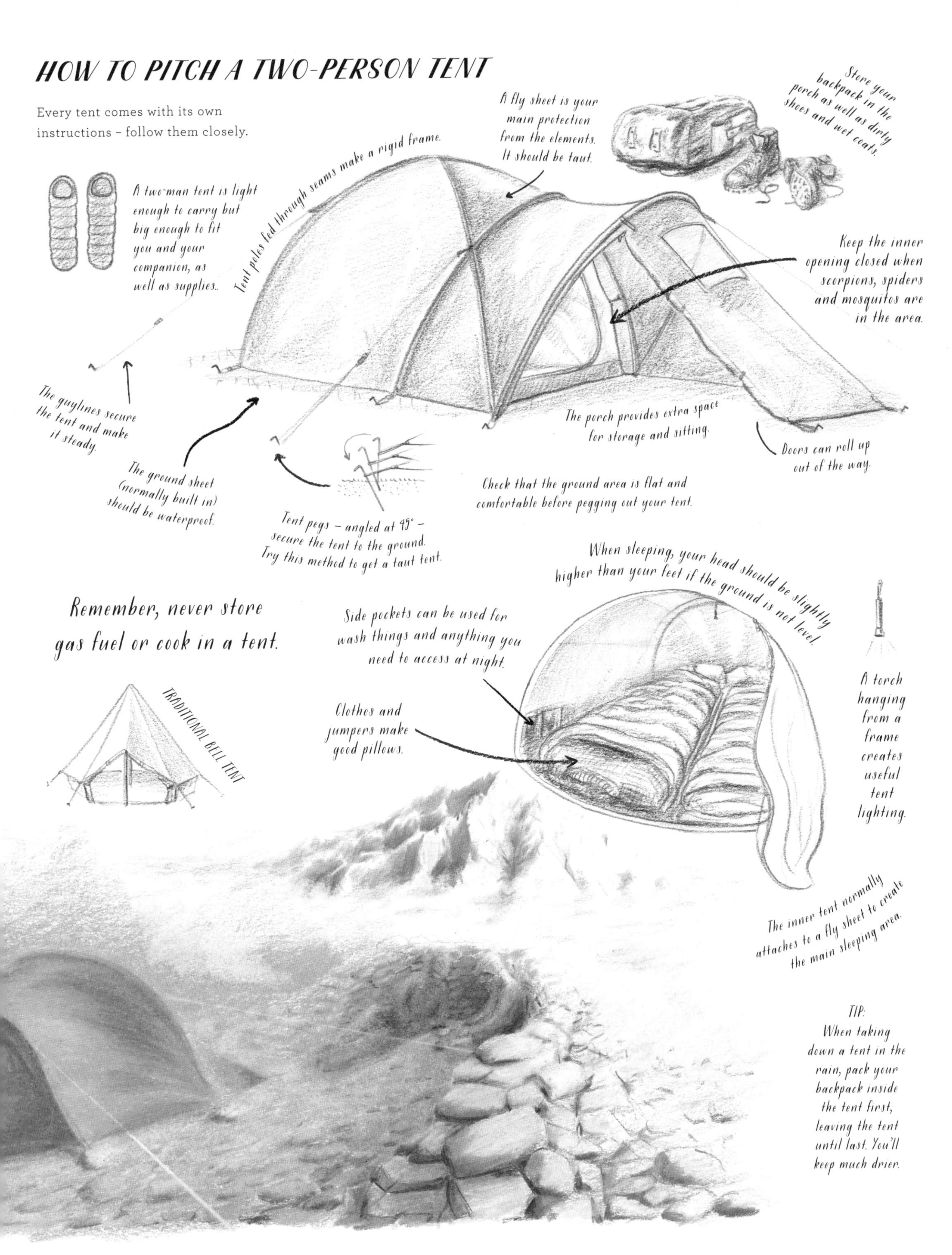

CHOOSING A PLACE TO CAMP

Sniffing out a good camp spot is something every adventurer enjoys. Over time you'll pick up a sixth sense for it just by scanning a landscape or a map. Sometimes you'll have the luxury of choice – like below – sometimes you won't, but with a bit of knowledge and good planning your wild camp will be a success.

CAMP SPOT CHECKLIST:

* Flat, open ground;

* Sheltered from wind;

* Near water source if needed;

* Clear from risks and obstacles – flash floods, run off, falling rocks.

* Avoid dips and depressions where rain water could collect;

* Stay away from unhealthy trees.

* Avoid fields where cows are present.

CAMPING BY WATER

* Assess if the water poses a hazard for your group;

* Always camp well above water level;

* Do not camp where there's chance of flash flooding;

* Know the animal life – avoid rivers and lakes inhabited by crocodiles and hippos.

MOSQUITOES AND FRIENDS

TIP: The blighters generally don't like high ground, wind or smoke.

In mosquito and midge season try and avoid rivers. Wear repellent and keep tent doors closed. And pray.

If scouting for a site as you go, take time to consider your spot carefully. Don't be too fussy, but don't be too casual. A good night's sleep is worth the effort.

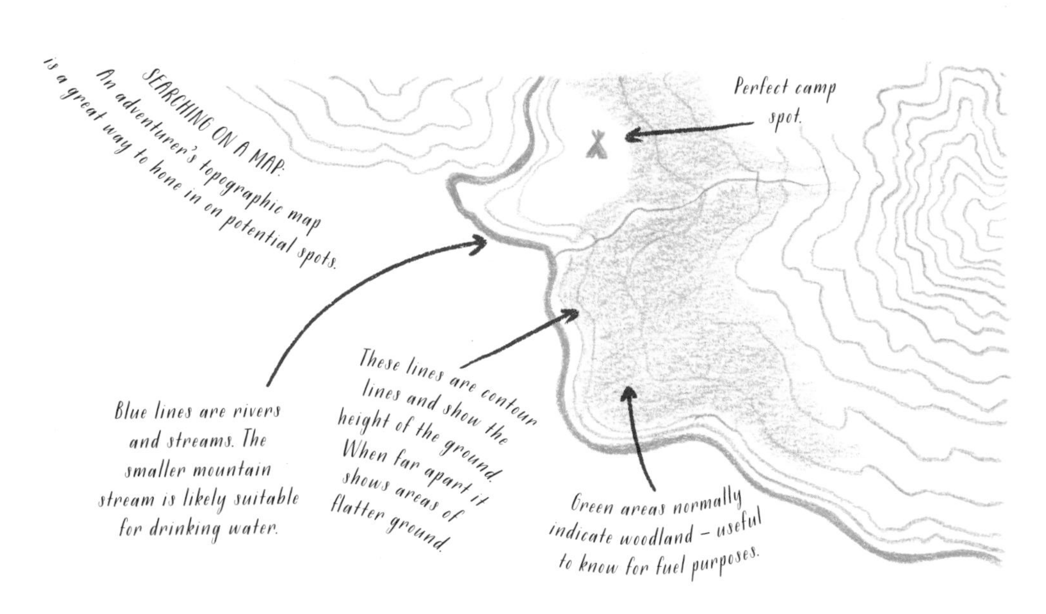

USEFUL TIPS FOR GETTING TO SLEEP:

* Make sure the ground beneath the tent is as flat as possible – remove any sticks and stones;
* Ear plugs are handy especially when camping with snorers or beside waterfalls;
* Empty your bladder before going to bed to avoid the need later;
* Don't get too hot or too cold – if cold, wear extra clothes inside the sleeping bag;
* Contemplate the universe – I find it helps.

Great camp spots have a habit of getting superglued to your memory.

The delicate flicker of the flame reached a dry twig, and then another... and so it grew.
Small smokey clouds circled the damp moss and leaves.

The fire hissed and popped as it bore fresh flames that leapt upwards into the night.
This captivating spectacle is something I've experienced many times, and it never disappoints.

FIRE MAKING

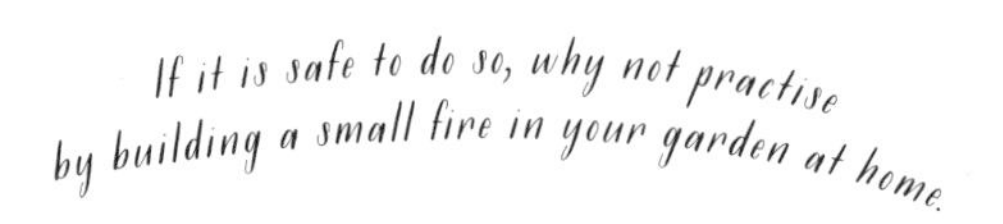

Warming yourself in the wild beside a good fire that you have made yourself is one of life's great rewards. Here are some basics on how to build a fire, where to build it, and how to do it safely.

WHERE TO BUILD:

* Find an open, flat area with enough space;
* Keep the fire away from tents and trees;
* Avoid any tripping hazards like roots and rocks;
* If windy, position the fire downwind of your camp area;
* Setting up a fire in a sheltered dip or out of the wind will help when lighting and tending the fire. Dig a shallow hole if necessary.

BUILDING YOUR FIRE

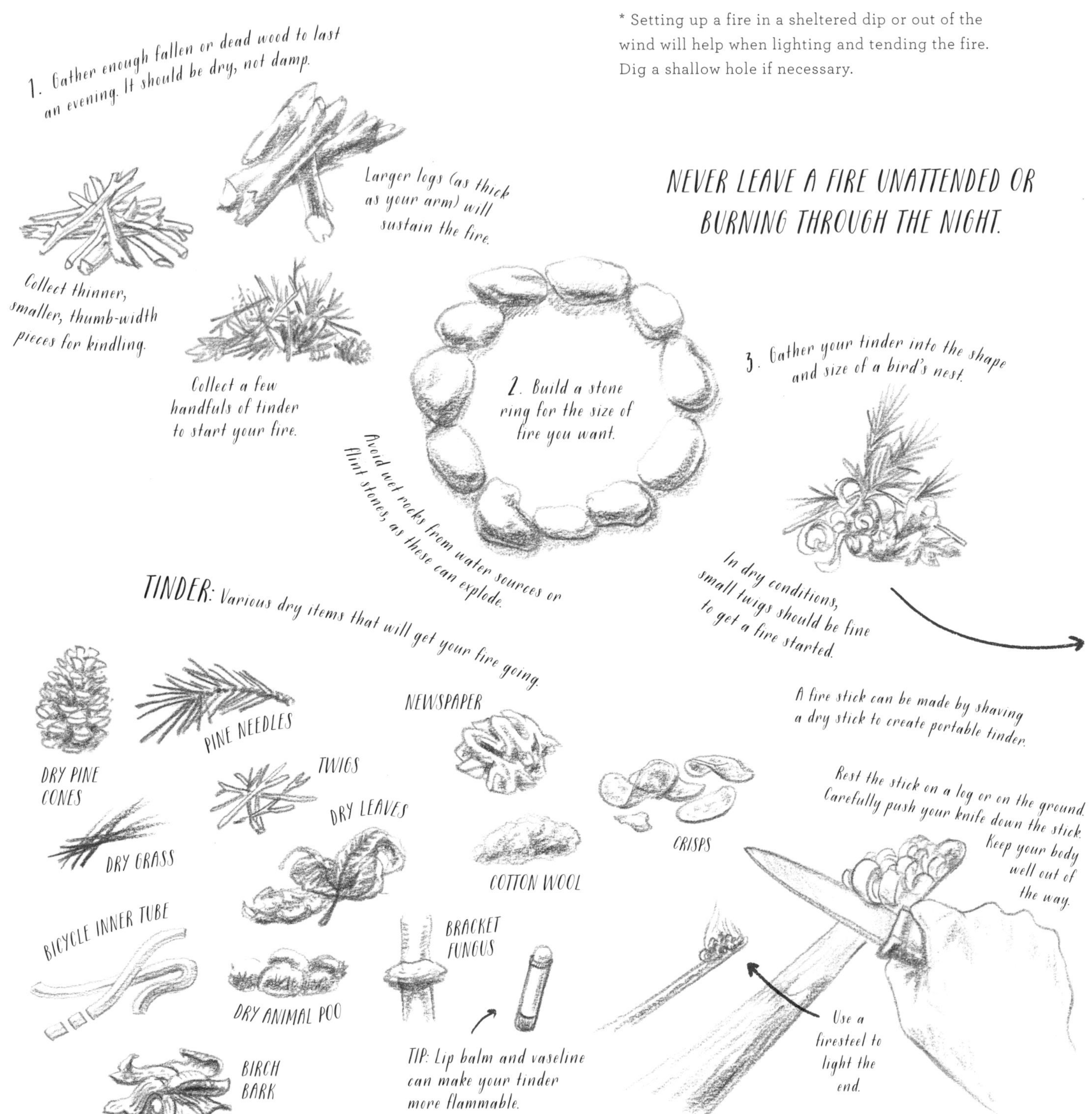

If water is scarce, sand or soil can also put out a fire.

FIRE COMMANDMENTS:

* Never start a fire in places it is forbidden;

* Do not start a fire in very dry and hot conditions where there is a risk of sparks landing in some grass or trees;

* Never go to sleep with a fire still going or leave it unattended;

* Avoid overhanging trees, like eucalyptus.

Always have some water ready to extinguish your fire.

BUILDING A FIRE WITH WET WOOD

Sometimes, dry wood is hard to find. In these situations, find the driest wood you can and collect good tinder.

Start small and slowly build up your fire. Once it is going, slowly dry out wet wood around the edges of the fire.

A good wooden poking stick will help manage the fire.

6. Once the fire is going, add dry logs and branches. Keep adding logs when needed.

4. Build up a teepee shape with kindling.

Leave space for the flames to breathe.

TIP: Have more tinder and kindling ready to add as the flames grow.

5. Use your fire-lighting tool to set the tinder alight. If needed, gently blow or fan the embers to get the fire going.

Always put out the fire when you go to sleep. Keep water or earth nearby for this.

FIRE-LIGHTING TOOLS

Choose waterproof survival matches if you can. You can strike them almost anywhere.

I always carry a lighter, but only as a back up.

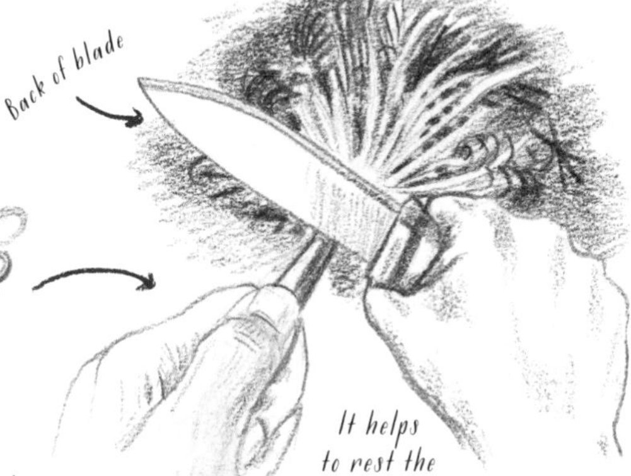

Firesteel produces hot sparks.

It helps to rest the firesteel on the ground or a stable log.

Strike down with the back of your fixed knife blade or striker to create sparks. Angle the firesteel to apply strong pressure. Repeat until the tinder catches. You may need to blow gently on the embers for it to catch.

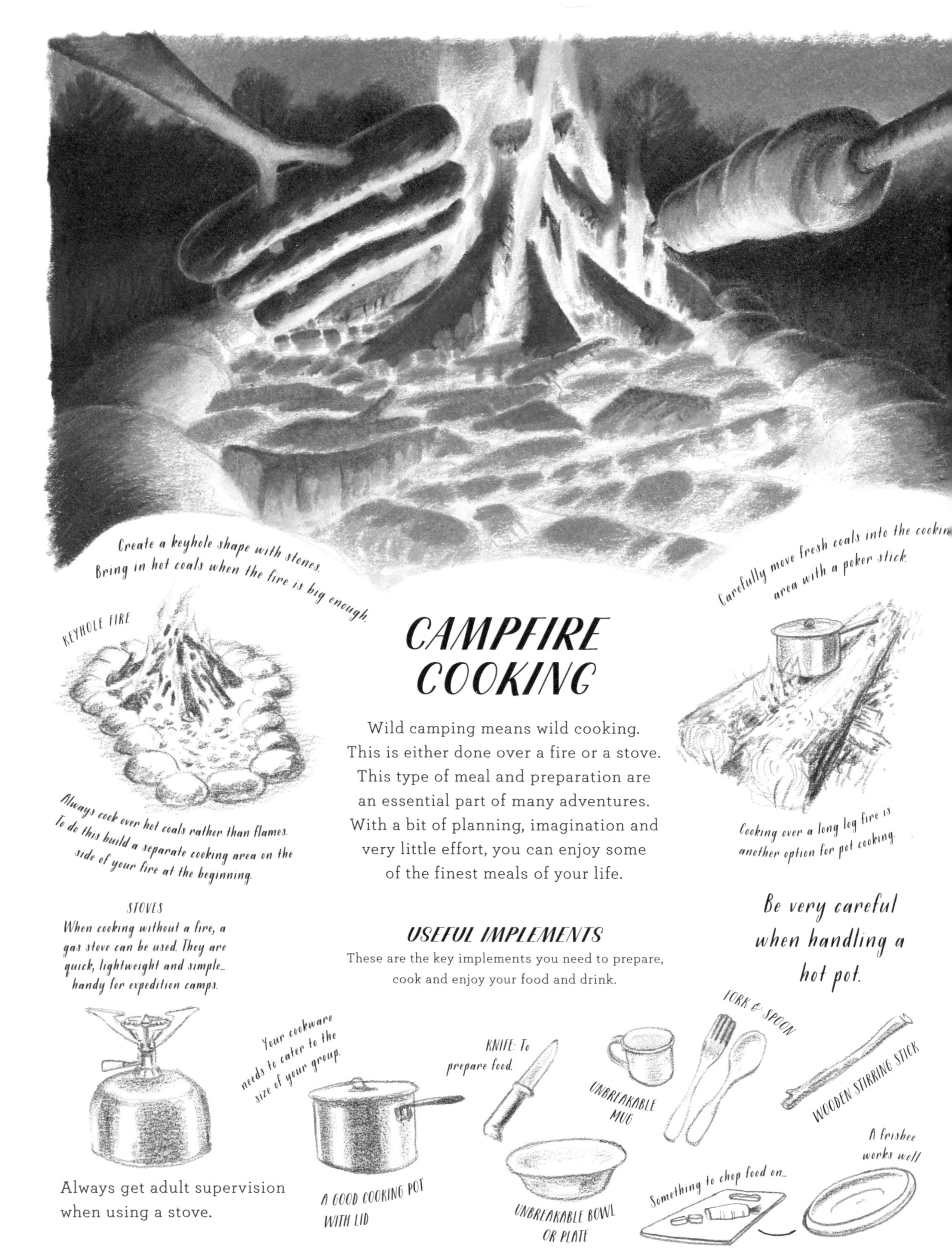

CAMPFIRE COOKING

Wild camping means wild cooking. This is either done over a fire or a stove. This type of meal and preparation are an essential part of many adventures. With a bit of planning, imagination and very little effort, you can enjoy some of the finest meals of your life.

USEFUL IMPLEMENTS

These are the key implements you need to prepare, cook and enjoy your food and drink.

Always get adult supervision when using a stove.

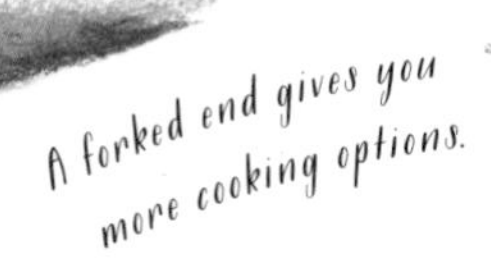

A forked end gives you more cooking options.

IDEAL COOKING STICK:

Thin and long, but not too bendy.

Find greener fresh wood that won't burn.

COOKING WITH A STICK

This is a fun and easy way to cook over fire.

FIRE-GRILLED SAUSAGES:

1. Find a good forked stick and skewer some sausages.

2. Cook above hot coals, not a flame. Turn them when one side is done.

Secure the stick by pushing it into the ground and support it with rocks, like this. Make sure the sausages are well-cooked inside.

KEBABS:

Impale meat such as lamb along with mushrooms, peppers and onions. Hold over hot coals until well-cooked. It's great for cheese like halloumi, too.

A stick is all you need to roast a fish over the fire.

A 'V' in the stick stops the fish from sliding down.

BAKING

Baking over fire is one of life's greatest treats. With tin foil you can create your own makeshift oven. Simply wrap your item in foil and place in the hot embers.

FIRE-BAKED POTATO:

Cook for 45 mins – 1 hour. Keep the hot coals topped up all around your potato.

FIRE-BAKED BANANA AND CHOCOLATE: Cooks in 10 mins.

FIRE-BAKED CORN IN THE HUSK:

Simply roast on hot coals until it's nicely blackened. Remove the husk and enjoy.

CAMPFIRE BREAD

It's easy to make bread over a fire. Here are two simple and effective methods I use in the wild.

FIRST, MAKE YOUR DOUGH

A bowl, pot or bag can be used for mixing.

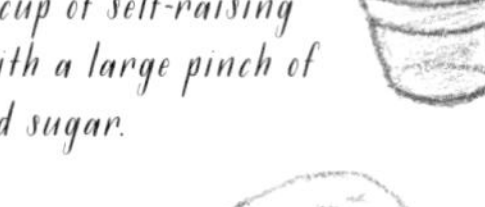

1. Mix 1 cup of self-raising flour with a large pinch of salt and sugar.

2. Add 1/2 a cup of water and mix with your hands until you have a good dough. It shouldn't be crumbly or sticky.

FLATBREAD

1. Flatten small handfuls of dough into round shapes.

2. Lay on a hot, smooth rock at the edge of the fire. Or cook in a pan over hot coals until golden brown.

Add cooked sausage or another filling to make a delicious meal.

BREAD TWISTS

1. Break the dough into small pieces.

2. Roll these into thumb-width lengths, 15–20 cm long.

3. Wrap around the end of a stick. Pinch the ends to make it grip.

4. Roast above hot embers until it turns golden brown, roughly 5–10 mins.

5. Once it has cooled, carefully remove from the stick. It tastes good with jam if you have some.

DESPERATE MEALS

When you commit to real adventure, you're bound to encounter foods of many kinds. These are two of my most memorable meals to date. Please do not try this at home.

Once, in Brazil, we roasted these tarantulas on sticks over the campfire. Crunchy in texture, the abdomen tasted a lot like peanut butter.

FIRE-ROASTED GOLIATH BIRD-EATING SPIDER

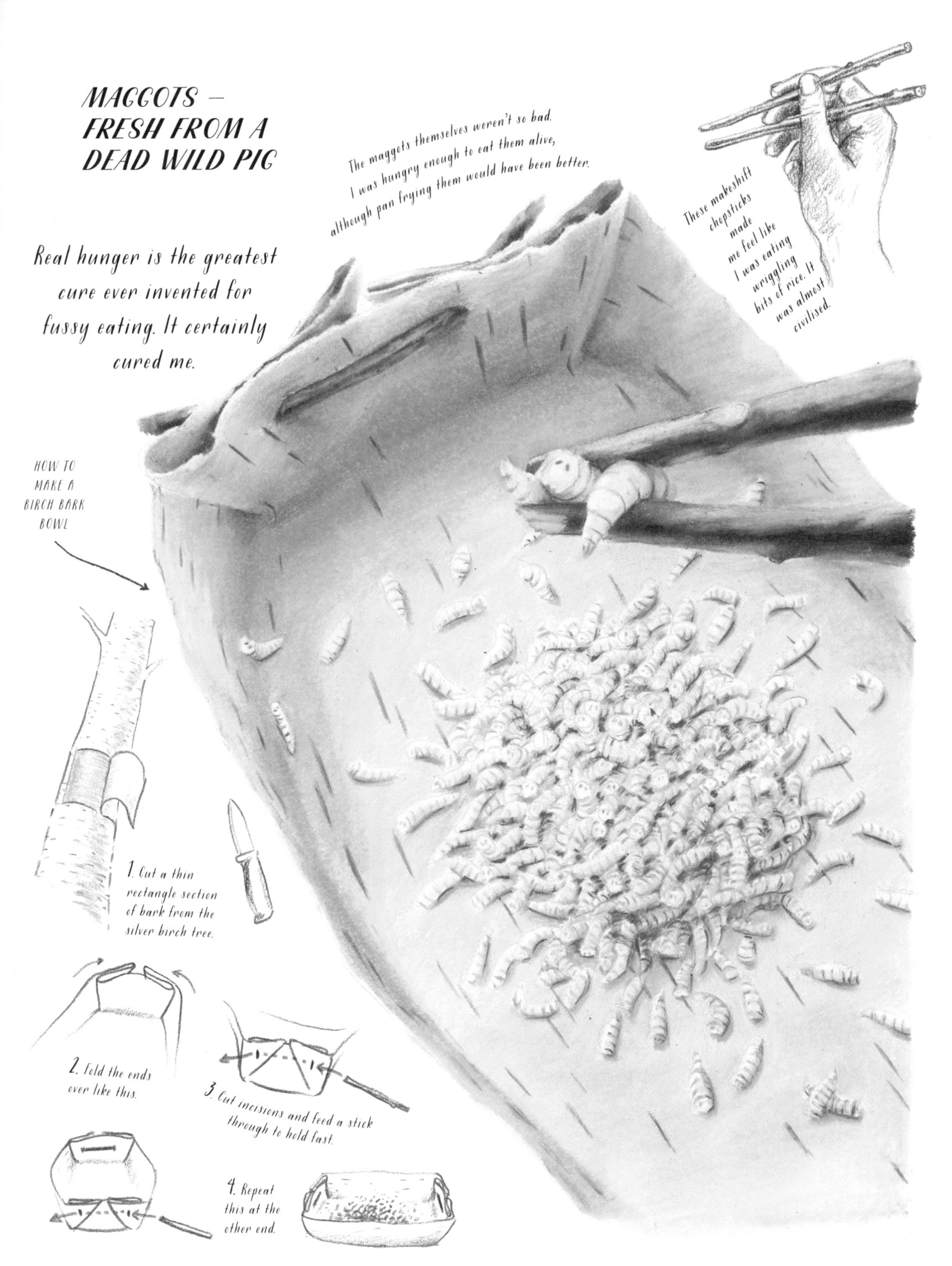
MAGGOTS –
FRESH FROM A
DEAD WILD PIG
The maggots themselves weren't so bad.
I was hungry enough to eat them alive,
although pan frying them would have been better.
These makeshift
chopsticks
made
me feel like
I was eating
wriggling
bits of rice. It
was almost
civilised.
Real hunger is the greatest
cure ever invented for
fussy eating. It certainly
cured me.
HOW TO
MAKE A
BIRCH BARK
BOWL
1. Cut a thin
rectangle section
of bark from the
silver birch tree.
2. Fold the ends
over like this.
3. Cut incisions and feed a stick
through to hold fast.
4. Repeat
this at the
other end.

POOING IN THE WILD

Here's everything you need to know when nature calls.

This is an ancient rite of passage that every adventurer must go through.

CHOOSE A GOOD LOCATION:

* Secluded and well away from footpaths and camp;
* Good supply of large-leafed trees and plants;
* Rocks and logs can be used as perches;
* At least 100m from any water source, and downstream from camp.

WIPING MATERIALS AND METHODS

Always gather wiping materials beforehand.

THINGS TO AVOID

TECHNIQUES

DISPOSAL

With a stick or trowel, dig a hole 15 cm deep before you go to the toilet.

Don't forget to wash your hands.

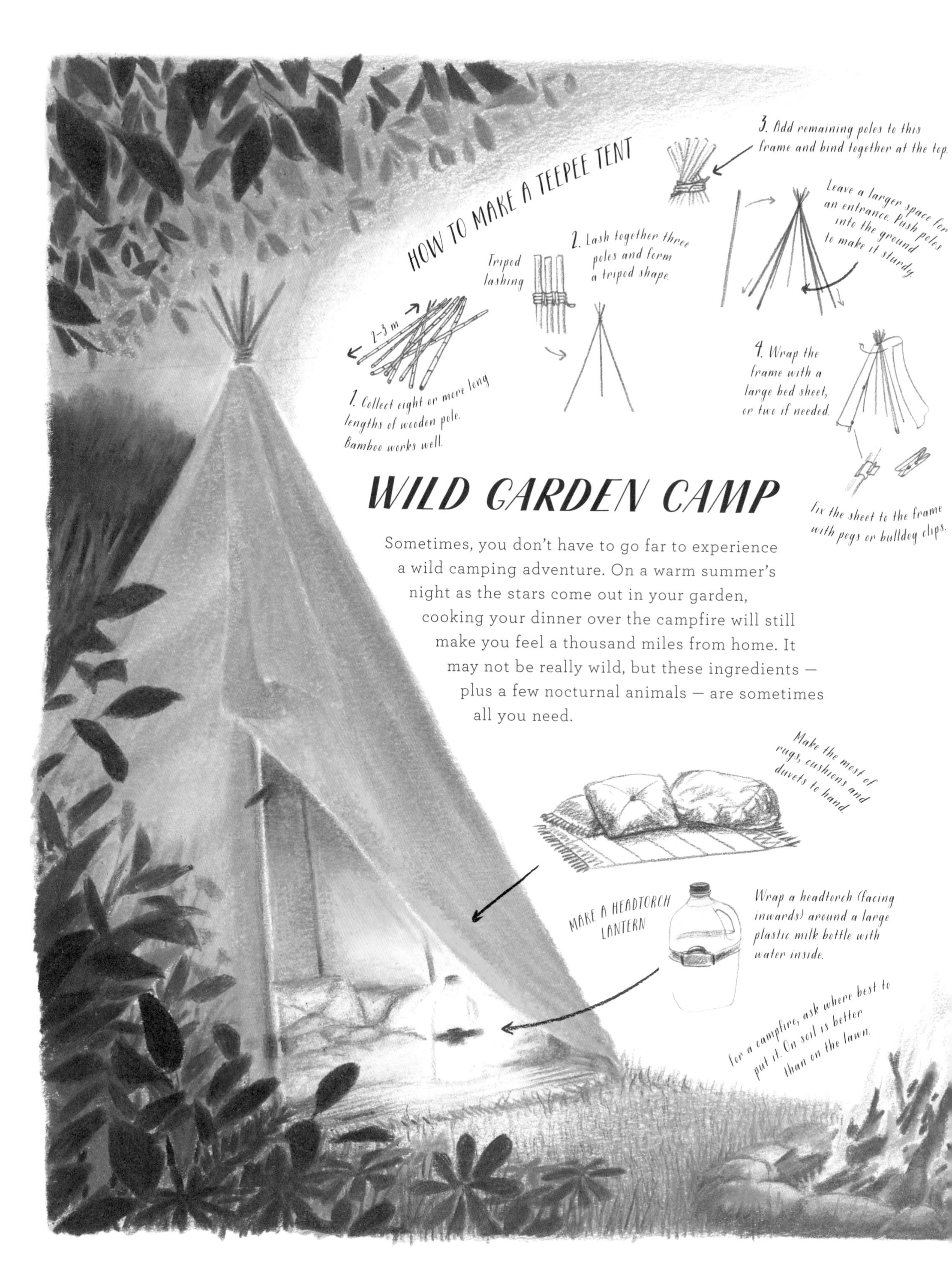

WILD GARDEN CAMP

Sometimes, you don't have to go far to experience a wild camping adventure. On a warm summer's night as the stars come out in your garden, cooking your dinner over the campfire will still make you feel a thousand miles from home. It may not be really wild, but these ingredients — plus a few nocturnal animals — are sometimes all you need.

GARDEN CAMP CHECKLIST:

* Make yourself a teepee, sleep in a hammock or put up a tent;
* Invite a friend or two to join you;
* Cook dinner over a campfire;
* Have a midnight feast;
* Make duvet sleeping bags (if you're short on real ones);
* Keep watch and listen for nocturnal animals;
* Have a cold wild shower;
* Invite the cat and dog to join you;
* Count shooting stars and explore the surface of the moon.

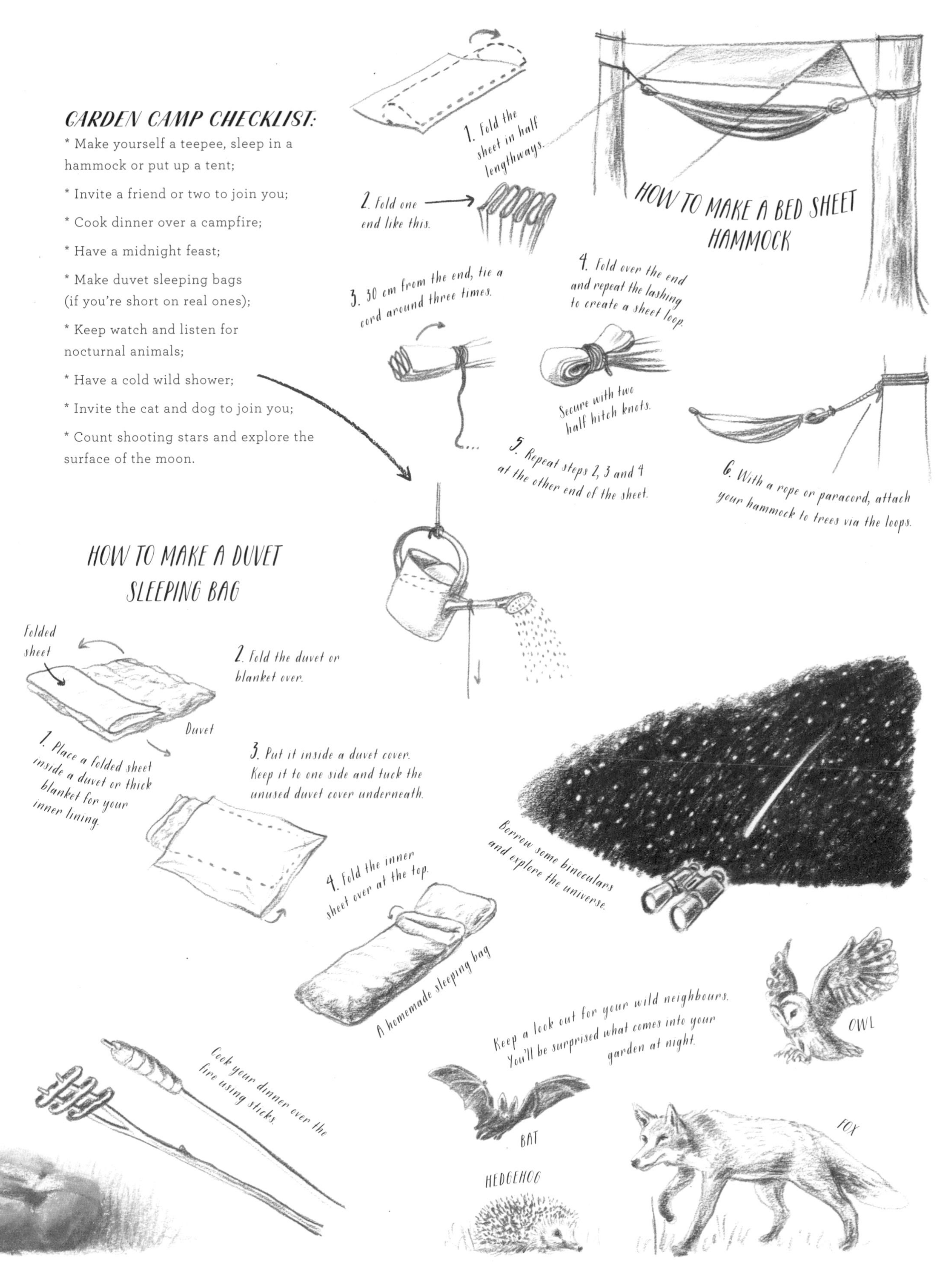

EYES IN THE DARKNESS

On my right leg there is a scar. It arcs over my thigh before criss-crossing my kneecap in a patchwork of shiny, jagged lines. This is the story of how it came to be there.

Many years ago, my sister and I had been exploring the vast and wild Okavango delta in Botswana. Although we were in big game territory we felt confident the local wildlife would let us be. As night started to fall, we set up camp and started a good fire — making sure we had enough wood to last through the night. As we settled down we heard a few noises coming out of the darkness, but nothing unexpected for this part of the world. We talked. We ate. The big night sky showed off its wonders as it always does in this region. But exhaustion soon took over. Our eyelids closed before we'd even made it to our tent.

What seemed like moments later, I woke up with a start, confused and in the darkness. For a moment I thought it was a dream then I felt the stoney ground scraping along my back and saw the dark, hunched shape of a hyena, its jaws gripped around my right leg. I could hear the excited whines of the others, their eyes glinting in the darkness. I tried to yell but nothing came out. I had gone into shock. I struggled, kicked, and punched as hard as I could but it was useless. I was being slowly dragged into the night.

Then, for a moment, the sky lit up. Out of nowhere a burning log came crashing down on the animal. It struck three times. Sparks and the smell of singed hair filled the air. Finally I felt the jaws release their grip. It was gone.

My sister hauled me back to the safety of the fire where she treated my wounds with our first aid kit and kept watch. It was a long night waiting for the sun to rise. The next day, by a stroke of luck we found an old mekoro (dug out canoe) by the river which we promptly requisitioned. Eight hours later we made it to the small town of Maun and a much needed doctor, feeling very lucky be alive.

The greatest discoveries

start with a voyage.

RAFTS

Imagine stepping onto an uncharted island where nobody has ever set foot, or exploring sunken shipwrecks beneath the waves. Imagine following a river's current as it takes you deep into wild places, where each bend uncovers a new wonder.

Of all the ways to travel in remote places, the raft is by far the most exciting. Before you begin, you need to source and scavenge your materials. Then you'll need to build it.

This is where the adventure really begins.

A pallet raft from a recent voyage along a wild estuary. We were mid-build when I drew this; the tide rose just when we needed to launch the raft.

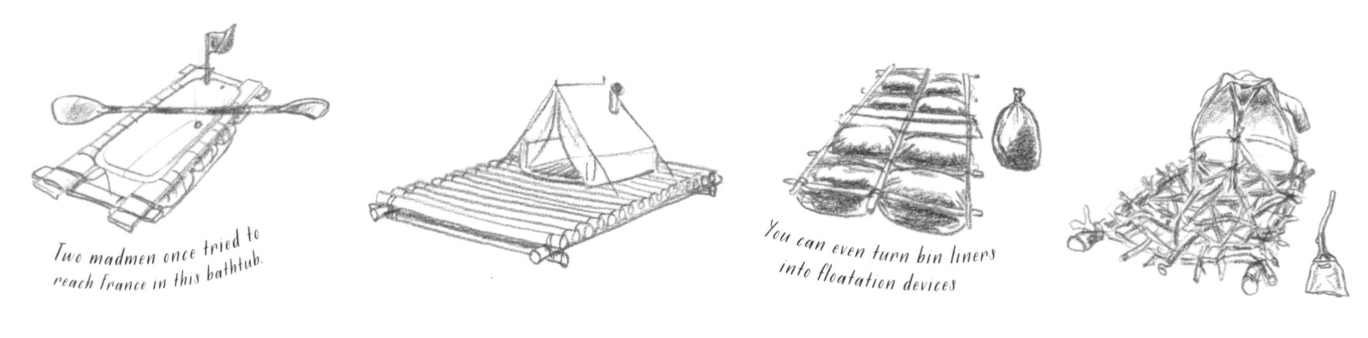

Two madmen once tried to reach France in this bathtub.

You can even turn bin liners into floatation devices

Raft: A buoyant structure of timber or other materials fastened together, used as a boat or floating platform, often in a survival situation.

THE ANATOMY OF A RAFT

The type of raft you build depends on your environment, materials and how much time you have. Many designs share common characteristics – these two examples show the essential elements for a simple structure (like the driftwood) and a more complex one (like the catamaran).

FRAME

Nearly all rafts need a strong and rigid frame. This base forms the platform which everything else can then be added to.

Rafts can be heavy. Build it next to the water unless you have the means to transport or carry it.

DRIFTWOOD RAFT

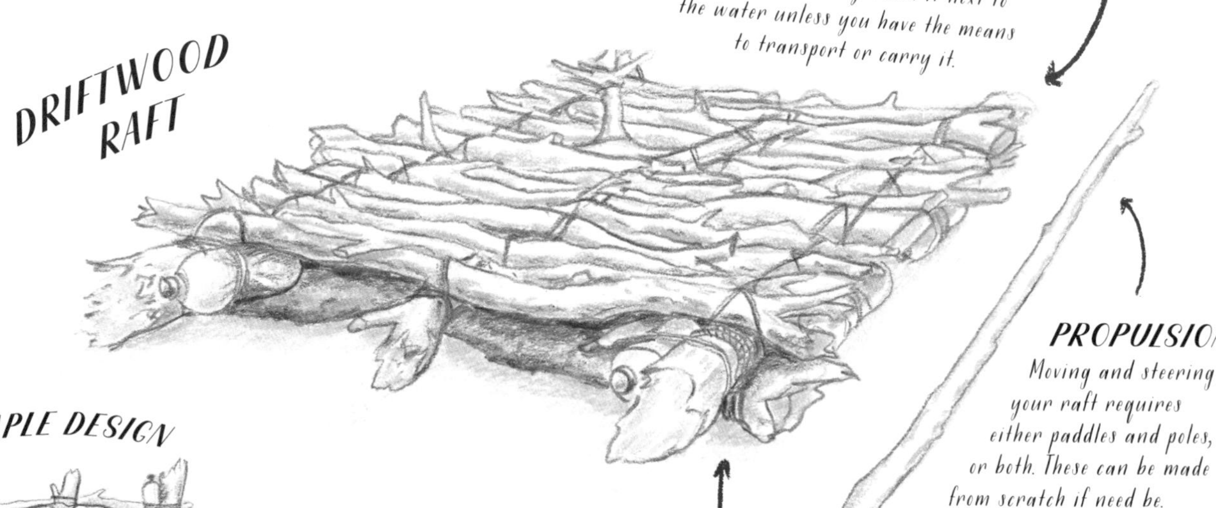

PROPULSION

Moving and steering your raft requires either paddles and poles, or both. These can be made from scratch if need be.

SIMPLE DESIGN

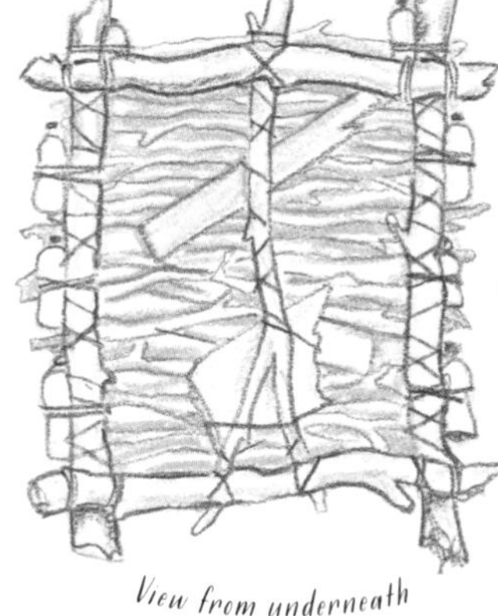

View from underneath

Working with what you have often involves making very simple designs. This driftwood raft is made from beached wood, washed-up plastic bottles and some rope.

ROPE AND KNOTS

Raft making involves fixing and lashing materials to each other. Rope and cord are ideal for this. Duct tape, bicycle inner tubes and cable ties are also useful.

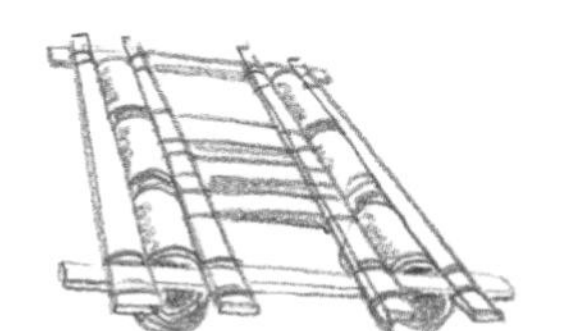

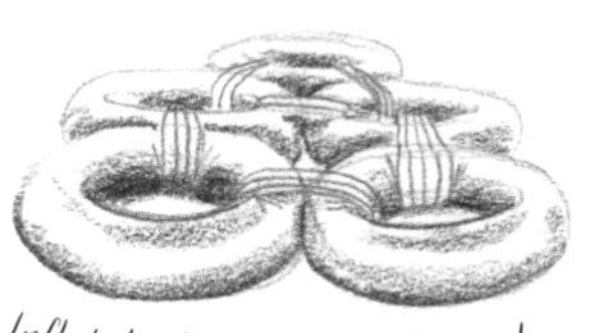

Inflated vehicle inner tubes make incredible, lightweight raft designs.

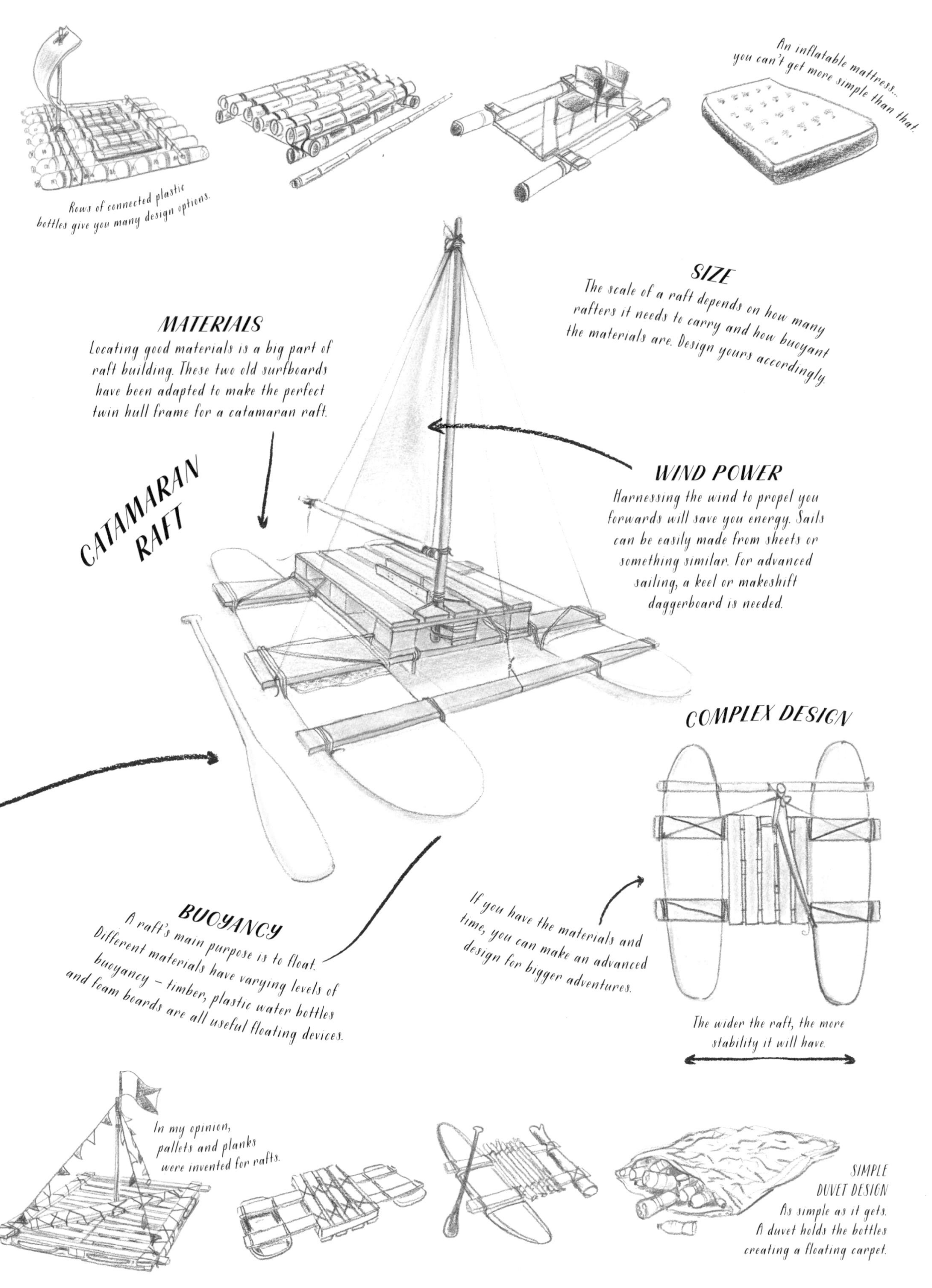
Rows of connected plastic bottles give you many design options.
An inflatable mattress... you can't get more simple than that.
SIZE
The scale of a raft depends on how many rafters it needs to carry and how buoyant the materials are. Design yours accordingly.
MATERIALS
Locating good materials is a big part of raft building. These two old surfboards have been adapted to make the perfect twin hull frame for a catamaran raft.
CATAMARAN RAFT
WIND POWER
Harnessing the wind to propel you forwards will save you energy. Sails can be easily made from sheets or something similar. For advanced sailing, a keel or makeshift daggerboard is needed.
COMPLEX DESIGN
BUOYANCY
A raft's main purpose is to float. Different materials have varying levels of buoyancy – timber, plastic water bottles and foam boards are all useful floating devices.
If you have the materials and time, you can make an advanced design for bigger adventures.
The wider the raft, the more stability it will have.
In my opinion, pallets and planks were invented for rafts.
SIMPLE DUVET DESIGN
As simple as it gets. A duvet holds the bottles creating a floating carpet.

RAFT INGREDIENTS

These materials are the ingredients of your raft. Some are like gold dust — others, like plastic bottles, are more common. Unless you are in a real survival situation, take time to track down and gather your ingredients. What you unearth will inspire the raft you push out into water.

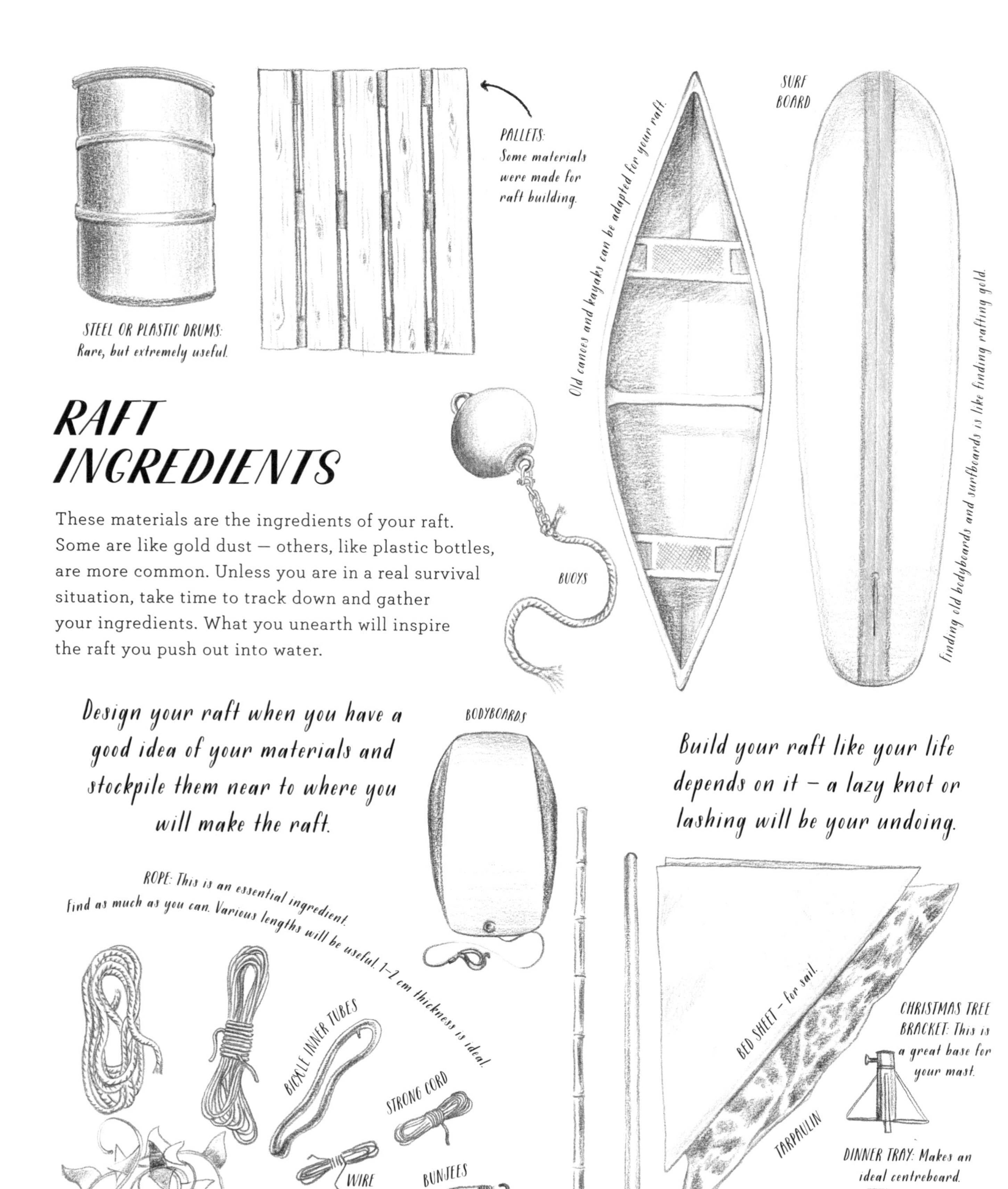

Design your raft when you have a good idea of your materials and stockpile them near to where you will make the raft.

Build your raft like your life depends on it – a lazy knot or lashing will be your undoing.

Remember, you can never have too much rope.

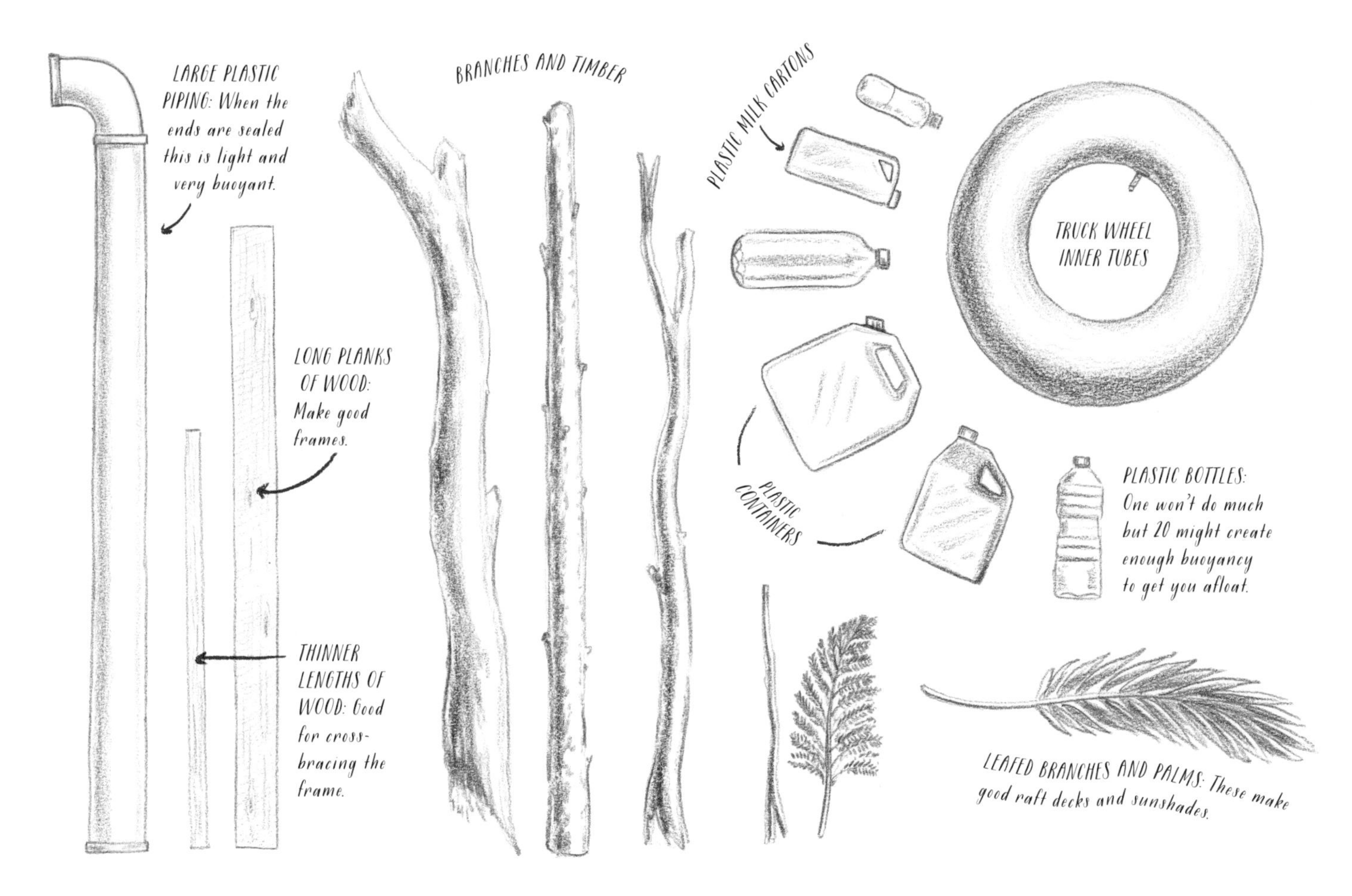

Here are the makings of a million rafts... imagine what you could build with all this.

KIT ESSENTIALS

On tidal waters make sure you have a tide timetable.

When you are planning an expedition, pack your food and supplies in a waterproof container or dry bag.

RAFTING

There are three ways to travel by raft: paddling, punting and sailing. You can also drift your raft along with the current, but you will still need paddles or poles to manoeuvre it.

Being able to propel and steer your raft is important — you always need confidence that you can reach safety. That's why you should always have paddles and poles on board. Bear in mind that your raft may be heavy and unwieldy so you'll need at least two paddlers.

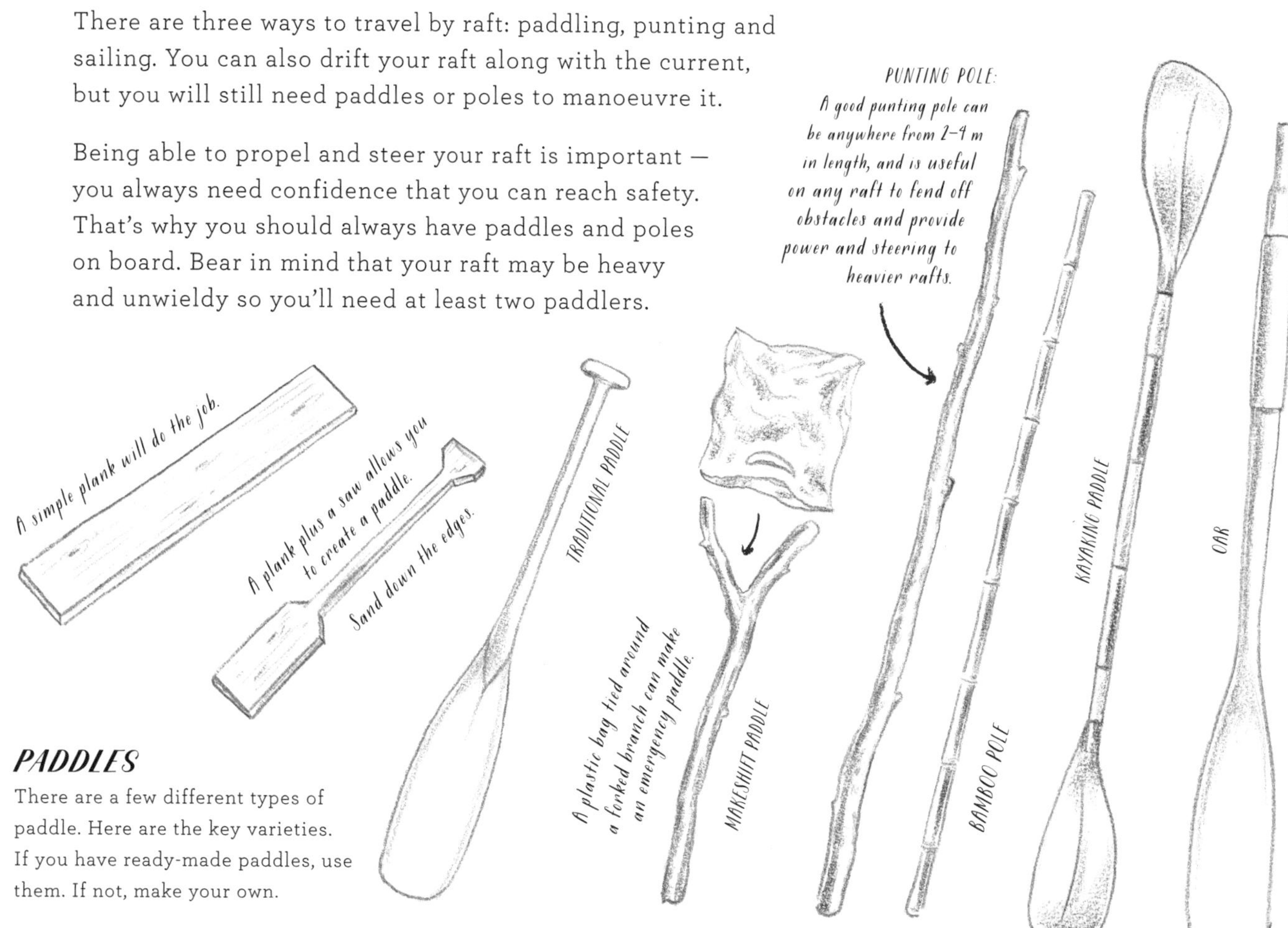

PADDLES

There are a few different types of paddle. Here are the key varieties. If you have ready-made paddles, use them. If not, make your own.

On land: left and right; on water: port and starboard.

PADDLING

Most rafts will be propelled from opposing sides by different paddlers. You can either sit down or try kneeling on one or two knees for stronger strokes. Avoid standing up at any point whilst on a raft (unless it is required).

PADDLE TECHNIQUE

For the forward stroke, dip your paddle in front of you and pull back towards you, with your hands roughly an arm's length apart.

TIP: Kneel on foam or another suitable material to protect your knees.

GOING FORWARDS

Paddlers on both sides need to find a rhythm that keeps the raft going straight.

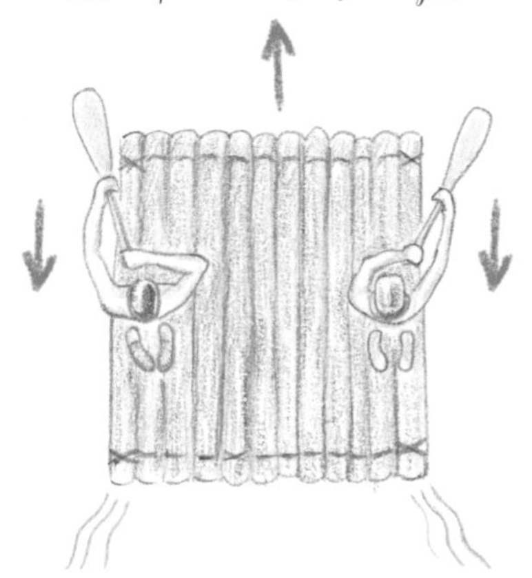

STEERING YOUR RAFT

Here the raft is turning to port (left).

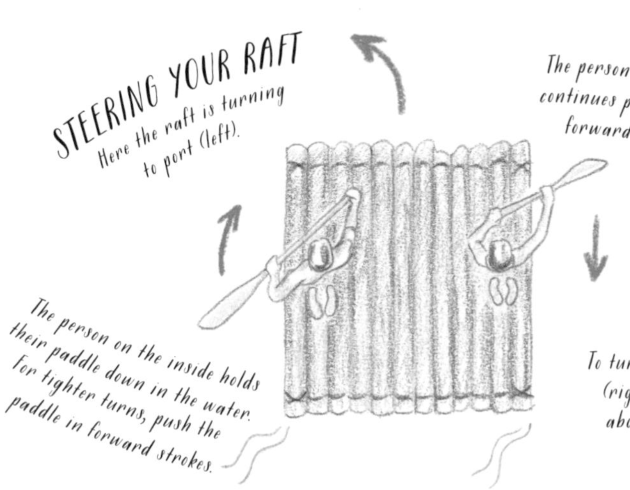

The person on the outside continues paddling with forward strokes.

The person on the inside holds their paddle down in the water. For tighter turns, push the paddle in forward strokes.

To turn to starboard (right), swap the above procedure.

USING THE PADDLE AS A RUDDER

A paddle can be used like a rudder on rivers to steer the raft. This is useful if there are three or more rafters.

Hold the paddle firmly in position on the side you wish to turn to.

Keep the paddle blade edge-side up in the water.

POSITION

The punter is normally positioned towards the back of the raft. If more than one, take a side each.

Keep your hands an arm's length apart and push the pole down to the ground.

Experienced rafters often punt standing up.

PUNTING

Punting is the means of using a long pole or length of wood to push down and propel your raft. This is most useful for canals and water where you're no deeper than the length of your pole. Always have back-up paddles on board in case you lose your pole or enter deep water.

Beware of getting your pole stuck in the mud or riverbed. If possible, connect the pole to the raft with a length of cord.

Then lean on the pole and push backwards away from the direction of travel. Use your bodyweight to gain more power.

If there's a breeze why not add a sail to your raft.

SAILING

Imagine feeling the invisible power of the wind drive you through water with nothing more than a sail you've cobbled together from a wooden stick, a bed sheet and some string. You may not go fast or be able to tack into the wind, but you've used your brain to harness nature's energy. This is sailing at its elemental best.

Making a sail doesn't need to be complicated and it can let you put your feet up and rest your paddle arms. Try a simple design first. Get used to how it affects your raft. Here, I've laid out the basics of raft sailing, from a simple design to something more advanced.

YOU WILL NEED

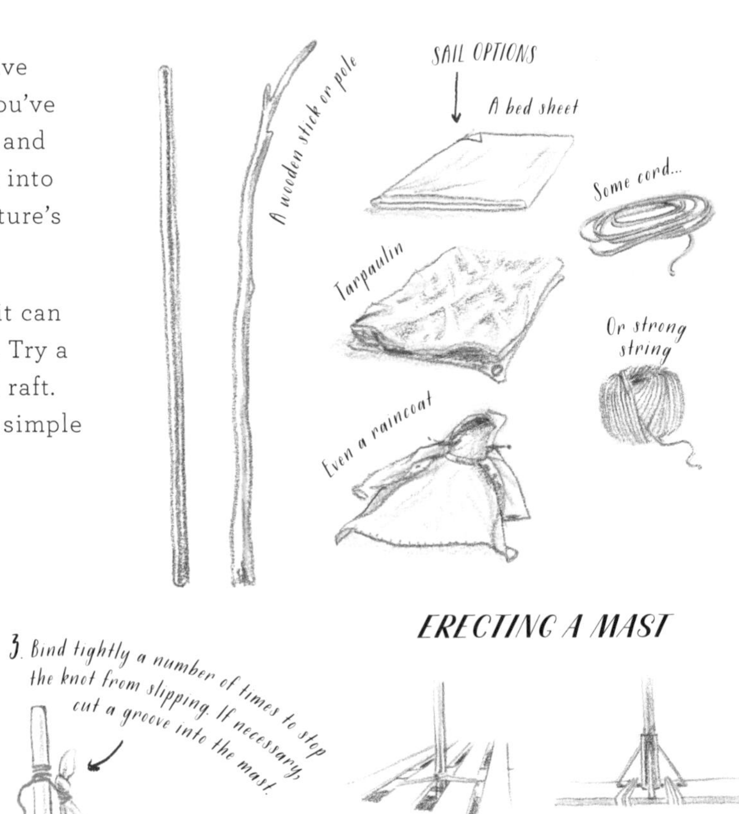

SIMPLE MAINSAIL

You can use any suitably-sized fabric to catch the wind. Here a bed sheet has been cut into a triangle.

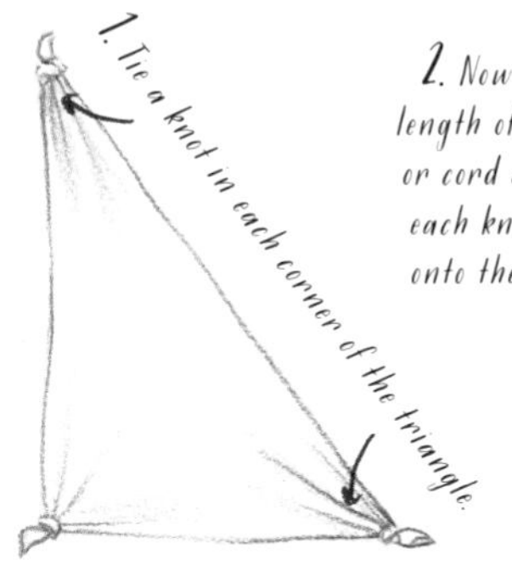

1. Tie a knot in each corner of the triangle.
2. Now tie a length of string or cord around each knot and onto the mast.
3. Bind tightly a number of times to stop the knot from slipping. If necessary, cut a groove into the mast.
4. Tie a long length of cord to the outer corner of your sail. Tie this down towards the back of your raft, pulling the sail taut.

TIP: A boom will help your sail keep its shape

ERECTING A MAST

1. Wedge the mast as best you can into a point along the centre of the raft towards the front and lash it to the frame.
2. If you have some kind of bracket, this can be a good support base. Lash it down well.

3. Attach three lengths of cord to the top of the mast and tie down each to the edges of the raft so that the mast stands firmly upright.

BOOMS

1. Simply roll up a suitable length of thin wood into the bottom of the sail, leaving the knots poking out.

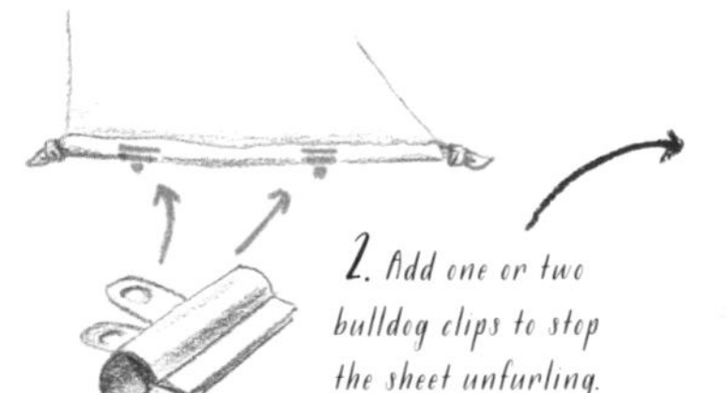

2. Add one or two bulldog clips to stop the sheet unfurling.
3. Tie to the mast as per the mainsail instructions.

SAILING LAW:

* Left = port; right = starboard;
* A sailing vessel has right of way over a motor-powered vessel but don't assume you have been seen;
* Oncoming vessels pass each other portside to portside.

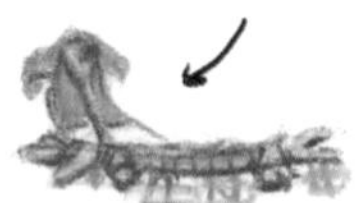

A daggerboard is a removeable board that slots vertically into the raft to stop sideways movement when you're sailing.

RUDDERS AND DAGGERBOARDS

A simple sail will allow you to travel in the direction that the wind is blowing. By adding a daggerboard or keel you will have more control of where your raft is heading.

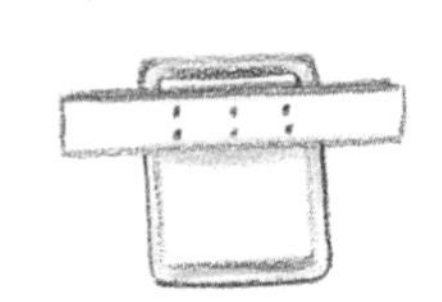

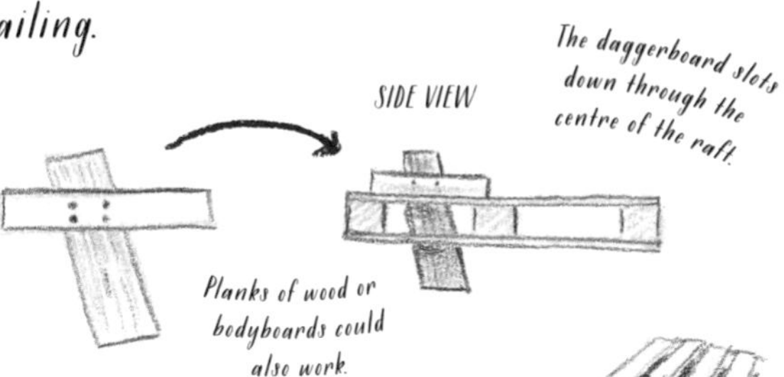

Remember to remove the daggerboard when you enter shallow water.

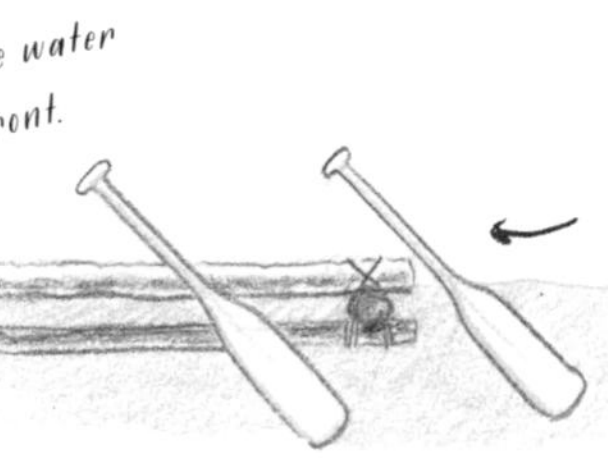

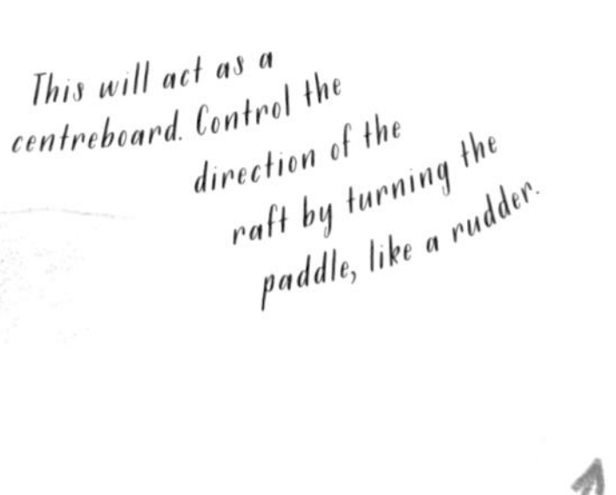

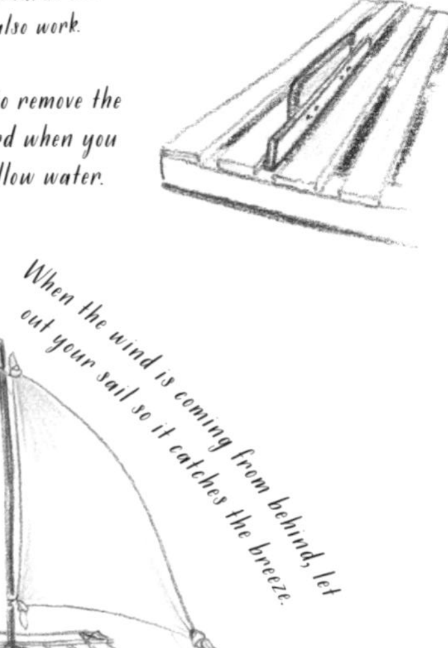

When it's not in use or you're paddling into the wind, wrap the sail around the mast and tie it in place with a hitch knot. Alternatively, keep your sail in line with the wind.

SAILING TECHNIQUE

Set your sail to catch the wind. Move the loose end of rope to do this. Once you're in a good position, tie it down or hold on to it. You can adjust the sail as needed during your journey.

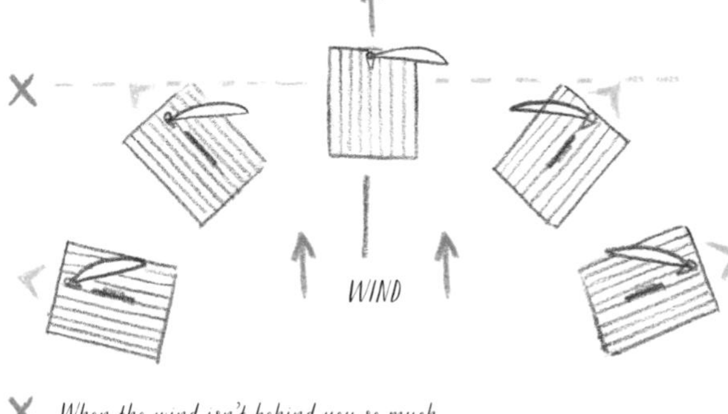

✕ *When the wind isn't behind you so much, a daggerboard is needed.*

I spotted this adventurer on a Pacific wave in her outrigger, harnessing Mother Nature.

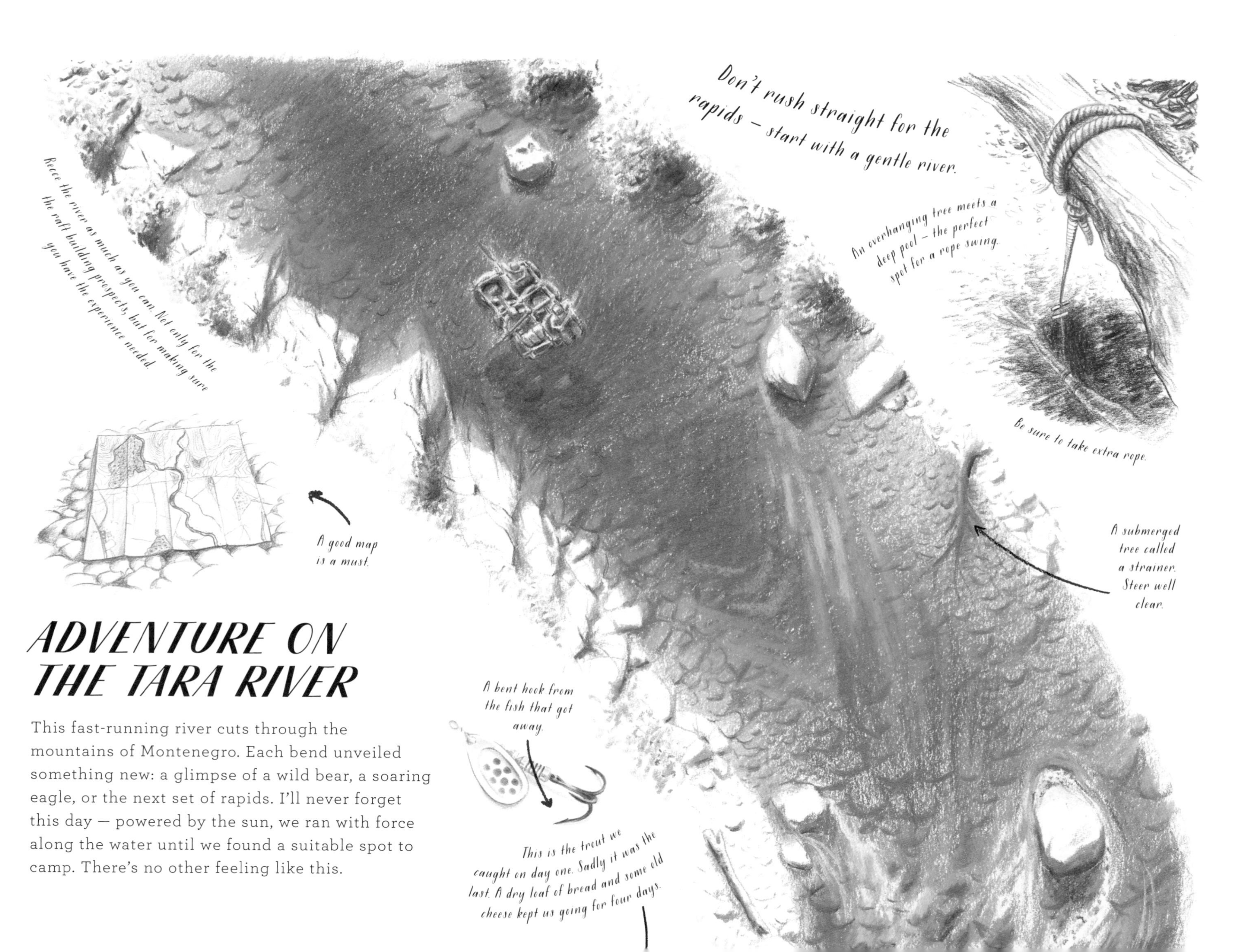

ADVENTURE ON THE TARA RIVER

This fast-running river cuts through the mountains of Montenegro. Each bend unveiled something new: a glimpse of a wild bear, a soaring eagle, or the next set of rapids. I'll never forget this day – powered by the sun, we ran with force along the water until we found a suitable spot to camp. There's no other feeling like this.

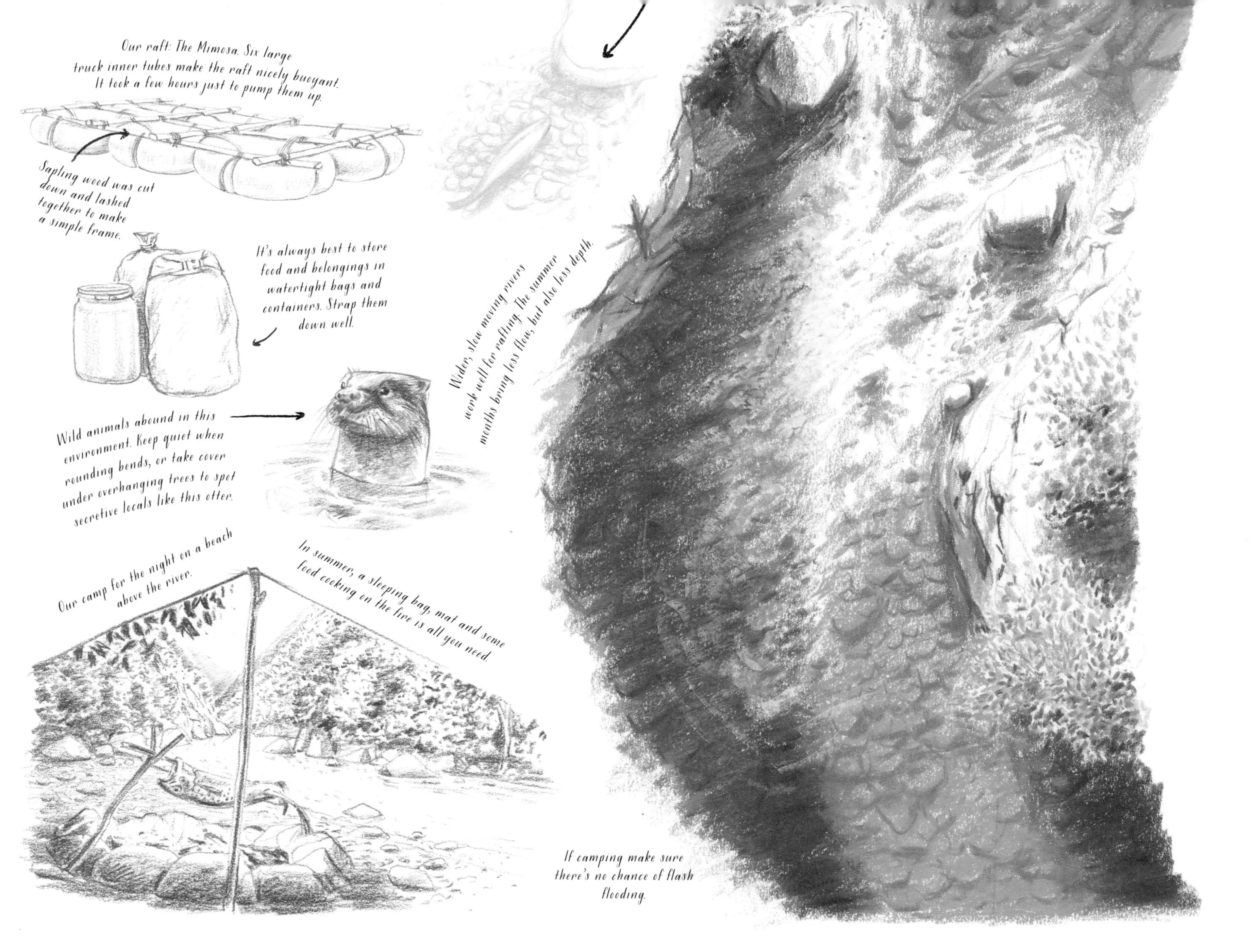
Our raft: The Mimosa. Six large truck inner tubes make the raft nicely buoyant. It took a few hours just to pump them up.
Sapling wood was cut down and lashed together to make a simple frame.
It's always best to store food and belongings in watertight bags and containers. Strap them down well.
Wild animals abound in this environment. Keep quiet when rounding bends, or take cover under overhanging trees to spot secretive locals like this otter.
Wider, slow moving rivers work well for rafting. The summer months bring less flow, but also less depth.
Our camp for the night on a beach above the river.
In summer, a sleeping bag, mat and some food cooking on the fire is all you need.
If camping make sure there's no chance of flash flooding.

SECRET ISLAND EXPEDITION

I've always been fond of lake exploration. Here in the remote north-east American wilderness we were enveloped by the morning mist. As we drew closer the island revealed itself. Huge boulders and ancient pine trees loomed over us creating a secret fortress, keeping out all but intrepid souls.

There are many lakes and islands out there waiting to be explored. Look at local maps. Do some research. You'll find something, and if you can't find any islands, you can explore the lake shore and river inlets or find a way to make a lake crossing.

As there are often woods near the lake shore I've included a log raft design to inspire you.

Build close to the water's edge, you don't want to be dragging a big raft.

TOOLS YOU WILL NEED

THE LOG RAFT

This is a classic raft design ideal for environments where wood is easily available. This example is made with pine wood, but it can work with most other wood as well as driftwood, which is useful if you don't have an axe or saw. Log rafts are heavy, so make use of available adults.

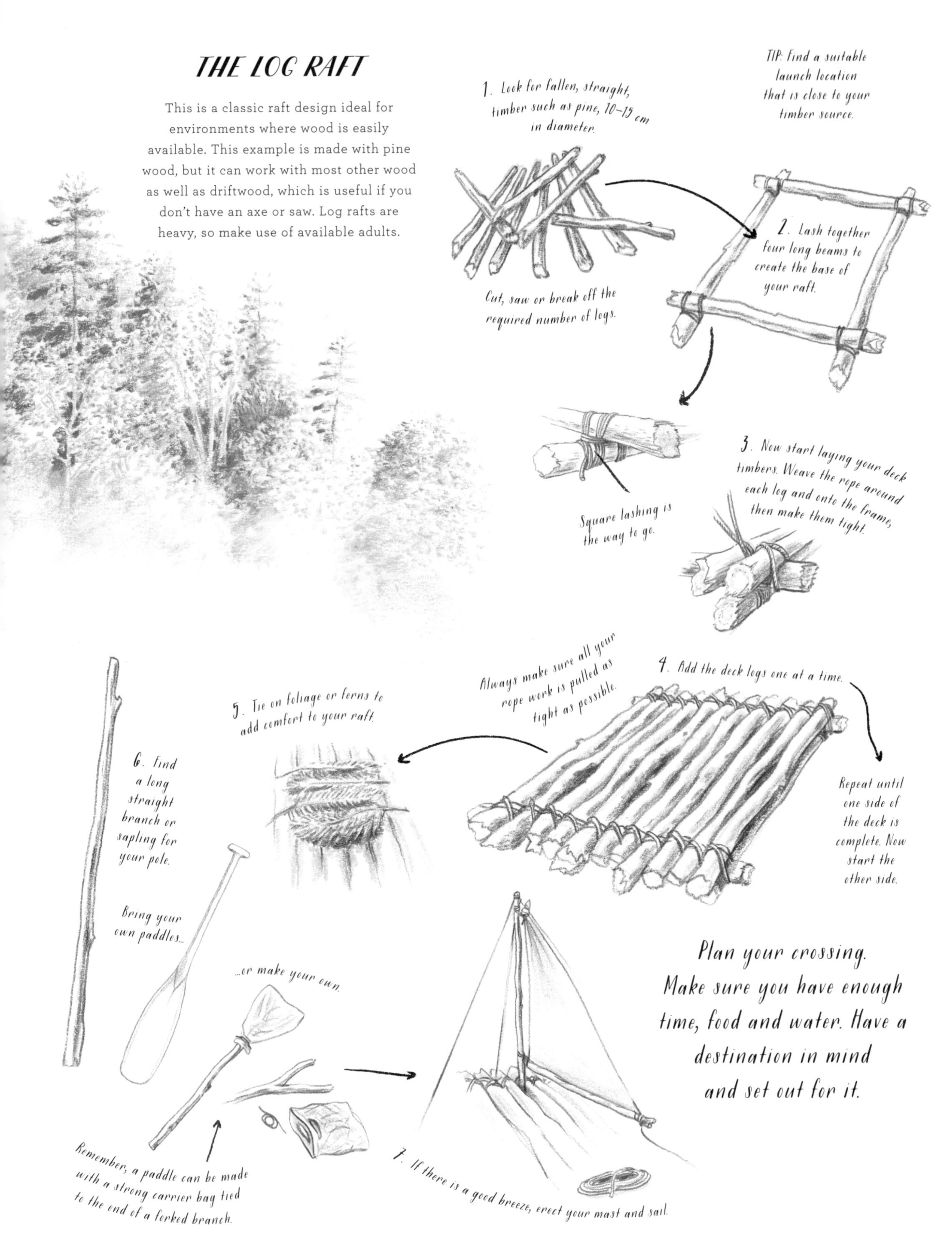

SHIPWRECK EXPEDITION

On this expedition, we caught the incoming tide up the estuary to a shipwreck. Our raft was made of pallets lashed together with planks and other materials. It was slow and heavy, but it made the perfect platform from which to explore the submerged vessel with snorkels and fins. As the tide turned, we caught the current back with a bounty of freshly-foraged mussels, and stories of sunken ships.

Your raft will take you on incredible adventures like this. Travel on it in safe, sheltered bays, where you can explore the underwater realm or rock climb on rocky ledges. In estuaries, use the currents to your advantage and venture along creeks.

Sea caves are often dotted around the coast. Many were once used as smuggler's dens. No doubt some still hold various treasures.

Work your design around what pallets and materials you have.

As there are risks in this environment, you should always take an experienced adult with you who knows the water.

Do your research on shipwrecks. Find one that is close to shore and go and explore.

THE PALLET RAFT

Pallets make good rafts if you can find them. By adding bottles, foam boards and other buoyancy, you will have a good platform. Lashing longer lengths of wood on top creates the rigid frame needed.

WHAT YOU'LL NEED:

* Pallets – as a guide, you'll need roughly two per adult;
* Four or five long pieces of wood (scaffolding planks and decking were used here) for the main frame;
* A pole for the mast;
* As much floating material as you can find;
* Plenty of rope for lashing;
* Large cable ties are also handy.

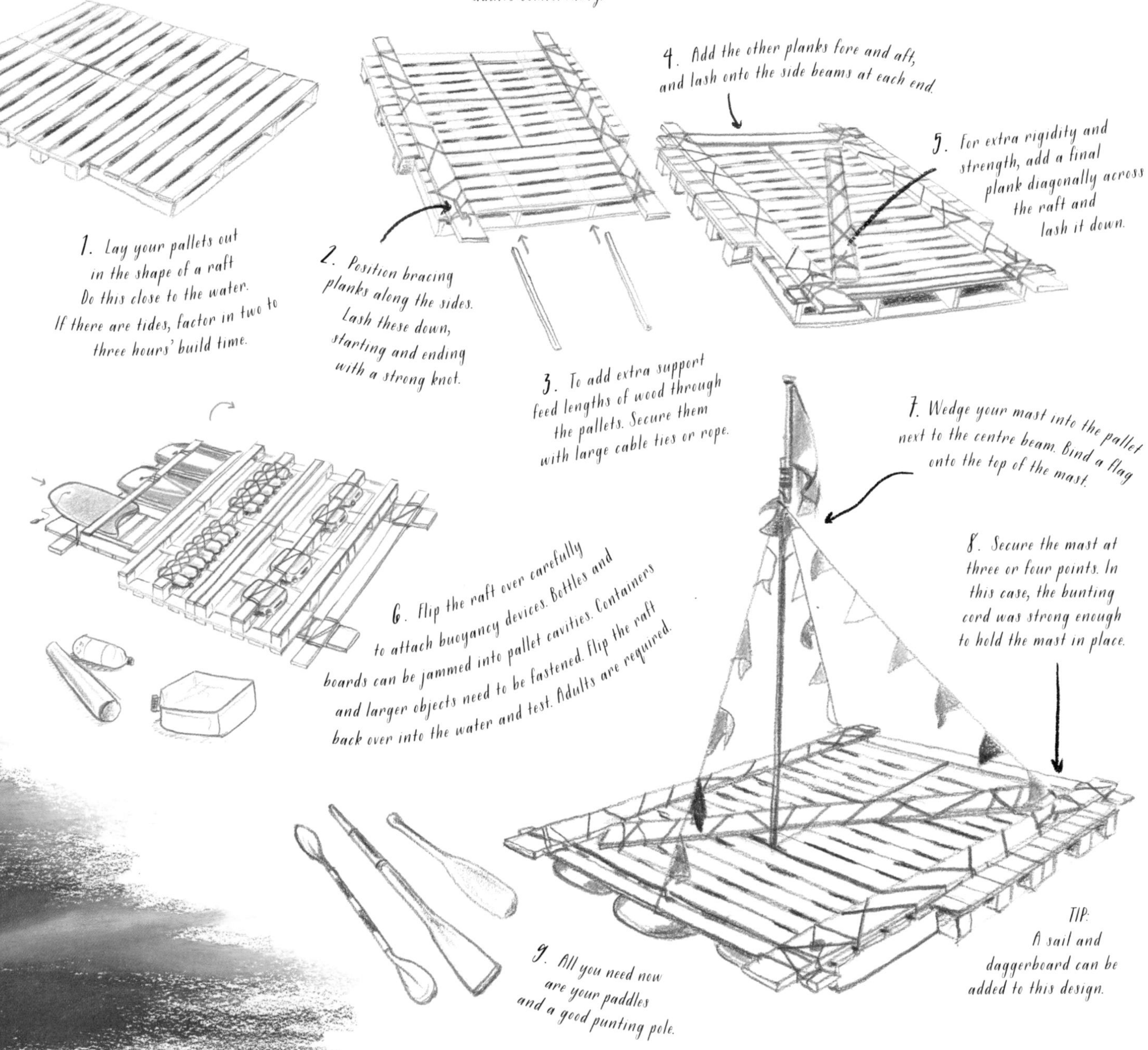

YOU WILL NEED

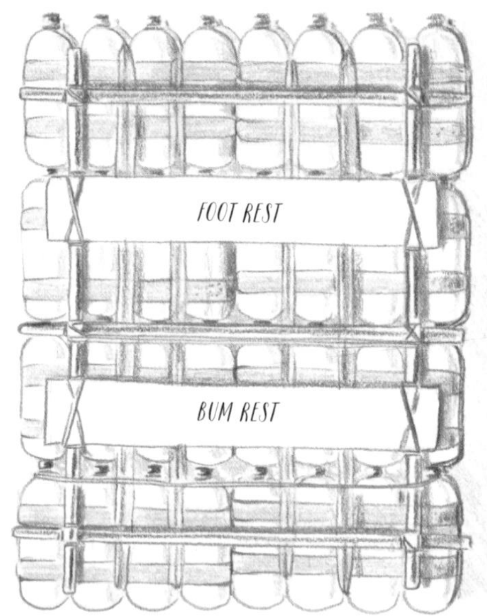

This raft was made from a total of 64 bottles, and suited one small paddler.

PADDLEBOARD RAFT

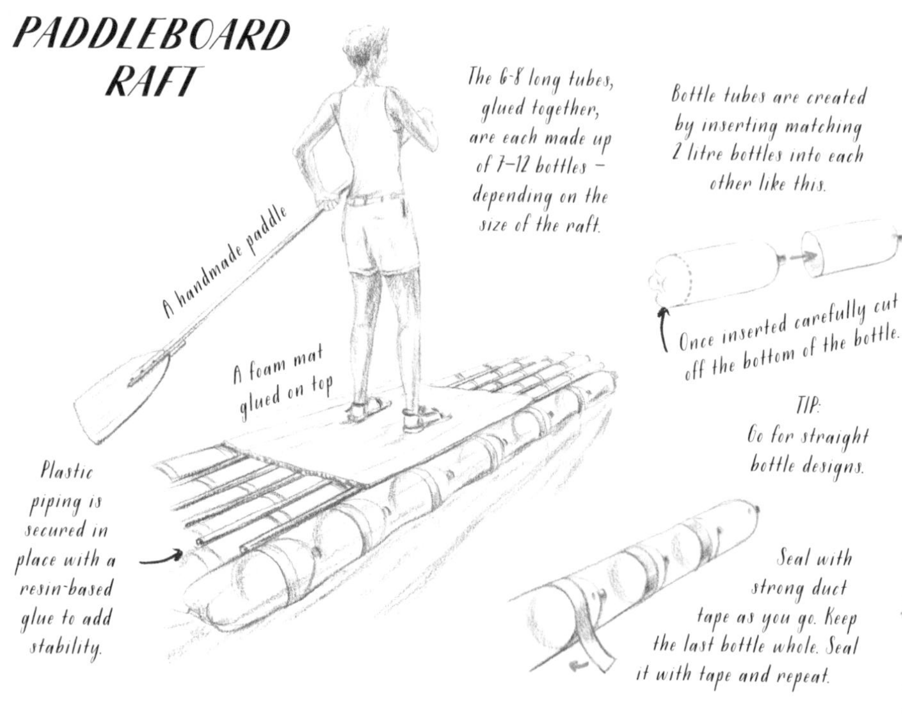

GREAT CANAL JOURNEY

Cities may seem far away from wild places, but try exploring one by raft. This canal journey passed straight through London Zoo. Here, in the heart of this great city, I was surrounded by the familiar noises of the jungle. The macaws squawked, the monkeys chattered and I thought I heard a lion roar. Gliding through the morning mist in one of the world's biggest cities, I felt at home.

If you can get to a canal, do so. Navigating the ancient waterways through secretive cities or exploring the wild landscapes of the countryside is special. Due to their slow and shallow waters, canals are ideal for paddling and punting on something that is lightweight — like these bottle rafts.

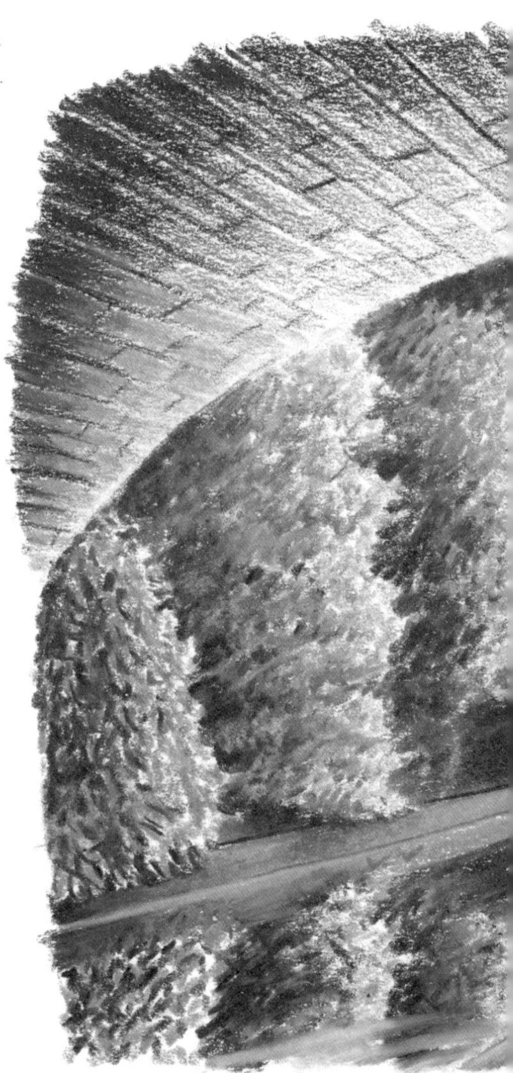

HOW TO MAKE A BOTTLE RAFT

Paddle boarding down the Regent's Canal, London

If you're going rafting, chances are you're going swimming.

WILD SWIMMING

Stepping into the water – be it lake, river or ocean – is like stepping into the wild kingdom. You are completely in its embrace and it feels magical.

ADVENTURERS KNOW THIS:

* Always swim with an experienced adult;
* Only swim in water you would consider easy;
* Wear a life vest or jacket if needed;
* Always check where you are swimming is safe;
* Don't swim in fast currents;
* Never jump into murky water;
* Don't go swimming alone.

REMINISCENCES OF A VERY LUCKY ESCAPE

EXPEDITION TO SRI LANKA, APRIL 10TH

I've had a lucky escape today.

Yesterday whilst hunting, I stumbled upon a beautiful lake about two hours walk into the jungle. I noticed a good variety of animal life – including geese on the far side of the lake. I hadn't eaten for a couple of days and badly needed to stock up on food supplies. The only way to reach them was to cross the water.

Back at camp I set about designing a raft. By a stroke of luck, there was an old, single engined, float plane nearby, long past its flying days. I managed to cut away one of the floats that made a good canoe-like hull for an outrigger raft. My plan was to drag the float through the jungle – storing my machete, rope and provisions inside – and build the raft at the water's edge.

I set out this morning just as the silhouettes of the trees appeared from the darkness. After removing a number of leeches (that had hitched a ride through the jungle) I proceeded to cut some good bamboo lengths for the raft, which I lashed to the float. A suitable palm log completed the outrigger design, and the stem of a palm frond made a half decent paddle. I scanned the far side of the lake with my binoculars. Crocodiles. About 200 metres away lay about six of them, their beady eyes bobbing above the water's edge. They seemed subdued enough... and I was really quite hungry.

I stepped carefully into the raft to test its buoyancy then started paddling out into the open water.

Things started to go wrong about 300 meters from the shore. The main float started taking on water – the jungle trek had obviously taken its toll on the fibreglass. This was not part of the plan. I picked my gear from the water-filled hull and started paddling back to shore with some urgency. Within a minute the crack had opened up.

One of the crocodiles on the lake shore.

I wasn't going to make it. I abandoned ship and swam towards a nearby tree, reaching up out of the water. It must have been quite a sight – me perched on a branch, stranded, scared stiff and feeling pretty stupid. I took a deep breath and lowered myself into the water – all my senses were now in survival mode. My only focus was the lake shore.

After a minute, something brushed my stomach. My whole body clenched up. Then something caught hold of my foot. I pulled hard but it wouldn't let go. I looked beneath the surface expecting the worst. But rather than a crocodile, my foot was knotted in some long, rope-like weeds. After a few breaths I swam down and managed to free myself by removing my jungle boot. For the next four minutes I got caught again and again. I then noticed that the blood from the leech wounds was filling the water. Surely the crocodiles were circling now.

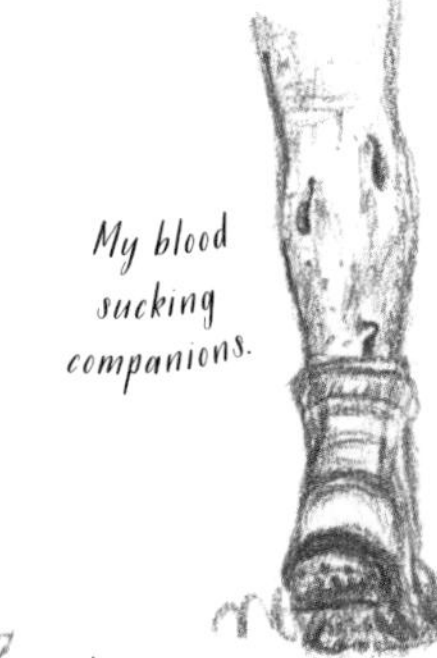

My blood sucking companions.

I held my breath and swam for my life, thinking only of reaching the safety of the shore. Finally, as I lay on the sand breathing heavily, I looked out across the lake. A dark shape moved along the water where I had just been.

This had been a case of the hunter becoming the hunted.

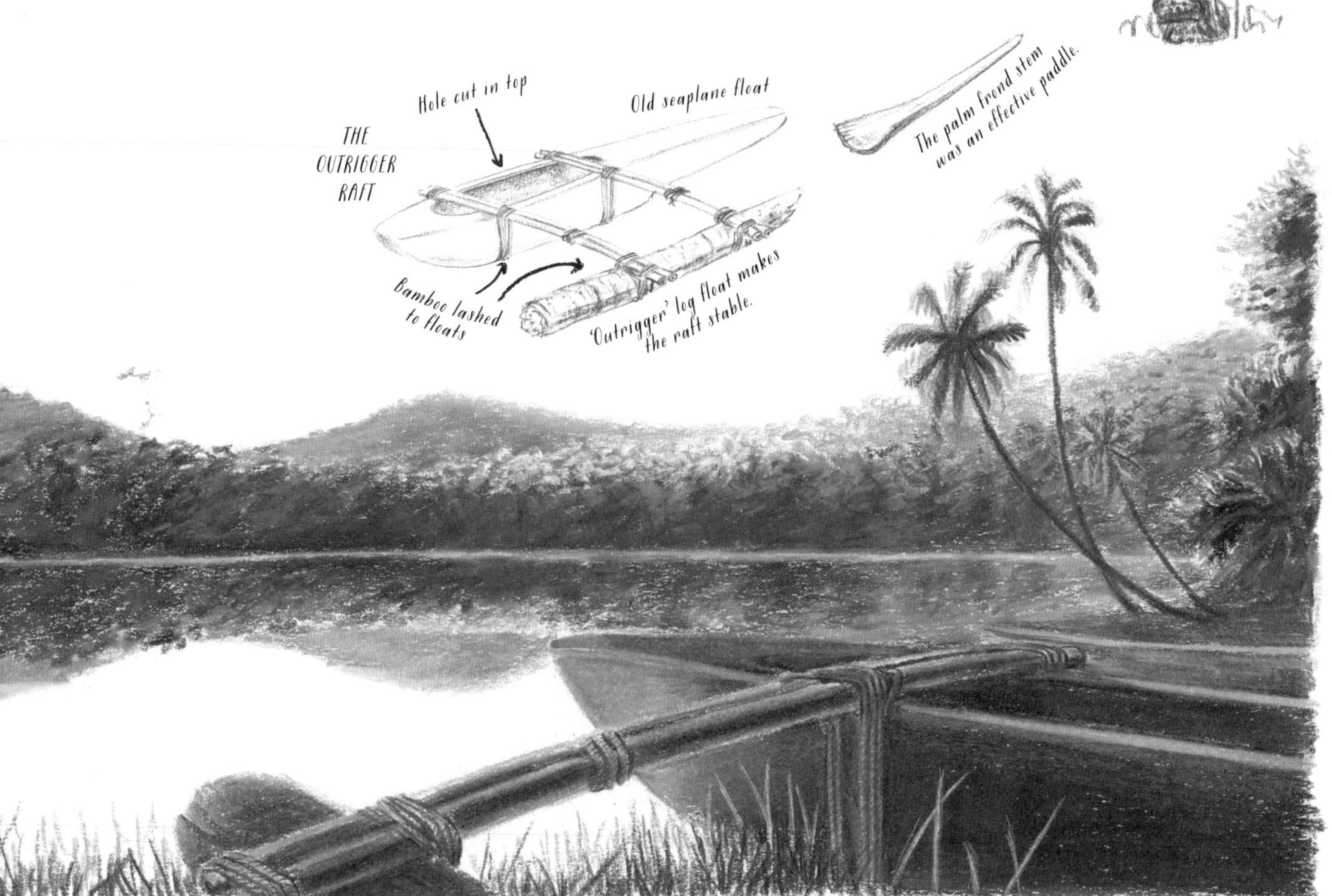

Where
there's shelter,
there's home.

SHELTERS, DENS AND TREEHOUSES

Imagine building a shelter with your bare hands.

With every interlocking branch and layered stick, you harness the power of nature and make it your own.

With a shelter, anything can be tamed: raging storms, wild animals, immense cold or heat.

You may need a shelter for a survival situation – maybe you're lost in the forest or shipwrecked – or you may need it for something more permanent, like a hideout or treehouse. In each instance, you're creating your own private kingdom – a skill every adventurer must know.

For what it's worth, here's a lifetime of shelter-building knowledge – now it is yours.

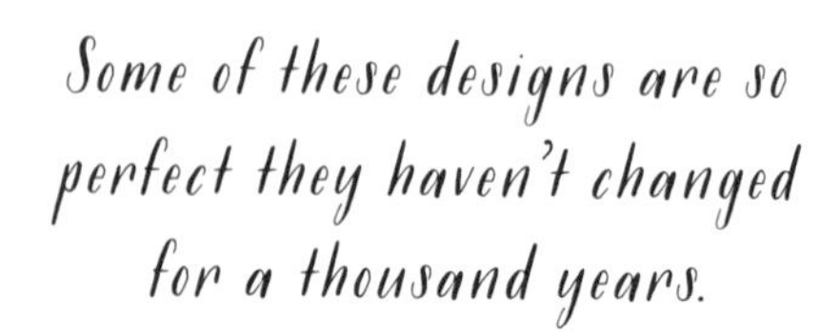

Some of these designs are so perfect they haven't changed for a thousand years.

SNOW HUTS

Crawling into an Inuit igloo in the far north. Snow is one of the best building materials to be found and is surprisingly warm. With just a saw, an experienced builder can erect one in an hour... although it took me considerably longer.

An abandoned whalebone shelter I came across in Alaska. These were made by the Tikigaq people up until quite recently. The whalebone walls and roof were covered in earth and grass for insulation – an ancient design that dates back thousands of years.

WHALEBONE SHELTERS

TENTS OF THE SAHARA

A Bedouin-style tent is perfectly suited to the hot desert. It can be neatly packed on the back of a camel when the time comes to move on.

FLOATING ISLANDS

Strong totora reeds are woven into thick platforms that can be moved around the lake or moored to the lake bed.

Even the boats are made entirely out of reeds.

In the high Andes mountains in South America lays Lake Titicaca. On its deep waters are the Uru people's incredible floating houses made from the local reeds.

These homes are completely sustainable – they work with the planet, not against it.

MEET THE MAKERS

Here are a few of the shelters and homes I've come across on my travels among indigenous and nomadic peoples. Even though they may look different, they share similar thinking. Each is handmade from local materials and is perfectly suited to the needs of its makers. They are a masterclass in ingenuity and resourcefulness. Let them – and their architects – inspire you.

JUNGLE SHELTER

This is a simple shelter I came across in the Amazon, most likely built by an uncontacted tribe. It was beautifully simple – just a few palm fronds stuck into the ground.

A Nenet reindeer herder posing in front of his chum (pronounced 'choom').
Reindeer skins are sewn together to make a warm and tough covering for the tent.
TEEPEES AND CHUMS
Tent designs travelled around the world as humans migrated across the planet. They were perfect for nomadic peoples who needed to travel between pastures with their herds of animals, or to new hunting grounds.
A great shelter speaks the language of its environment.
TREEHOUSES
Deep in the Papuan rainforests live the Korowai, who have mastered the art of treehouse building and push architecture to the limit.
GERS AND YURTS
A ger on the remote Mongolian Plateau. These large and friendly homes exist across central Asia and have been a welcoming sight on a few adventures. The walls are latticed wood that can be folded up. Rope holds down the canvas or animal skin roof.
STILT HOUSES
I've come across a few stilt houses around the world, but the ones off the coast of Malaysia are unique. They belong to the Sama-Bajau, a people who have migrated from the Philippines and brought their seaborne lifestyle with them.

TAKING SHELTER: MEMORIES FROM SIBERIA TO PAPUA

Caught in a snow storm deep in the Arctic Circle – one of the rare occasions when digging has made a problem better.

Every shelter has its own character, moulded by the materials and climate of its environment. The hot humid jungle is no exception.

Building materials come in all shapes and sizes. In this case, I stumbled across the skeleton of a North Atlantic right whale on the Alaskan peninsula. People have used whale bone as a shelter building material for thousands of years.

A SHELTER TO SURVIVE

You rarely plan a real survival shelter. It's more likely to just happen, which is why you should sharpen your skills now.

After an emergency landing in the Amazon rainforest, it took a week for the rescuers to determine the location of my pilot, Petr, and I. In that time, our shelter protected us from downpours, insects and leeches, and it gave us comfort. With it, we knew we could survive.

HOW TO MAKE A LEAN-TO SHELTER

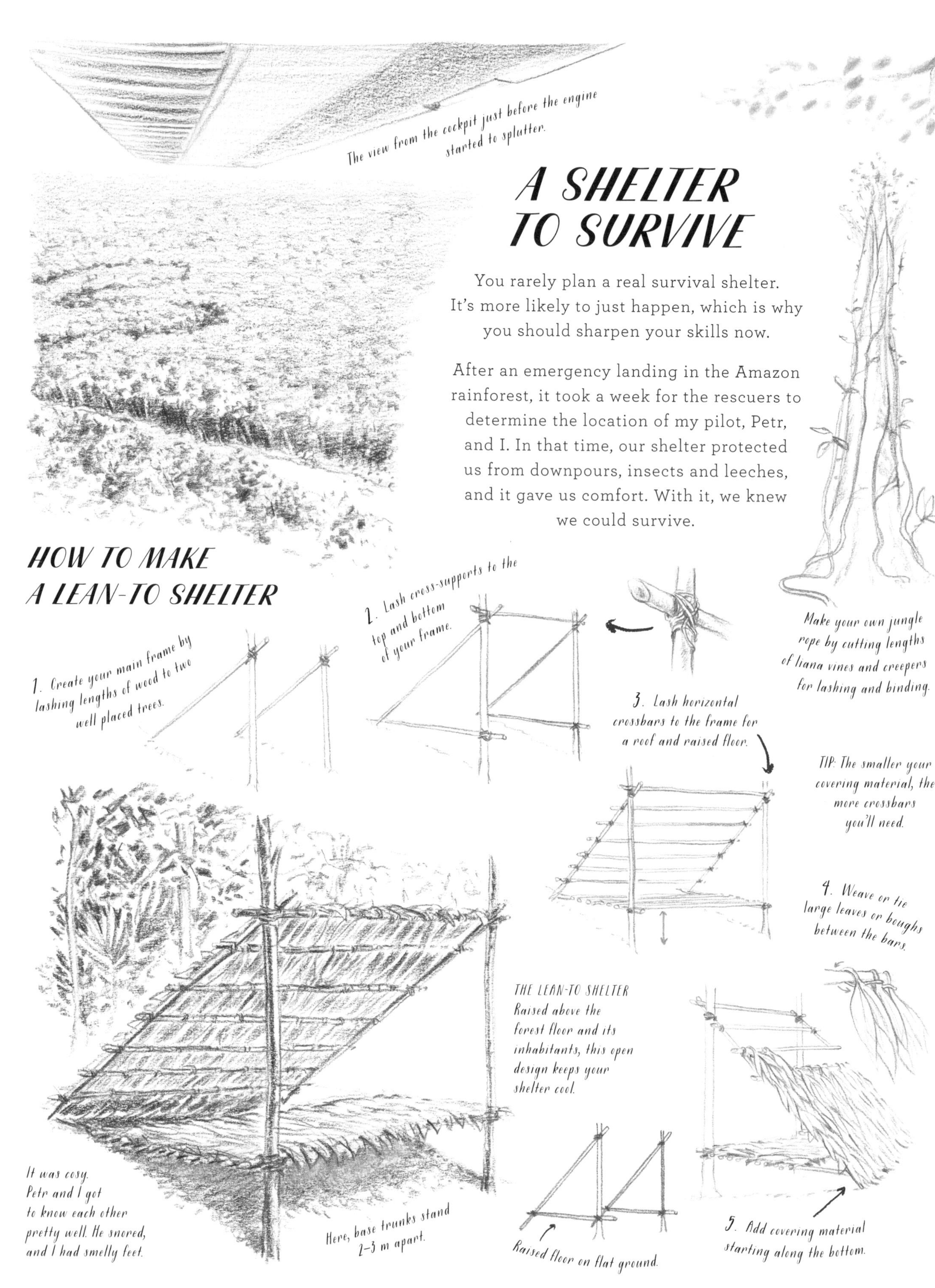

In survival mode your to-do list is reduced to what matters right now. Shelter building is at the top of that list.

NIGHTS AMONG THE NOMADS

Few places conjure the feeling of wilderness more than Arctic Siberia. And few people understand home building like the Nenet people. Their chum – similar to the North American teepee – is designed to survive the cold weather and be portable as they travel between pastures with their reindeer. This wikiup shelter is based on a similar design: a living space, not just a survival space.

Siberian wolves were a growing problem for the reindeer herders. If I'm honest, the sound of their howls in the night gave me the shivers.

There's no better way to travel through snow than on a reindeer sleigh.

COLD WEATHER TIPS:

* Pile snow over fir to create extra insulation;
* Face the entrance away from oncoming wind;
* Insulate the ground with a natural carpet;
* A small hearth fire keeps the cold at bay.

Water thrown up into the cold air instantly became ice crystals.

As the night settled in, the reindeer became restless. Wolves were nearby. We stayed out by the fire all night.

HOW TO MAKE A WIKIUP

1. Gather 10–15 long tree stems or branches for the mainframe. Here, birch and pine are used.

2. Lash together three lengths to make a sturdy tripod frame. Forked branches can be interlocked without the need for lashing.

In larger wikiups, allow for an opening at the top for smoke to escape when having a fire.

3. Rest your other stems around the tripod – all the way around. Leave space for an entrance.

4. For an extended entrance, build a frame as shown. Forked branches make it much easier.

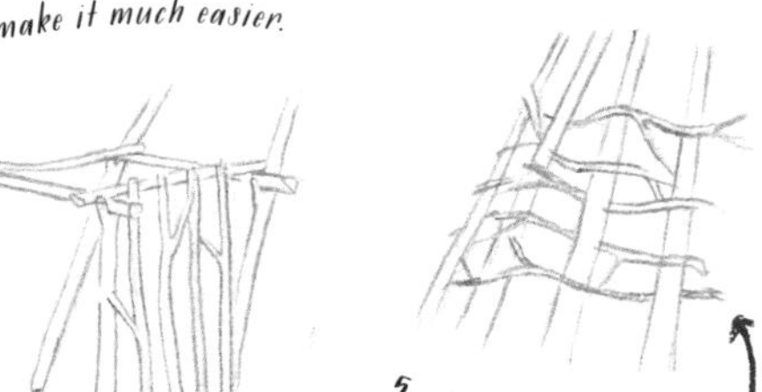

5. Interweave thinner branches horizontally through the vertical frame all around the structure.

Make your covering with ferns, fir boughs or other foliage to hand.

6. Weave your covering through the thinner branches, starting at the base of the shelter.

You can make many shelters like this without any tools or rope, just by interlocking branches.

ALL KINDS OF SHELTER

I've put together a few other types of wood-based shelter here. Maybe you'll see something you want to make or maybe you want to invent your own design – the main thing is to get out there and start building.

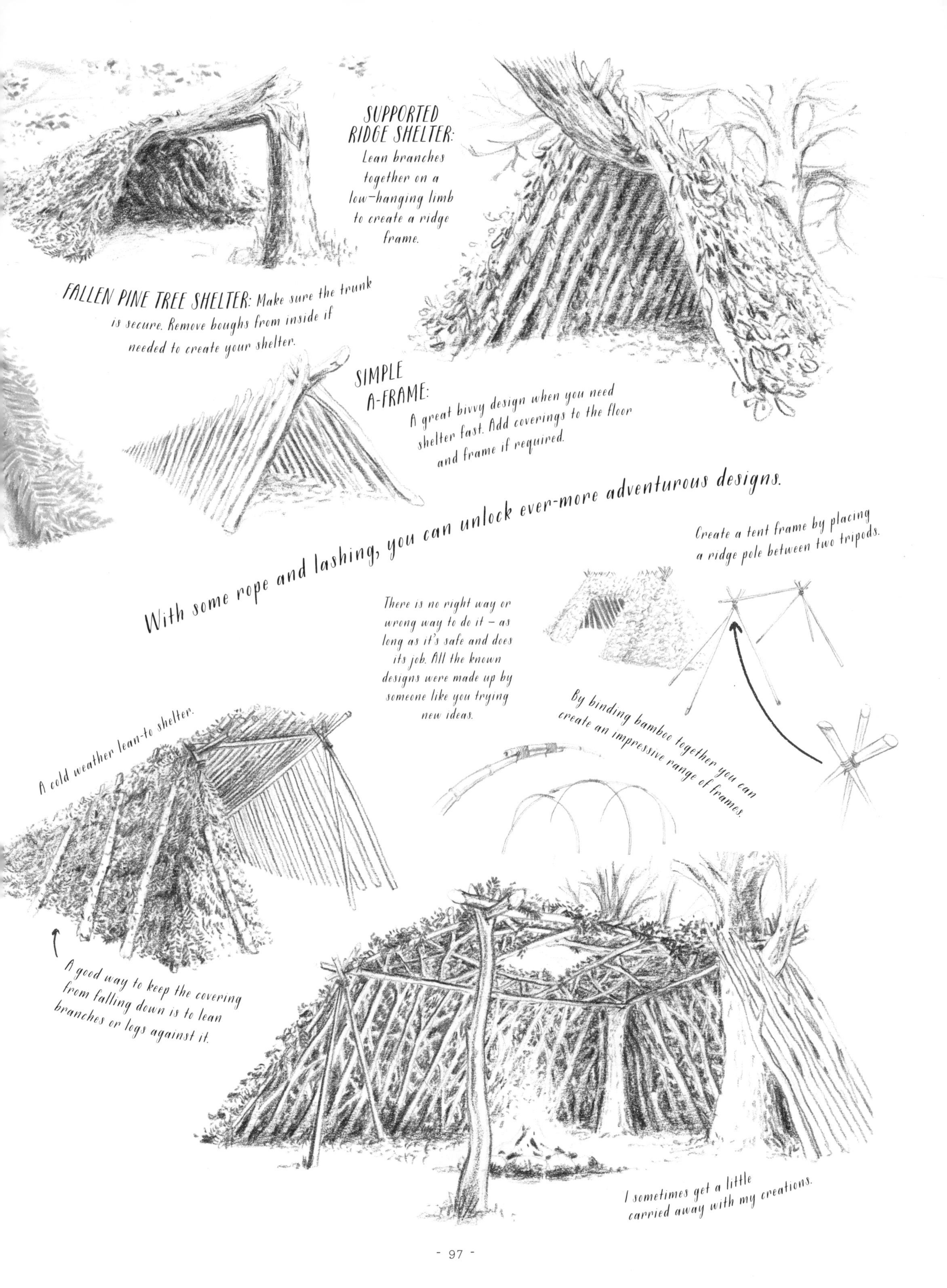
SUPPORTED RIDGE SHELTER: Lean branches together on a low-hanging limb to create a ridge frame.
FALLEN PINE TREE SHELTER: Make sure the trunk is secure. Remove boughs from inside if needed to create your shelter.
SIMPLE A-FRAME: A great bivvy design when you need shelter fast. Add coverings to the floor and frame if required.
With some rope and lashing, you can unlock ever-more adventurous designs.
Create a tent frame by placing a ridge pole between two tripods.
There is no right way or wrong way to do it – as long as it's safe and does its job. All the known designs were made up by someone like you trying new ideas.
By binding bamboo together you can create an impressive range of frames.
A cold weather lean-to shelter.
A good way to keep the covering from falling down is to lean branches or logs against it.
I sometimes get a little carried away with my creations.

COVERINGS, COMFORT AND CAMOUFLAGE

"However tough you may be, you're just stupid if you turn down comfort." I overheard this simple truth when trekking through Siberia. Here are just some of the techniques I encountered to make your shelter truly comfortable.

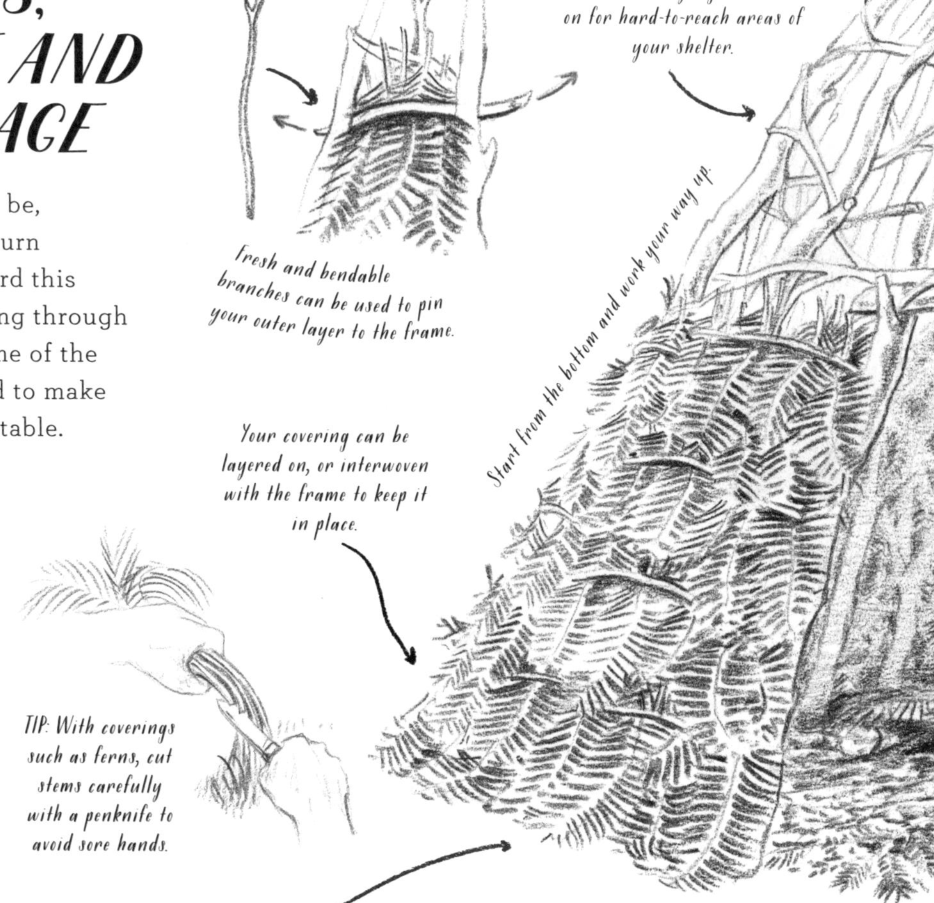

COVERINGS

The outer layer of a shelter is often the most overlooked, but this is what will keep out the cold and wet. Depending on your environment, there are a number of options open to you.

Your shelter should protect you from:

* Wind;
* Rain;
* Sunshine;
* Cold.

MATERIALS	FIR BOUGHS	FERNS/BRACKENS	LARGE LEAVES/PALMS	FOLIAGE	BARK
INSULATION /5 →	4	3	3	3-4	3
DURABILITY /5 →	5	3	4	3	5
EASE OF USE /5 →	5	4	4	3	3
COMFORT /5 →	4	4	4	3	3

Collecting your covering material can take time.
If in a group, have someone out gathering straight away.

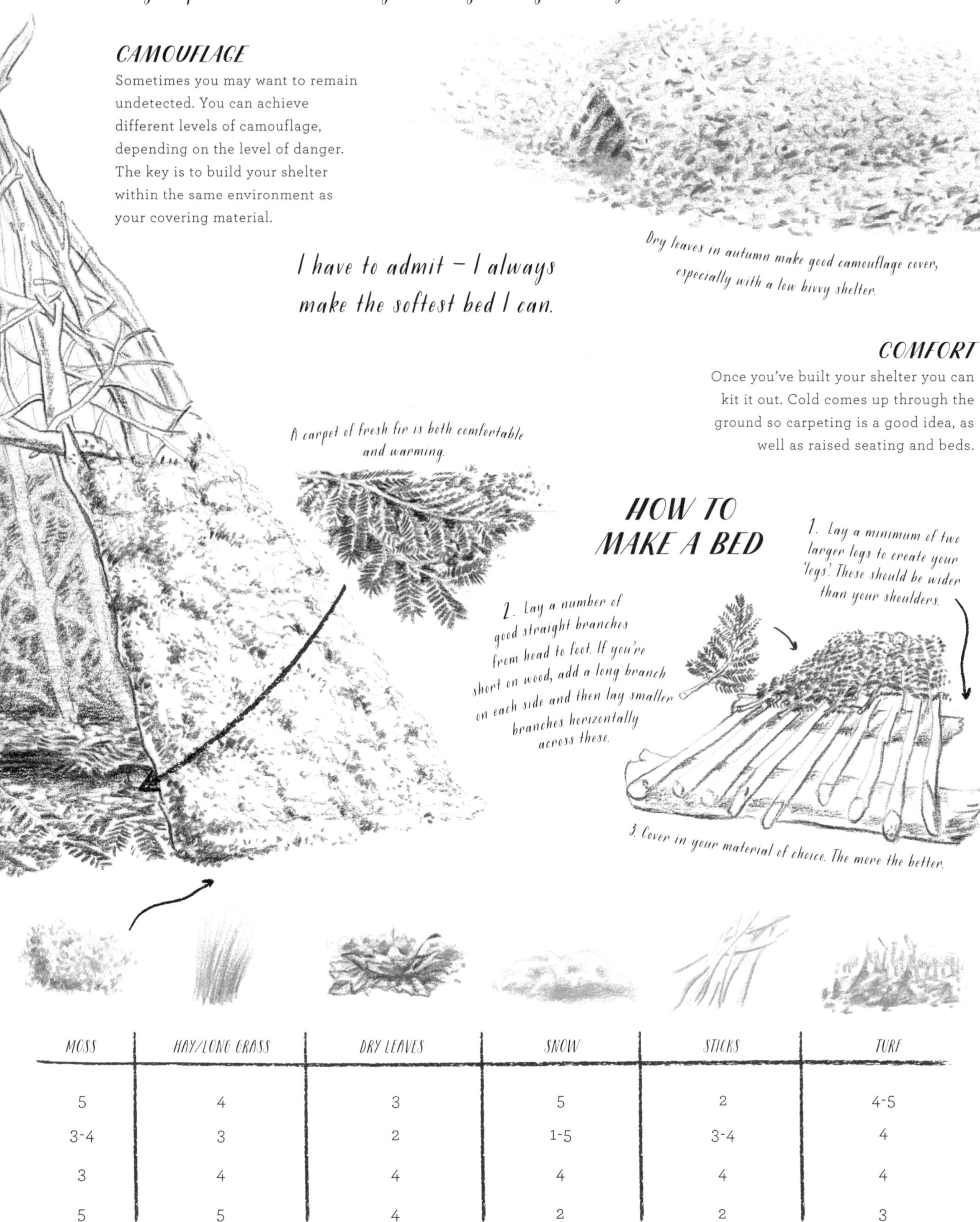

CAMOUFLAGE

Sometimes you may want to remain undetected. You can achieve different levels of camouflage, depending on the level of danger. The key is to build your shelter within the same environment as your covering material.

Dry leaves in autumn make good camouflage cover, especially with a low bivvy shelter.

I have to admit – I always make the softest bed I can.

COMFORT

Once you've built your shelter you can kit it out. Cold comes up through the ground so carpeting is a good idea, as well as raised seating and beds.

HOW TO MAKE A BED

MOSS	HAY/LONG GRASS	DRY LEAVES	SNOW	STICKS	TURF
5	4	3	5	2	4-5
3-4	3	2	1-5	3-4	4
3	4	4	4	4	4
5	5	4	2	2	3

A FALLEN-TREE DEN

Just like shelters, there's a den for every environment – one of the best utilises the natural frame of a fallen tree like this one. An intricate layout of 'rooms' and corridors can be made around the branches – sometimes encompassing the entire tree.

DENS vs SHELTERS:

* A shelter is normally finished when it's habitable. Dens often continue to grow and evolve;

* Shelters often need be erected quickly whilst on the move. Dens are more like bases from which to set out on adventures;

* Shelters normally follow a tried and tested design. The only rule for dens is that they're safe. Everything else is up to your imagination;

* Shelters are always outdoors and normally made from natural materials. You can build a den anywhere from nearly anything.

The den is like the shelter's unruly cousin that makes up its own rules.

In terms of honing your shelter-building skills, you can't beat den making.

THE SHELTER THAT BECAME A HOME

Although it was many years ago, it feels like yesterday that this small island was my home. After my sailing boat's mast was lost in a storm during a solo Pacific crossing I was incredibly lucky to be near a remote island atoll. Sadly it was uninhabited. This here is the note that would eventually lead to my rescue from what I later discovered to be the island of Takutea. The bottle and message were discovered on a beach 320 kilometres away by a young girl who took it to her parents. If it hadn't been for that inquisitive girl I would still be living in this shelter to this day. And you would not be reading this.

CONTAINERS AND DRUMS

Buried beneath the sand, this drum stores emergency drinking water and is used as an anchor for the shelter.

Open walls to allow constant viewing for ships.

Plastic bottle floats

Repaired fishing net – my main means of catching food.

Lashed stones acted as weights.

This is the message I wrote down with an old biro I'd discovered. This pizza menu was the best thing I could find to write on.

I named my bottle Livingston, after the seagull, not the explorer. I adapted him so he would sail, as well as look unusual enough, for someone to pick up.

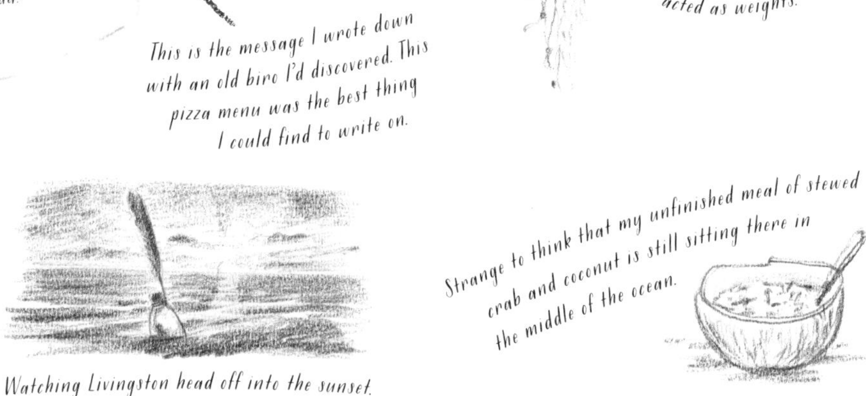

Watching Livingston head off into the sunset. I wondered where his voyage would take him.

Strange to think that my unfinished meal of stewed crab and coconut is still sitting there in the middle of the ocean.

THE DEN

This was my home for six months. I called it The Den. It was made entirely from the washed-up junk which our oceans are so full of. It's amazing what you can make from things you find lying about when you use your imagination.

SHELTERS OF THE SAHARA

With the right knowledge you can tame the most hostile places. Here, during an expedition into the Sahara desert, I discovered the wonder of the Bedouin tent and how it is uniquely designed to suit the climate. I also learned how it can be packed up on the hump of a camel. And how it can turn an inhospitable desert into an oasis of calm and comfort.

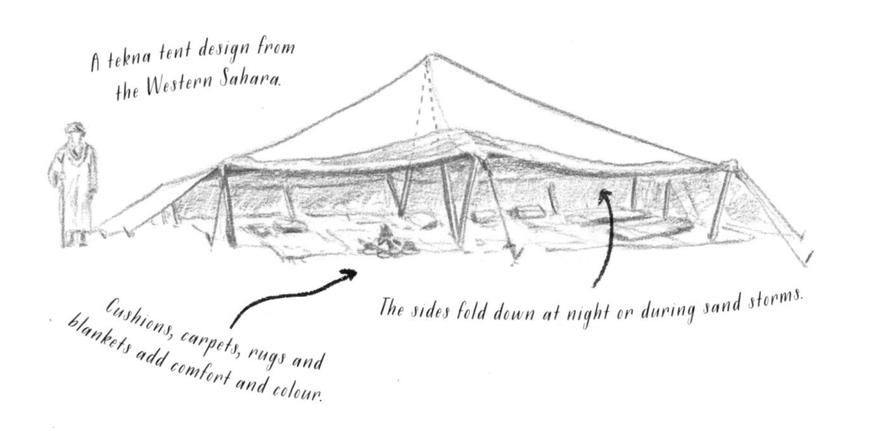

HOW TO MAKE A BEDOUIN TENT

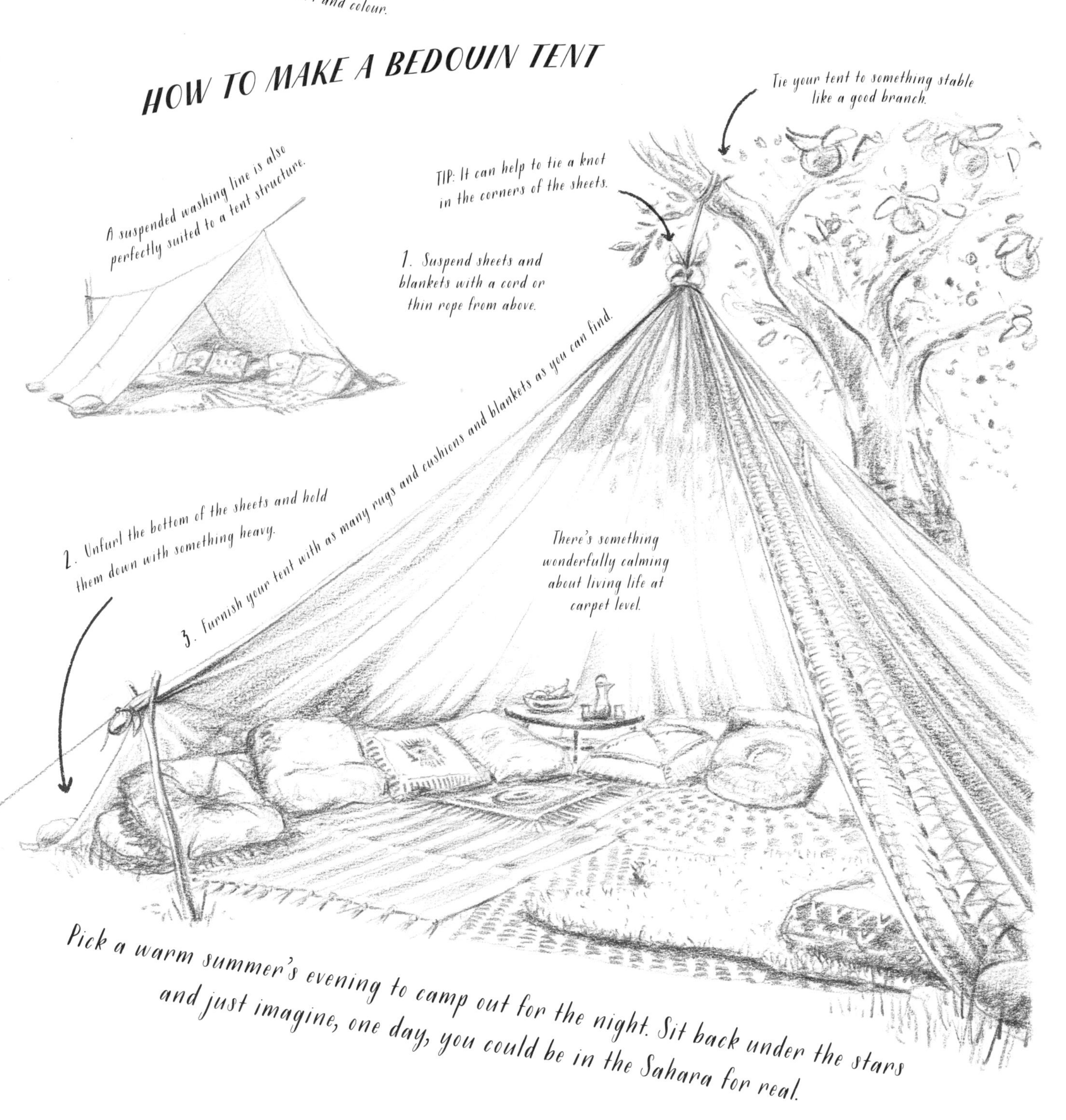

Pick a warm summer's evening to camp out for the night. Sit back under the stars and just imagine, one day, you could be in the Sahara for real.

NIGHT IN A SNOW HOLE

We've dug into the slope about 4 m to avoid a nasty blizzard. The entrance is blocked by backpacks but the roar outside continues. The thermometer reads a balmy -30 degrees. I should probably stop writing as I can't feel the pen I'm holding.

A snow shovel or a good spade is indispensible when working with snow.

The morning after the storm, breakfast was brewing.

Do not attempt to make a snow hole without an experienced adult.

FROSTBITE

My companion's unnaturally long toes had succumbed to frostbite. That night I slept with his smelly left foot in my smelly armpit. He still has his ridiculously long toes.

SNOW SHELTERS

Cold environments have a habit of testing your survival skills. Luckily snow is one of the best shelter-building materials there is. Here are a few snow shelters that I've had to make over the years.

TREE BASE SNOW SHELTER

After heavy snowfall, the low-hanging branches of some conifer trees create the perfect shelter.

SNOW TRENCHES AND TUNNELS

A favourite among adventurers where there is deep snow, snow trenches are simple and effective. You will also build up strong arm muscles from all the digging.

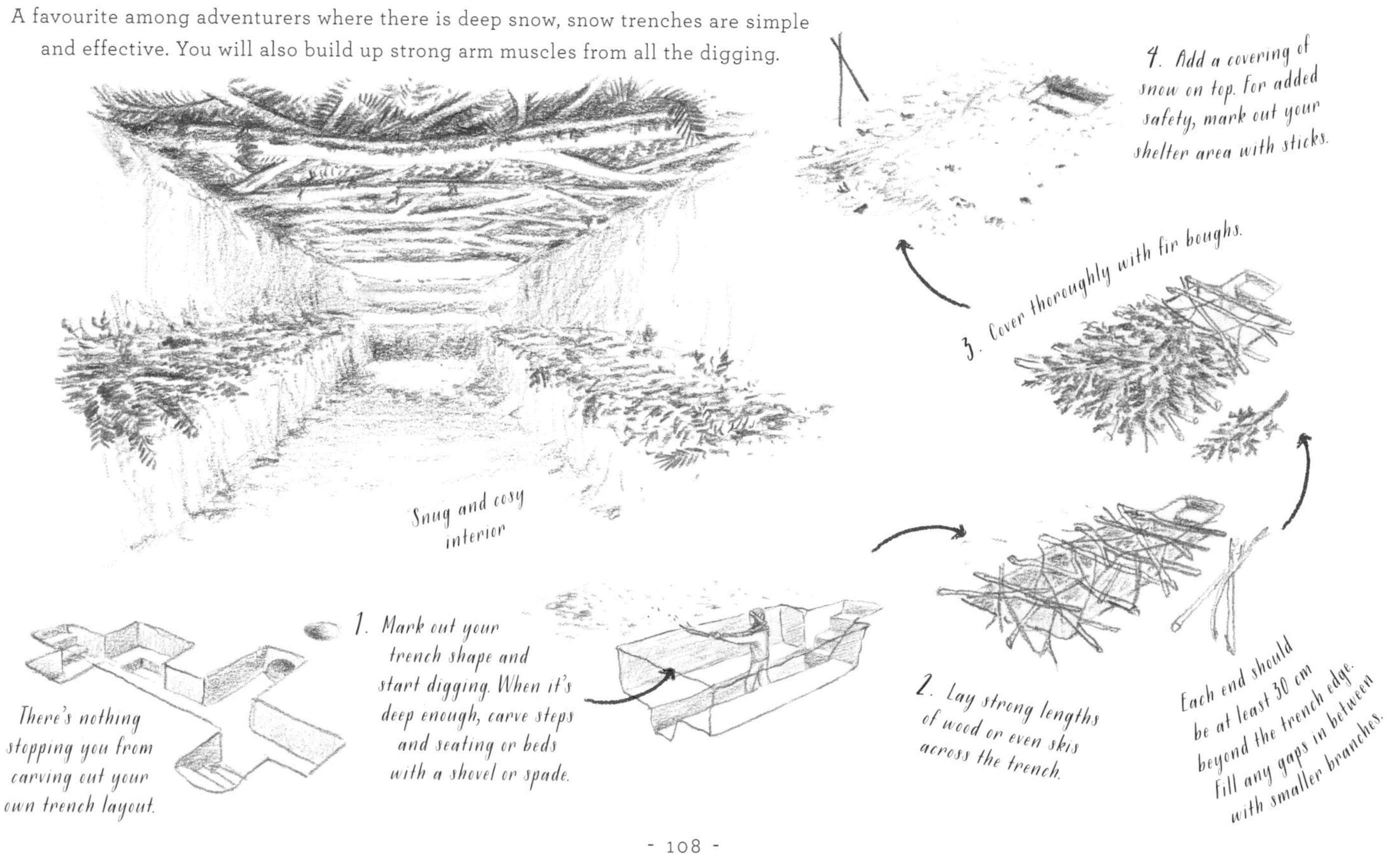

Don't wait until you're exploring the Arctic – when it next snows heavily, get out there and start building.

Not only can you carve out your shelter, but also your seating, beds, shelves and steps.

MAKE A QUINZHEE

A quinzhee is a cross between an igloo and a snow hole, and it's easier than both to make. You'll need two people or more and it will take up to half a day to build it. Be sure to get an adult to help with this.

These shelters may look cold but snow is a surprisingly good insulator.

1. Mark out a circular area that will fit two people lying down.
2. Pile up a large mound of snow within your designated area, approximately 1.8 m high.
3. Shape it and pack it down. Then leave it for an hour or two to sinter (harden).
4. Collect a number of thin sticks – about 45 cm in length – and push them into the mound by 30 cm.
5. Start digging out an entrance with a shovel. As person one digs further inside, person two should remove the extracted snow from the entrance and keep watch.
6. Inside, carefully excavate ceiling snow with gloved hands or shovel until you hit the sticks.
7. Once done, carefully remove the sticks and create a breathing hole in the top.

When sleeping inside make sure you have cold weather sleeping bags and mats or a cosy fir carpet.

Up here in the canopy,
surrounded by birds,
I felt like I had entered
a secret world.

SOARING ABOVE PARADISE

In a far corner of the world, deep inside the Papuan rainforest, you can find real tree houses. On this expedition, I stayed amongst the Korowai (or Kolufo) tribe, the great treehouse architects. Some of their creations reached high into the canopy, and were originally designed to protect them from warring tribes. Just sleeping in their homes was an adventure of a lifetime.

THE GREATER BIRD OF PARADISE
My sketchbooks soon became full of incredible wildlife, some of it hard to believe.

My company at night. A pet dog was a surprising find so high up.

Tree bark sleeping mat

Papua, one of the most unspoilt habitats on Earth.

The sunset touched the highest leaves. From here to the horizon, the rainforest glowed warm and pink. Beneath the canopy, the cool darkness gathered.

Looking down through the bark floorboards at the jungle floor far below felt surreal. Not the place to go sleepwalking, I reminded myself.

THE PRINCIPLES OF TREEHOUSE BUILDING

Warning – building at height can be dangerous – always seek the help of a skilled adult.

Every tree and treehouse is unique, but there are a few things they all have in common:

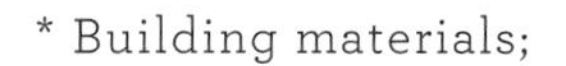

* Building materials;

* A strong and stable platform;

* Ways of fixing materials together;

* A ladder of some kind;

* Ingenious contraptions;

* Safety features and tree health.

RAW MATERIALS

SMALLER BRANCHES

FENCING

PALLETS

OLD DOOR

BOARDS AND OFF-CUTS

PLANKS

LONG PLANKS

4X4 TIMBER

NATURAL ROUNDED TIMBER

STRONG BRANCHES

These are good for platform and structural supports.

BAMBOO

Great treehouses are made of imagination. Scavenge around for good materials.

TOOLS

Dependent on design – use adults as required:

* Saw;

* Knife;

* Hammer;

* Drill and screwdriver;

* Wrench.

FIXINGS

NAILS (optional)

SCREWS

LAG BOLTS

ROPE

Go for natural manila rope or weather resistant nylon rope around 10–15 mm thick.

LADDER

A good ladder is needed to build at height.

FIXING METHODS

There are a few ways to create your platform and frame. Research which one is right for your tree and design.

When lashing to branches, protect bark with some sacking or rubber.

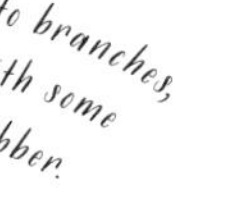

LASHING

Square lashing with rope is a simple and effective way of joining your elements together.

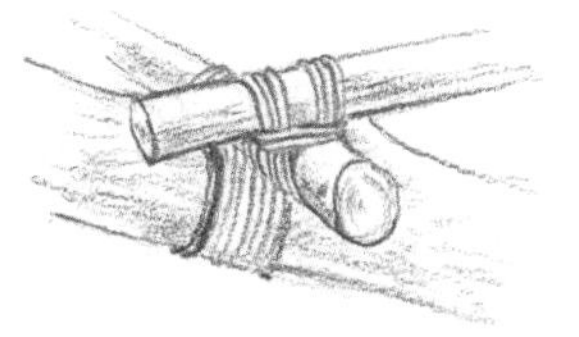

Lashing is good for rounded timber and branches.

WEDGING

Where possible, wedge your main support beams into suitable 'V' shapes between branches.

This causes less damage to the tree.

BOLTING

Better for larger and long-term treehouses.

LAG BOLT

One or two lag bolts can support a lot of weight. These should be used with brackets which allow for tree growth.

A bracket ready to be fixed to the timber beam.

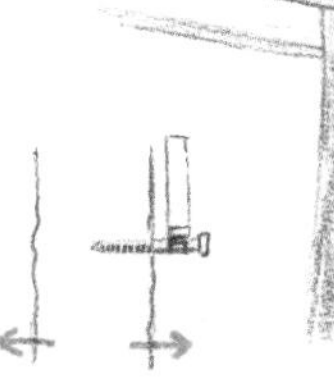

As the tree grows outwards there is space available.

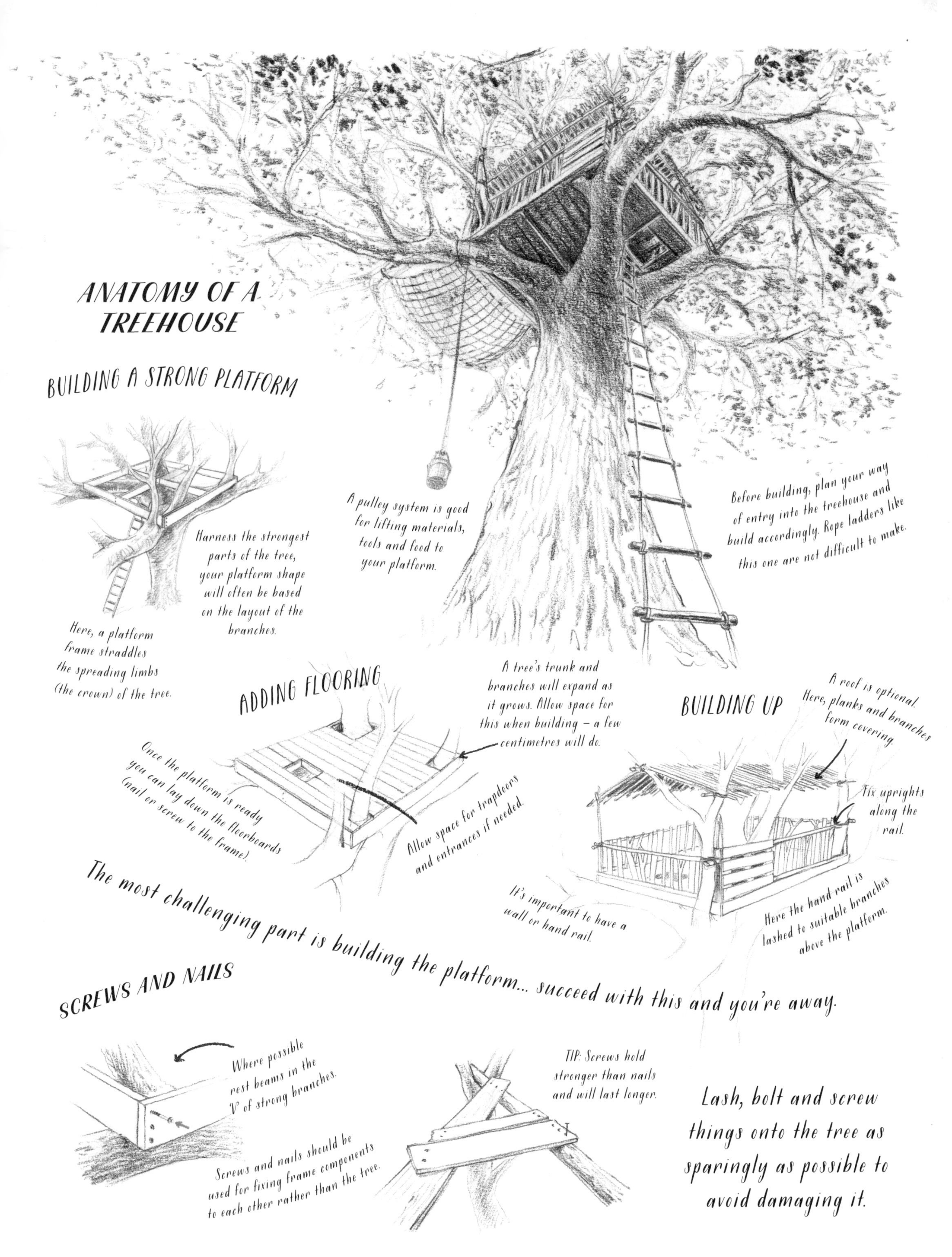
ANATOMY OF A TREEHOUSE
BUILDING A STRONG PLATFORM
Harness the strongest parts of the tree, your platform shape will often be based on the layout of the branches.
Here, a platform frame straddles the spreading limbs (the crown) of the tree.
A pulley system is good for lifting materials, tools and food to your platform.
Before building, plan your way of entry into the treehouse and build accordingly. Rope ladders like this one are not difficult to make.
ADDING FLOORING
A tree's trunk and branches will expand as it grows. Allow space for this when building – a few centimetres will do.
Once the platform is ready you can lay down the floorboards (nail or screw to the frame).
Allow space for trapdoors and entrances if needed.
BUILDING UP
A roof is optional. Here, planks and branches form covering.
Fix uprights along the rail.
It's important to have a wall or hand rail.
Here the hand rail is lashed to suitable branches above the platform.
The most challenging part is building the platform... succeed with this and you're away.
SCREWS AND NAILS
Where possible rest beams in the 'V' of strong branches.
Screws and nails should be used for fixing frame components to each other rather than the tree.
TIP: Screws hold stronger than nails and will last longer.
Lash, bolt and screw things onto the tree as sparingly as possible to avoid damaging it.

NOTES ON OTHER TREEHOUSE DESIGNS

SUPPORTED TREEHOUSE

This design uses supporting stilts or other tree trunks to create a platform area. It's most suited to structures for small to medium-sized trees, where the branches are high up or insufficient. It's also a great structure to add contraptions to.

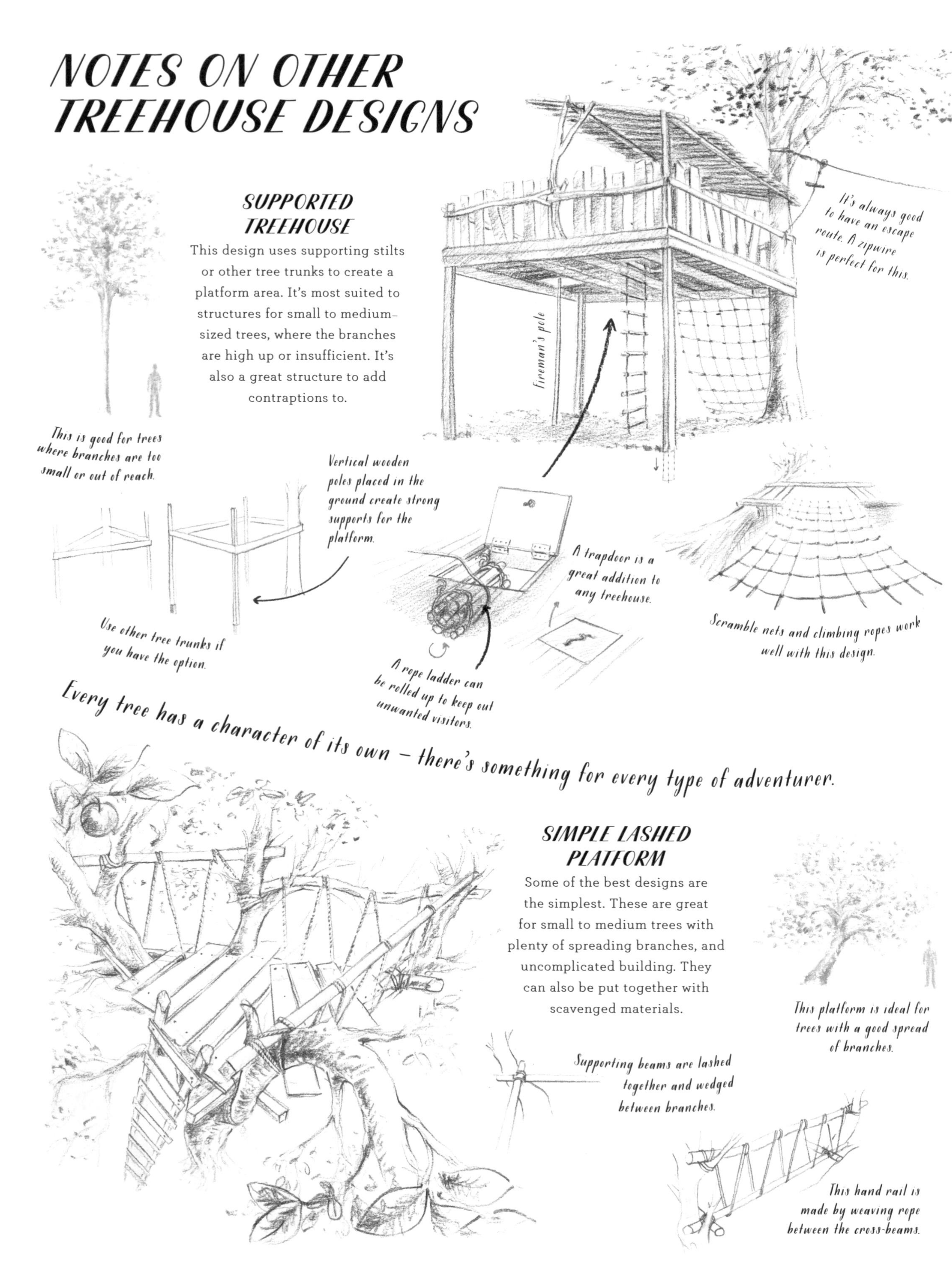

SIMPLE LASHED PLATFORM

Some of the best designs are the simplest. These are great for small to medium trees with plenty of spreading branches, and uncomplicated building. They can also be put together with scavenged materials.

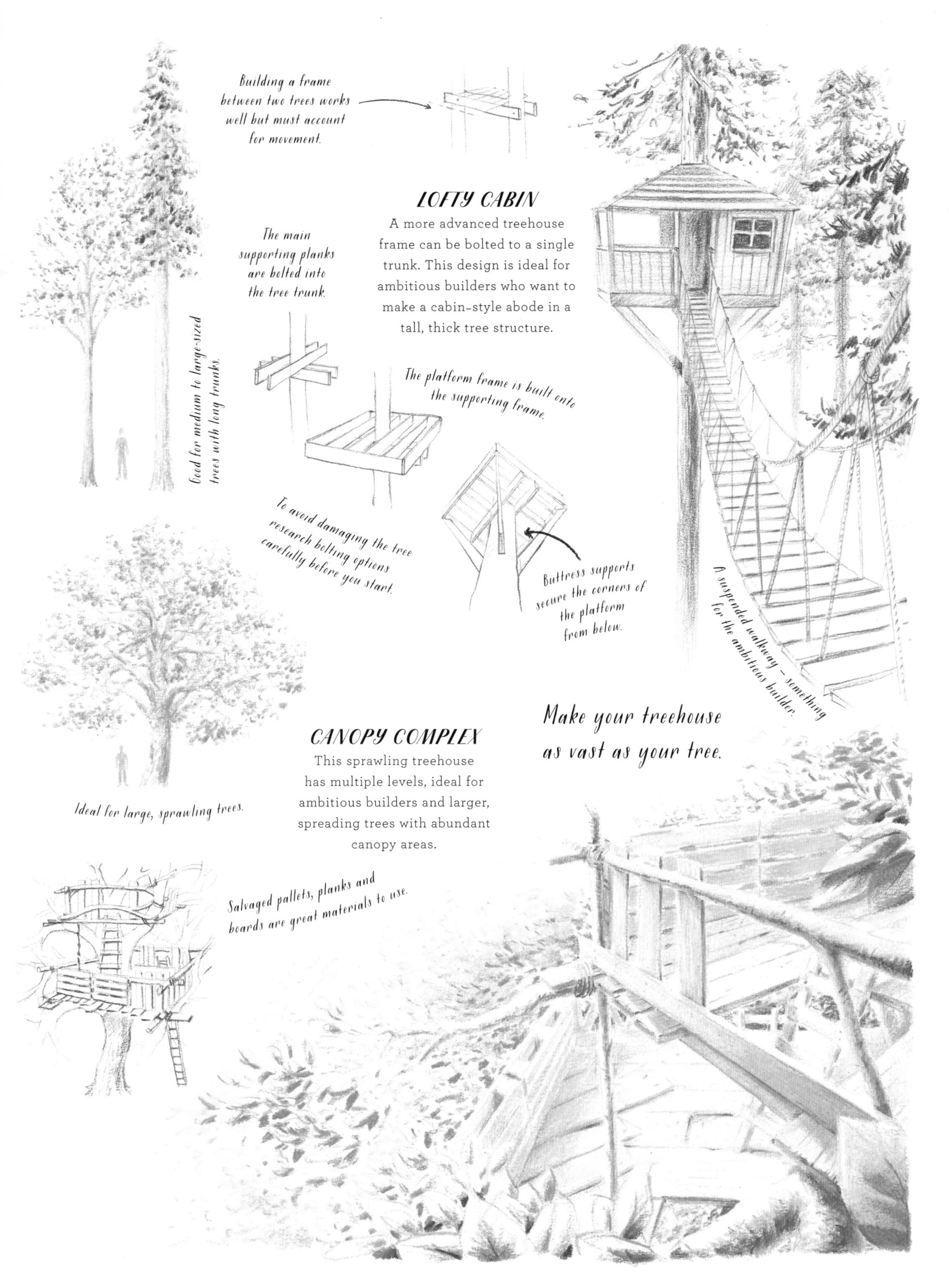

LOFTY CABIN

A more advanced treehouse frame can be bolted to a single trunk. This design is ideal for ambitious builders who want to make a cabin-style abode in a tall, thick tree structure.

CANOPY COMPLEX

This sprawling treehouse has multiple levels, ideal for ambitious builders and larger, spreading trees with abundant canopy areas.

PLANNING A NIGHTTIME FOREST SHELTER

Camping is fun, but building your own shelter and sleeping in it adds a wilder dimension to the adventure. A forest shelter is a great one to start with. It is a magical experience and you won't be short on materials.

Knowing you have a few hours to put something together before dark adds to the excitement.

CHOOSING A LOCATION:

* Research locally and look at maps;
* Find some woodland or forest you can access;
* If access is difficult build a shelter in the garden.

WHERE TO BUILD YOUR SHELTER:

* Near a good source of wood;
* On flat ground;
* In a clearing if having a fire;
* Away from unhealthy trees.

Check the weather forecast. Rain and cold will mean that you need more covering material and insulation.

KIT AND SUPPLIES

FOOD AND DRINK

WARM CLOTHES

CAMPING GEAR

If cooking on a stove, pack the necessary apparatus and utensils.

HOW TO MAKE A RIDGE FRAME SHELTER

In a group, give everyone a task – collecting covering material can begin right away.

Track down strong and long stems and branches– these are the most important ingredients.

TIP: Wait until you have a good idea of your materials before you decide on a shelter type.

1. Mark out an area to fit the number of sleeping occupants before building your frame.

This shelter was made with just our bare hands and a penknife to cut the fern covering.
Waking up after a night in the wild like this, you'll know you are a real adventurer.
2. Start by erecting the main frame.
Interlock the branches to make your desired shape.
Make sure it is strong and stable.
3. Lean branches against the frame to create your walls. Then interweave smaller branches to create a lattice for your covering.
TIP: Pack some paracord or rope in case you need to do some lashing.
5. Carpet the inside with comfortable coverings such as leaves, ferns or fir boughs. Remember, the deeper the carpet, the better.
4. Add your chosen covering, working your way up from ground level.

The 300-metre-high wall of sand and dust approached. Before it engulfed us we secured the tent as best we could, unaware of the sheer force that was about to hit us.

SWALLOWED BY THE STORM

I had heard of the Saharan dust storms or 'haboobs' as they're sometimes called, but never experienced one first hand. Yesterday, just after 2pm, the camels started to become restless. There was something in the air – a heaviness you could feel as you breathed. It wasn't long before signs of the storm appeared along the eastern horizon. Soon, a huge wall of dust stretched as far as the eye could see.

We got to work lashing down our possessions. The normally-calm camels were on their haunches. Having wrapped our 'tagelmust', or turbans, tightly around our heads and faces, we tied the tent shut as tight as we could and waited.

The storm hit us with the force of a physical object. It felt as if it was a roaring giant, tearing up everything in its path. Within seconds, the air was filled with choking sand and dust and we held on to the wooden supports with all our strength. Before long, a corner of the tent became untethered and we struggled to tie it back down. Above us opened a scene from hell — the sky was painted fiery red. It felt like we'd been swallowed alive by the dust as it dug into our eyes and nostrils. I could only just make out the ground at my feet. At that moment, the canopy flipped and disappeared into the red dust.

I lay there, heaving into the sand, seriously questioning whether the pursuit of adventure was worth this misery. But the storm did finally pass... as did my sulking. Two days later we discovered our tent gracing a sand dune. It had travelled over 65 kilometres.

Are you ready to step

into the unknown?

At the foot of the
mighty Utchi Falls.
The sight and sound
of it was deeply
overwhelming...
especially after what
we had been through.

EXPLORATION

Have you ever wondered what was beyond that far hill or looked up a winding river and pictured what world lay beyond that distant bend? These unreachable, out of bounds places we're told we should not go – they pull at our curiosity, they put ideas of exploration in our heads... but sadly most of us never take the first step.

The great polar explorer Ernest Shackleton once wrote, "It is in our nature to explore, to reach out into the unknown. The only true failure would be not to explore at all." I believe he was right.

Luckily, with a bit of courage and some basic skills and planning, all those lost worlds are yours to be discovered.

THE MISSION...

At the heart of an exploration adventure is the mission or purpose. Each mission has its own character and comes down to what you want to discover – what unknown do you want to explore? It could be a challenging climb up a mountain to see the world above the clouds, or to explore a deep forest and track wild animals.

Follow the path that gets you most excited. Here are a few ideas.

...AND THE WAY

With a choice of different environments you have a few ways in which to explore them. Some you already know, some may well become lifelong passions, but each one will lead you on incredible adventures.

GET READY FOR THE UNEXPECTED

Always know the risks and plan for them before you set out on any adventure.

...and set off a breathtaking, underwater firework display as they hunted down a shoal of fish.
An old lady applying iodine to my buttock after a run-in with a mountain dog... An episode I'm sure neither of us thought we'd be experiencing that day.
The bum is actually a good place to take a bite. But always keep clear of aggressive animals and find another way around.
Alone on a remote ridge in Italy as the side of the mountain erupted into a million multi-coloured wings. Exploration is filled with pockets of magic like this.
"What's that noise?" Probably the most important question I've ever asked – my friend stopped and turned. As he did so, the path in front of him simply disappeared in a wall of rock, trees and dust.

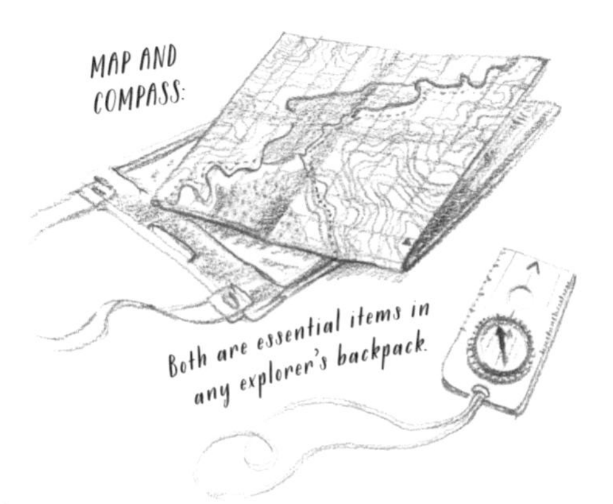

MAP AND COMPASS: Both are essential items in any explorer's backpack.

EXPLORER'S KIT AND SUPPLIES

Depending on where you are venturing and by what means, your kit needs will change, but here are a few useful and essential things that are packed into most explorer's backpacks.

CAMPING GEAR: If you are camping out, remember to pack your camping gear.

Look inside any explorer's backpack and you'll find that every single object serves a purpose.

FOOTWEAR OPTIONS

If you are planning to use hiking boots, be sure to 'wear them in' first to avoid blisters on long hikes.

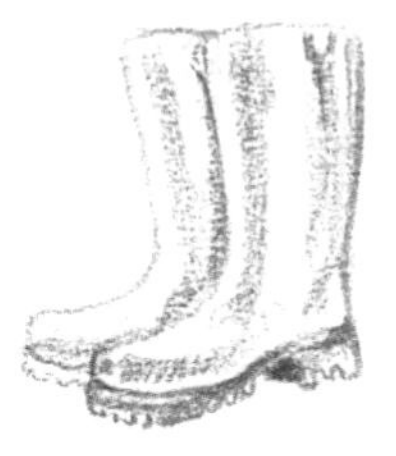

BOOTS: Good for shorter journeys in wet weather.

SPORT SANDALS: Ideal for rivers and coastal exploration.

OLD TRAINERS: These are good all-rounders.

HIKING BOOTS: Solid ankle support and grip when trekking with a backpack.

CLOTHING AND OUTERWEAR

Tips:

*Choose clothes that suit the weather and the adventure;

* Wear comfortable and breathable materials, especially if trekking;

* Cotton holds sweat and can chafe, particularly during long expeditions.

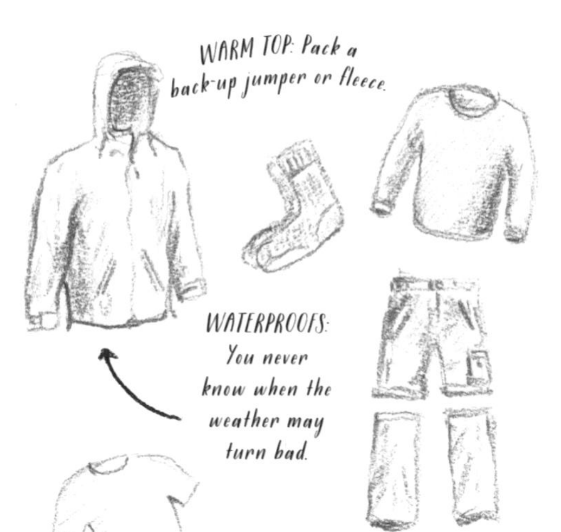

WARM TOP: Pack a back-up jumper or fleece.

WATERPROOFS: You never know when the weather may turn bad.

Some trekking trousers unzip to become shorts.

HATS AND GLOVES: To help you retain heat in cold weather.

SUNHAT: Gives essential protection against the sun.

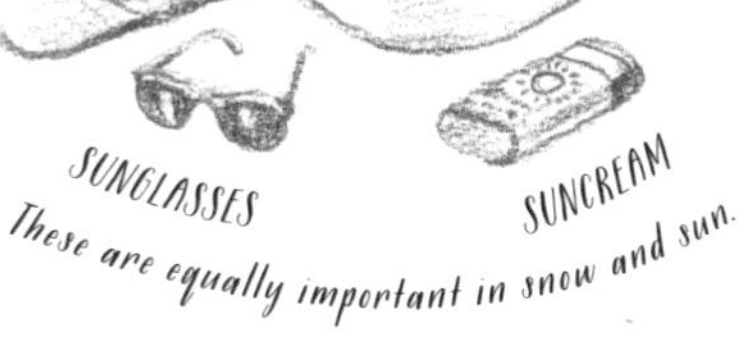

SUNGLASSES

SUNCREAM

These are equally important in snow and sun.

KIT

TORCH/HEADTORCH: Even for a daytime adventure (just in case you get lost).

EMERGENCY BLANKET: For protection against the elements.

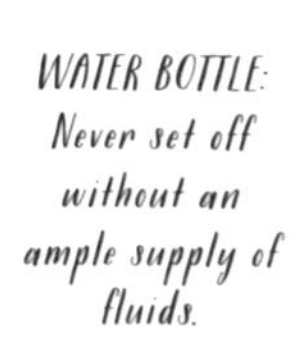

WATER BOTTLE: Never set off without an ample supply of fluids.

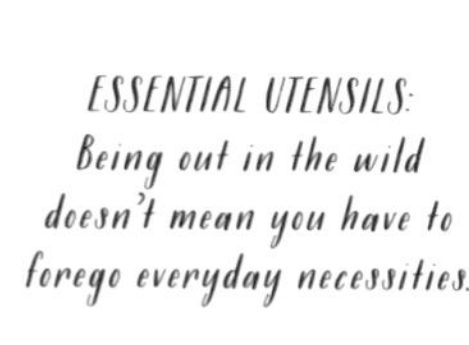

ESSENTIAL UTENSILS: Being out in the wild doesn't mean you have to forego everyday necessities.

WATCH

PENKNIFE/ MULTITOOL: Useful for all manner of tasks.

WHISTLE: To attract attention if you get into trouble.

FIRST AID KIT: One per group is enough.

SURVIVAL TIN

INSECT REPELLENT

SMALL CAMERA: You never know what unexpected sights you might want to record.

BINOCULARS: Great for spotting wildlife.

The packing of a backpack means only one thing – adventure is imminent.

THE BACKPACK

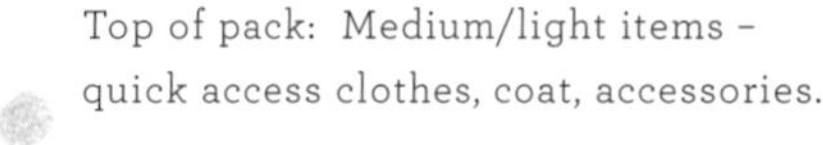

Top of pack: Medium/light items – quick access clothes, coat, accessories.

Middle (front): Heavier items – extra water, tent, cooking gear.

Middle (back): Medium/light items – clothes, food.

Lower pack: Bulky, lightweight items – sleeping bag.

SHOULDER STRAPS: Adjust these after you've done your waist belt.

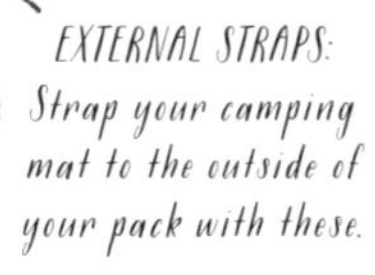

EXTERNAL STRAPS: Strap your camping mat to the outside of your pack with these.

WAIST BELT: This sits on top of your hip bone and should carry most of the weight.

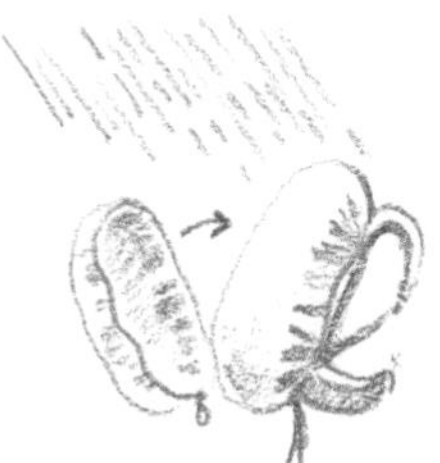

WATERPROOF COVER: Some backpacks come with very handy rain covers. They're not completely waterproof.

ESSENTIAL KNOWLEDGE:

* Make sure your backpack is set up comfortably;

* If it starts rubbing, readjust the straps straight away;

* Pack carefully – an unbalanced backpack can be dangerous;

* Backpacks come in a range of sizes. Go with something that's right for you and your adventure.

EXPEDITION BACKPACK

Extra large backpack for multi-day adventures.

These bags have a strong design.

It has extra space for camping equipment.

WEEKEND BACKPACK

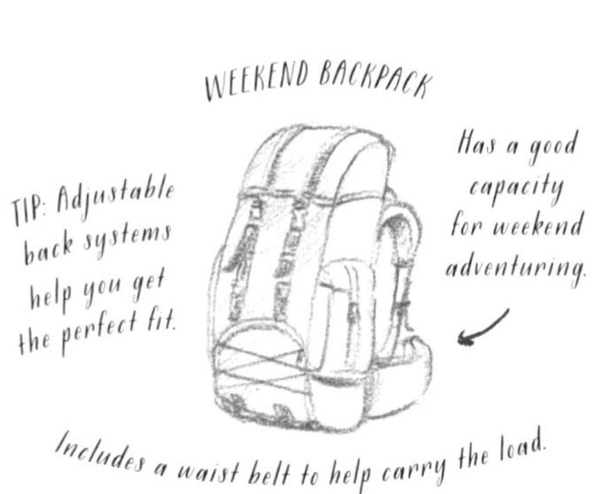

TIP: Adjustable back systems help you get the perfect fit.

Has a good capacity for weekend adventuring.

Includes a waist belt to help carry the load.

DAYPACK

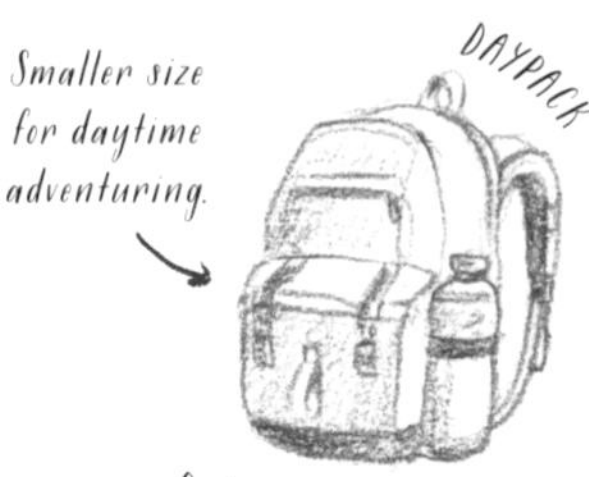

Smaller size for daytime adventuring.

Pockets for quick access make this ideal for bike adventuring and smaller expeditions.

TIP: You can also waterproof your backpack by putting the contents inside into a dry bag or a bin liner.

FOOD

Some things to think about:

* How many people do you need to feed, and how will it be prepared;

* Nutritious, lightweight foods that don't need to be in a fridge are ideal;

* For longer trips, or if you want to cook food, you'll need to make a separate plan.

LUNCH: Bread, cheese and and cured meats are great fuel.

PREPREPARED MEALS: Pack sandwiches or pasta in a robust tin.

SNACKS: Fruit and nuts are ideal for keeping you going.

EMERGENCY RATIONS: Sweets and chocolate are good for short-term energy boosts.

Always plan how you will top up water on your expedition.

WATER

You'll drink more than you think when exploring, so:

* Always take at least one bottle of water with you per person;

* On longer journeys or in hot weather, take back-up water for the group;

* Adventurers avoid fizzy drinks as they don't hydrate your body properly.

BECOMING A NAVIGATOR

Navigation is about being able to read the landscape and successfully find your way through it, normally using a map. Practise and get good at it – it will take away the fear of getting lost and will give you the confidence and experience to explore ever-more exciting places.

When the clouds descend and you can't see where you're going, a compass and map will guide you.

NAVIGATOR SKILLS:

* Being aware of landmarks and features around you and that you pass;
* Good map reading skills and being able to picture the land from above;
* Knowing how to find north (and therefore east, south, west);
* Know your geography – such as finding rivers in valleys;
* Good memory and sense of direction;
* An awareness of time.

THE FEATURES OF A LANDSCAPE ON AN ADVENTURER'S MAP

Woods & forests

Rivers & lakes

Types of terrain – like marshes

Valleys

Hills and mountains

The thin lines on a map are called contour lines. They show the height of the land above sea level.

The closer contour lines are together, the steeper the gradient.

This is a good way to picture how contour lines work to show the shape and height of a landscape.

HOW TO READ AND SET A MAP

1. Look for a stand out feature in the landscape and locate this on your map.

2. Compare this with other features in the landscape – like this lake.

3. Move the map around so that it is aligned with the landscape in front of you.

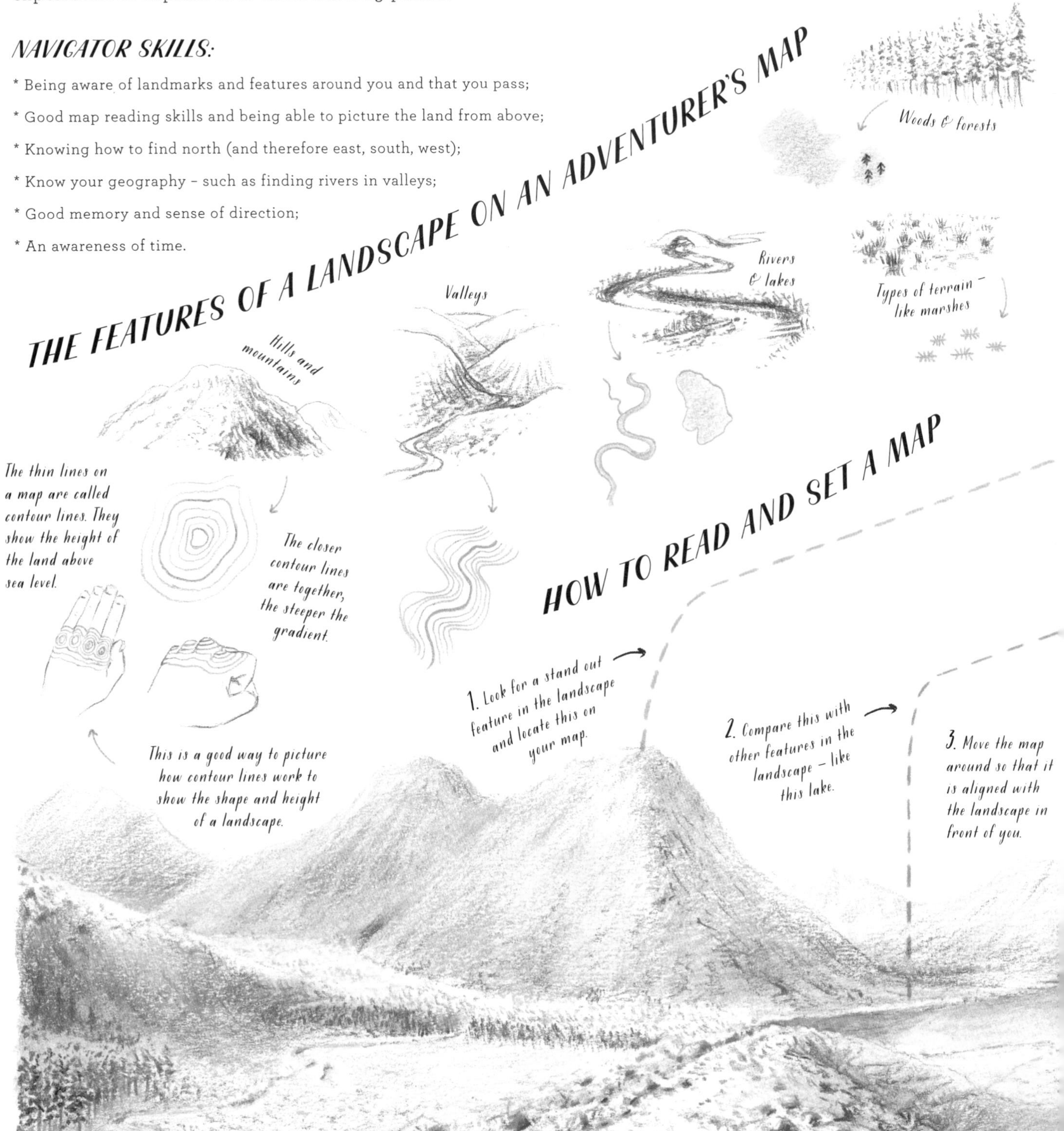

AN ADVENTURER'S MAP
ALSO KNOWN AS A TOPOGRAPHICAL MAP

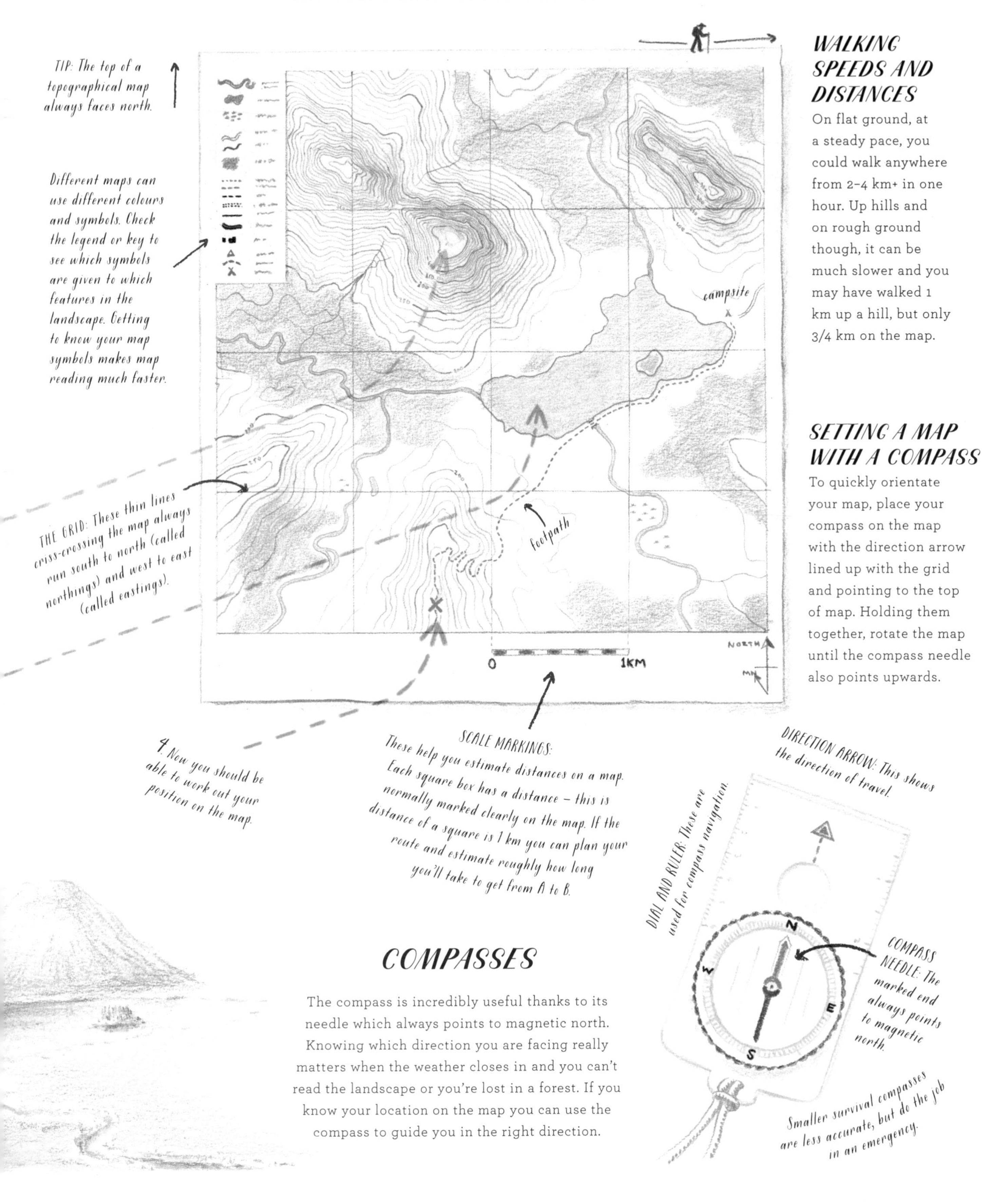

TIP: The top of a topographical map always faces north.

Different maps can use different colours and symbols. Check the legend or key to see which symbols are given to which features in the landscape. Getting to know your map symbols makes map reading much faster.

THE GRID: These thin lines criss-crossing the map always run south to north (called northings) and west to east (called eastings).

4. Now you should be able to work out your position on the map.

SCALE MARKINGS: These help you estimate distances on a map. Each square box has a distance – this is normally marked clearly on the map. If the distance of a square is 1 km you can plan your route and estimate roughly how long you'll take to get from A to B.

WALKING SPEEDS AND DISTANCES

On flat ground, at a steady pace, you could walk anywhere from 2–4 km+ in one hour. Up hills and on rough ground though, it can be much slower and you may have walked 1 km up a hill, but only 3/4 km on the map.

SETTING A MAP WITH A COMPASS

To quickly orientate your map, place your compass on the map with the direction arrow lined up with the grid and pointing to the top of map. Holding them together, rotate the map until the compass needle also points upwards.

DIRECTION ARROW: This shows the direction of travel.

DIAL AND RULER: These are used for compass navigation.

COMPASS NEEDLE: The marked end always points to magnetic north.

Smaller survival compasses are less accurate, but do the job in an emergency.

COMPASSES

The compass is incredibly useful thanks to its needle which always points to magnetic north. Knowing which direction you are facing really matters when the weather closes in and you can't read the landscape or you're lost in a forest. If you know your location on the map you can use the compass to guide you in the right direction.

JOURNEY TO THE LOST FALLS

Deep within the untouched rainforests of Guyana lies a mythical waterfall. At the time of our expedition, many believed it to be the highest in the world, but no one knew for certain. The pull of the unknown led a small group of us to attempt to reach the falls overland — something that had never been done before. Our aim was to explore the uncharted jungle and see if the myths of this mighty waterfall were indeed true. This was before the era of satellite navigation and the only help came from a hand-drawn survey map from 1952 – helpfully the estimated area of the waterfall on the map was missing. There was only one way to find out...

Finally, we stepped out of the jungle in the gathering dusk. Ahead of us the mighty Utchi Falls tipped into the abyss. The sound was like thunder.

The first step into the unknown. The feeling was electric. We said goodbye to the known world and headed into the dark rainforest, not knowing when we would return.

Why you should always set up a basha over your hammock...

1. Goliath bird-eating spider falls directly into hammock.

THE LILO RIVER SERVICE: I had brought along a lilo to much amusement, but it became a great way of crossing the deeper rivers. One of us would swim across with a rope then haul the individual and their backpack over on the inflatable mat.

Part of our badly damaged survey map – the only map in existence at the time.

We tried dropping rocks and branches down to gauge the height of the falls by counting, but to no avail as they'd disappear into the dense mist and spray. We ended up tying all our ropes together, plus a few liana vines. The final height was over 210 m – not as big as the myth suggested, but still a legendary waterfall.

The others posing for a portrait, dwarfed by the huge buttress-like base of the Mora tree. We were actually lost at this point, but then we heard a deep sound of thunder in the distance. Could it be the lost falls?

A typical scene, hacking through the undergrowth, always keeping a look out for snakes.

2. Aru realises what has fallen into his hammock.

3. Both escape unharmed and a bit wiser.

In the distance the Ilú-Tramen Tepui looms out of the savannah – beyond the top of the waterfalls another lost world was there waiting to be explored.

I reached up to another ledge. As I pulled my weight upwards I felt something wasn't quite right. I glanced up and there looking at me with its dark, red eyes was a bushmaster. The next two seconds slowed down completely. As my brain registered that I was just a few centimetres away from one of the most dangerous snakes on the planet, its coils twisted into strike mode. I let go of the rock face. As gravity pulled me down, the coils unfurled and the bushmaster bit into the air where my head had just been. Never has a fall down a cliff felt so pleasant.

A golden eagle captures a salmon for breakfast. The wildlife can be as extreme as the terrain.

PLANNING YOUR OWN ADVENTURE

You don't need to head to the ends of the earth to have an adventure – there are plenty of places to explore under your nose. The main thing is to get out there and get started. What environments would you like to explore? Let your mind wander. I've put down a few here to give you some ideas. Then maybe get the adults involved and put a plan together.

Always work to the ability of the most inexperienced in the group. Adventurers work as a team. No one gets left behind.

THE ESSENTIAL EXPLORER'S CHECKLIST

Before you embark, have you got the following:

* At least one experienced (adult) member;

* A good map of the area, a compass and clearly-marked route if required;

* An assessment of how much time is needed and any risks that may be encountered;

* An up-to-date weather forecast and the right kit, clothes, food and water for your intended expedition;

* A list of emergency telephone numbers;

* An adult not going who knows where you're headed, what route you're taking, and what time you're due to be back.

On some beaches you can uncover dinosaur fossils that haven't seen the light of day for more than 250 million years.

Do your research – there are many shipwrecks out there to explore.

Always know what the tide is doing – never get caught out.

EXPLORE THE COAST

Every coast has its own character, and each has something worth exploring. Low tide reveals hidden wonders from the deep, be it old shipwrecks or giant crustaceans in rock pools. Venture into dark caves carved out by the waves. Here, you'll find all sorts of treasures, washed up from distant lands.

There isn't a coast in the world which doesn't have incredible creatures waiting to be discovered.

EXPLORE A FOREST

Head deep into the world of giants as you explore ancient oak and beech woods. Look out for wild animals in the magic of a fir forest or climb up into the trees and explore the canopy above. Around every bend and branch the unknown awaits.

If you're quiet you can get close to the wild inhabitants. Elusive birds and beasts are there to be discovered.

Sometimes exploring requires an overnight shelter. The forest is the perfect place to build one.

Take a roll of string and try to find the tree with the biggest circumference.

Just imagine, some trees in the world need over 40 m of string to reach around them.

Look out for animal tracks and see where they go. If you see this one it's either a dog or a wolf.

EXPLORE THE TOP OF THE WORLD

If the hills and mountains talk to you then you aren't mad, you are lucky. With the effort to climb comes a reward which is hard to do justice to in a sentence. Up here though, you are at the edge of your comfort zone and as an adventurer that is often the most comfortable place you can be.

The joy of feeling infinitesimally small... This rock is a pebble compared to what's out there.

Until you're experienced, choose climbs with clearly marked footpaths like this.

HOW TO CLIMB A MOUNTAIN

Just being in the mountains is an adventure, but one day you'll want to visit those lofty summits above the clouds. You may even be ready right now. If you are, and you have experienced adults to hand, here's what you need to know.

ESSSENTIAL KIT CHECKLIST:

* Map and compass;
* Small backpack;
* Plenty of water;
* Energy snacks and food;
* Suitable footwear;
* Head torch (even in daytime);
* Survival blanket;
* Spare warm clothes;
* Sun hat and cream if required;
* First aid kit;
* Emergency telephone numbers.

Experience matters in the mountains – who would be your ideal guide?

WHERE TO CLIMB

There are many mountains out there ideal for a young mountaineer – do some research before setting out on your adventure. Carefully assess the length of the route, the difficulty of the terrain, the altitude and the equipment you have available, and cater the trip to the least able member of your group.

CHOOSING YOUR GUIDES

One or two experienced adults are needed when exploring in this realm. If friends or family aren't qualified for this kind of adventure, try groups like the Scouts, which are built for expeditions like this.

Cumulonimbus clouds – the potential gathering of a storm. Always keep an eye on the clouds and look for signs of change.

CHECKING THE WEATHER FORECAST

The weather can be especially changeable in the mountains and the risks can be severe. If the weather starts to deteriorate while you are climbing, don't keep going. Always head back down.

Start with something easier. This is too steep...

... but this could be okay.

When the adrenaline has subsided

You can't really 'conquer' mountains, but they can conquer you... in a wonderful way.

REACHING THE SUMMIT

Well done, you've earned this. Pat yourself – and your team on the back. Enjoy the view (unless you're in the clouds) and take some time to soak it all up.

ALLOW ENOUGH TIME

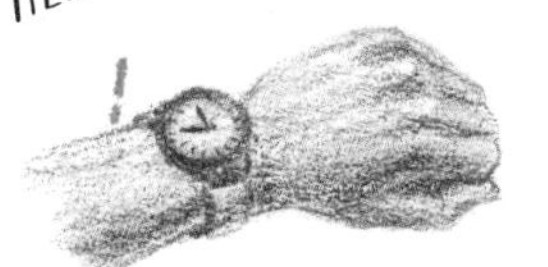

This is important and requires good planning. Know what time the sun sets and allow a few hours of extra daylight time to complete the trip. Always have a pre-agreed turn around time.

DOUBLE-CHECK YOUR KIT

Having enough water is absolutely essential for your safety on the mountain.

SUMMIT FEVER

This is a dangerous desire to reach the top of a mountain at any cost. Remember reaching the summit is only halfway. Real adventurers know when to turn around.

The symptoms of summit fever include:

* Ignoring bad weather;
* Moving too far ahead of team members;
* Thinking half a bottle of water will be fine;
* Having an inability to judge potential risks.

PLAN YOUR ROUTE

Choose a mountain with clear footpaths marked on your map.

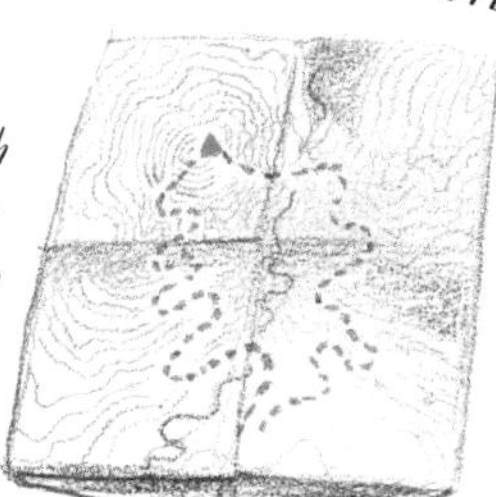

Check the path is suitable for the level of everyone in the group.

DESCENDING THE MOUNTAIN

As you head back down, stay focused. Most accidents happen on the descent when climbers get sloppy.

Always stick to the path. When two paths cross, double-check the map to make sure you take the right one.

take a moment. Sit, watch and think.

Always carry a map and compass in the wild.

They will help you get un-lost...

...and avoid getting lost in the first place.

POTENTIAL GETTING-LOST SCENARIOS AND HOW TO AVOID THEM

POOR WEATHER
Mist, cloud and rain can blot out the landscape leading you to become lost or split up from your group. Always keep close together. With a map and compass you can continue if the weather is not severe.

POOR LIGHT AND NIGHTFALL
Lack of visibility makes it easier for groups to get split up. Stay close together. Put headtorches on and make plans to camp out if need be.

MULTIPLE PATHS
Even with a good map, it's easy to be confused by multiple paths. This is how groups get split up when they're not together.

WOODS AND FORESTS
It's easy to lose your sense of direction here. Everything can look the same. Always keep close together and stick to the paths.

Before every adventure always agree on a plan for if the group gets lost or split up.

WHAT TO DO IF YOU GET LOST:

* Stop, sit down, take a few deep breaths and get your head clear;

* Take out a snack;

* Retrace the route you've taken in your head and discuss where you might have gone wrong if you are in a group;

* Look around you. Can you see any familiar landmarks? Can you hear any roads nearby or people calling? If you have a map, try and match it up with the landscape;

* Decide whether you're better to stay put or find your way out – there are some details here on both options.

FINDING YOUR WAY OUT

If you're lost as a group, or are confident of your destination, you can consider finding your way out.

1. It's normally best to retrace footsteps if you can.

2. Check your watch. Do you have enough daylight? If not, stay put until morning.

These are useful for retracing your steps and help people out looking for you to find you.

3. Leave markers with stones or sticks at regular intervals...

Use all your senses. Listen out for road traffic or voices.

4. High ground can provide a view to help you get your bearings.

5. Streams lead to rivers. Rivers generally lead to civilisation.

GETTING SPLIT UP AND WHAT TO DO

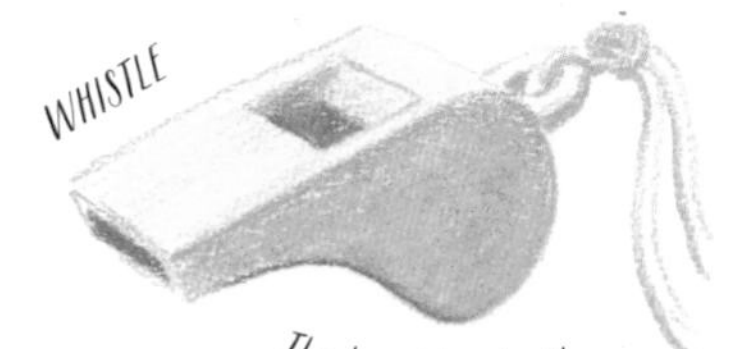

The humble whistle has saved many, many lives. Always keep one on you in the wild.

NO LANDMARKS
When the landscape looks the same all around you it's easy to get disorientated. Keep to the paths and keep together.

YOU FALL BEHIND
If you fall behind, you might choose a different path to the group ahead. If this happens and you are unsure of which path to take, stop, wait there and call ahead. When the group realise, they'll come back and find you.

YOU GO TOO FAR AHEAD
If you storm ahead of the group and choose one of multiple paths, the group behind you will have no idea which one you took. Stop at the junction and wait for your team to catch up.

NO PATHS
In densely wooded areas, paths can disappear and groups can be divided. Use your whistle or voice to locate others in your group. If this doesn't work, everyone should retrace their footsteps.

Above all remember to keep positive and be patient. People are on their way.

STAYING PUT AND GETTING FOUND

If you are in any doubt about your location, this is the safest option, especially if you are alone or split up. If you were with a group you'll be found quicker if you're not moving about.

Always carry a whistle. Blow it three times every 30 seconds.

This is when your survival tin goes from a fun item to a lifesaving support.

Flash three times to signal for help.

At night, use a torch. In the day, use a mirror or aluminium foil to reflect sunlight.

A good daypack should contain:

TORCH

BINOCULARS

SURVIVAL TIN

WATER

FOOD

SURVIVAL BLANKET

WARM CLOTHES

Look around for a large tree or rock. Make this your base.

Keep your spirits up. Stay positive, keep close if you are in a group, and keep warm.

If you need to camp out for the night, use your skills and kit to make a shelter and light a fire. Trust yourself, you've got this.

When you're sitting under a tree feeling sorry for yourself, it's comforting to know someone is aware of where you are, so remember, always leave your expedition plans with someone before setting off.

BIKE ADVENTURE THROUGH AFRICA

A small bike ride through Africa, led and organised by my fearless sister, Jo. I'll never forget the moment we pedalled away from home – the unbelievable excitement of heading off into the unknown, not even knowing where we were staying that night. The nine months that followed gave us a lifetime of memories, a thirst for adventure and a fair few lucky escapes.

The vast volcano of Kilimanjaro. It's so high that the snow blankets the higher slopes while the rest of us struggled in the heat.

Our bikes – simple but indestructible. They courageously carried us and our gear over 10,000 km.

Our secret weapon against any cyclist-eating mammals was a water bottle with some chilli sauce in it. It could fire over 6 m and it came in handy a few times.

chilli sauce

Our route

Jo racing giraffes... before she hit a pothole. Sometimes we wouldn't see a human soul for days. The silent pedalling let us hear the sounds from all around and get really, really close to the wildlife.

In Kenya we came back to our tent to find a cheeky vervet monkey impressively eating our snacks whilst balancing on our tent. Its friend was inside scattering food everywhere.

TIP: Wire up your zips when leaving camp.

Of all the modes of travel, the bicycle is the most friendly – it opens doors and brings smiles wherever you are.

After a heavy rain – riding gingerly along a track that was now a muddy river.

We arrived late to lake Malawi. We'd been told the hippos weren't in the area so we made camp and soon fell fast asleep. We were woken early by the sound of loud chomping right next to the tent.

For an hour we lay motionless, wondering whether we'd prefer to be squashed or chomped.

I've never opened a zip so quietly. There, just one metre away, was the most dangerous animal in Africa. I gulped and closed the zip. Luckily the hippos eventually headed back to the lake.

Never attempt what you see in this picture

MIKUMI
NATIONAL PARK
DANGER
WILD ANIMALS
NEXT 50KMS
STAY IN VEHICLES
A sign at the entrance helpfully reminded car drivers not to leave their vehicles...

Here you are looking down from above at the two of us pedalling like mad through the Mikumi nature reserve... in the dark. The huge shapes of the elephants, faintly lit by our bike lights, loomed up at our sides while we sang songs to make the lions' roars seem slightly more comforting. Lesson learnt: always make sure you allow enough time for any adventure before darkness falls.

Preparing for an off-road descent through unchartered forest.

Escapes don't come any better than when on two wheels.

Prepare to get muddy.

PLANNING A BIKE ADVENTURE

Few things beat heading into the wild on two wheels. You can cover good distances and explore more widely than on foot. There's the thrill of speed and riding off-road where your skills are put to the test. Then there's the freedom. You may be cycling locally now, but one day, just think — you might cycle around the world.

A CROSS-COUNTRY EXPEDITION

Sometimes the best adventures start from your own front door. Where could you get to? The coast? The hills and fields? A forest? Make a plan, explore the maps, ask for any support. Make it happen.

Riding off on adventure with friends and family into the sunset – where would you go?

After a few adventures your bike is no longer a bike, but a very close friend – I often talk to mine out loud.

A WEEKEND TRIP INTO THE WILD

Pack your bikes and camping gear and head off into the wilderness. There are many places with campsites and bike trails, or if you're feeling more adventurous, find your own secret spot. You'll need a means of transport and a useful adult or two.

In my mind, if you've ever explored on a bike, you've tasted freedom.

TRIP CHECKLIST:

* Always have a good map of the area;

* Choose a route to match your group's experience. Avoid roads if necessary;

* Always take a first aid kit, enough water and food, a puncture repair kit and helmets;

* Offload heavy gear onto the adults if needed;

* Do everything on your explorer's checklist before you go.

GET YOUR BIKE ADVENTURE-READY

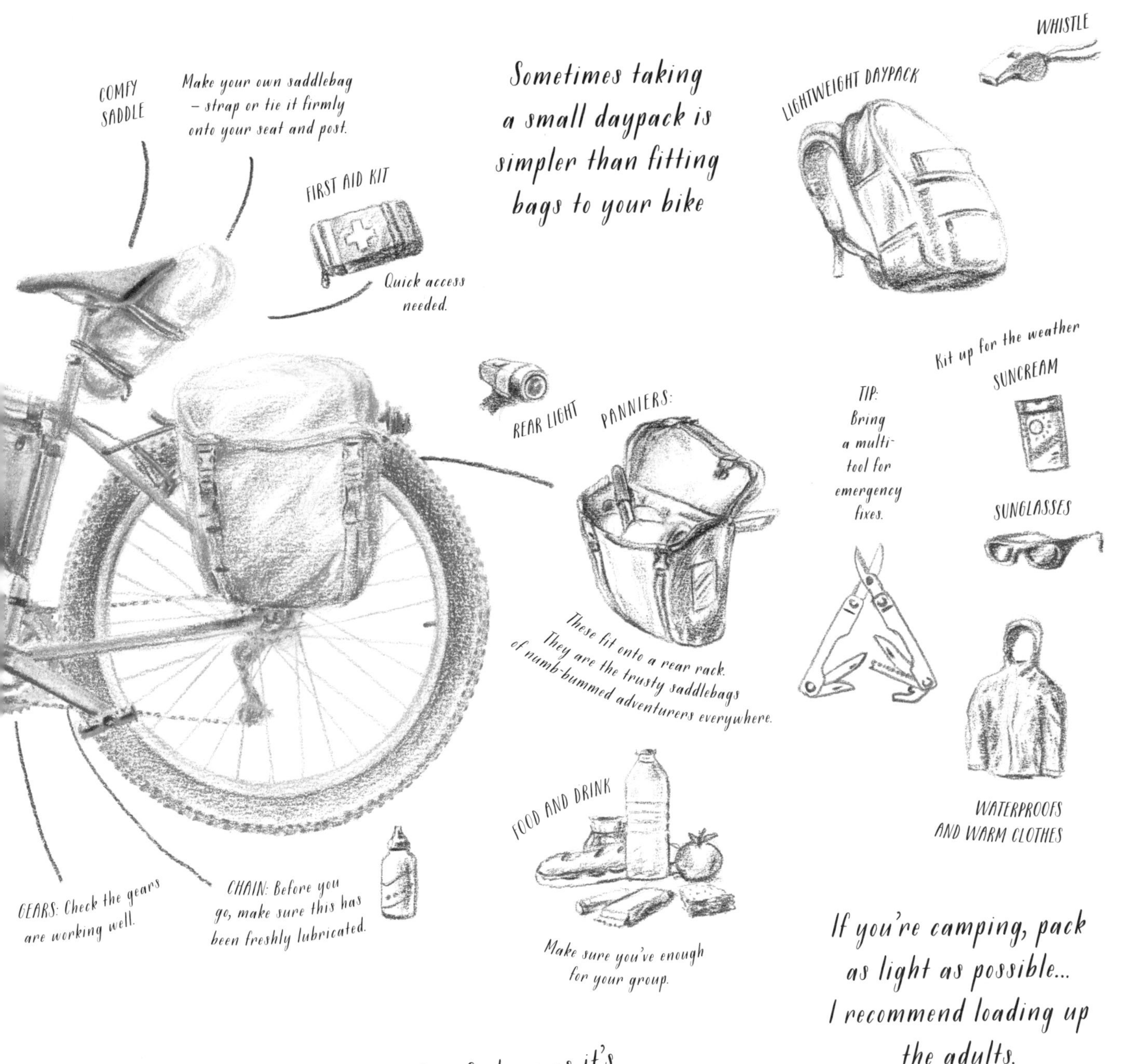

You can explore on any bike... So long as it's got two wheels and a chain you're good to go.

Apart from a few essentials and making sure your bike is in good working order, you don't need much to get going. Here are some useful pointers you might find handy depending on your adventure, for you to use or ignore as you see fit.

BMX: Raise the seat for longer journeys.

ROAD BIKE: Better on smoother paths and roads.

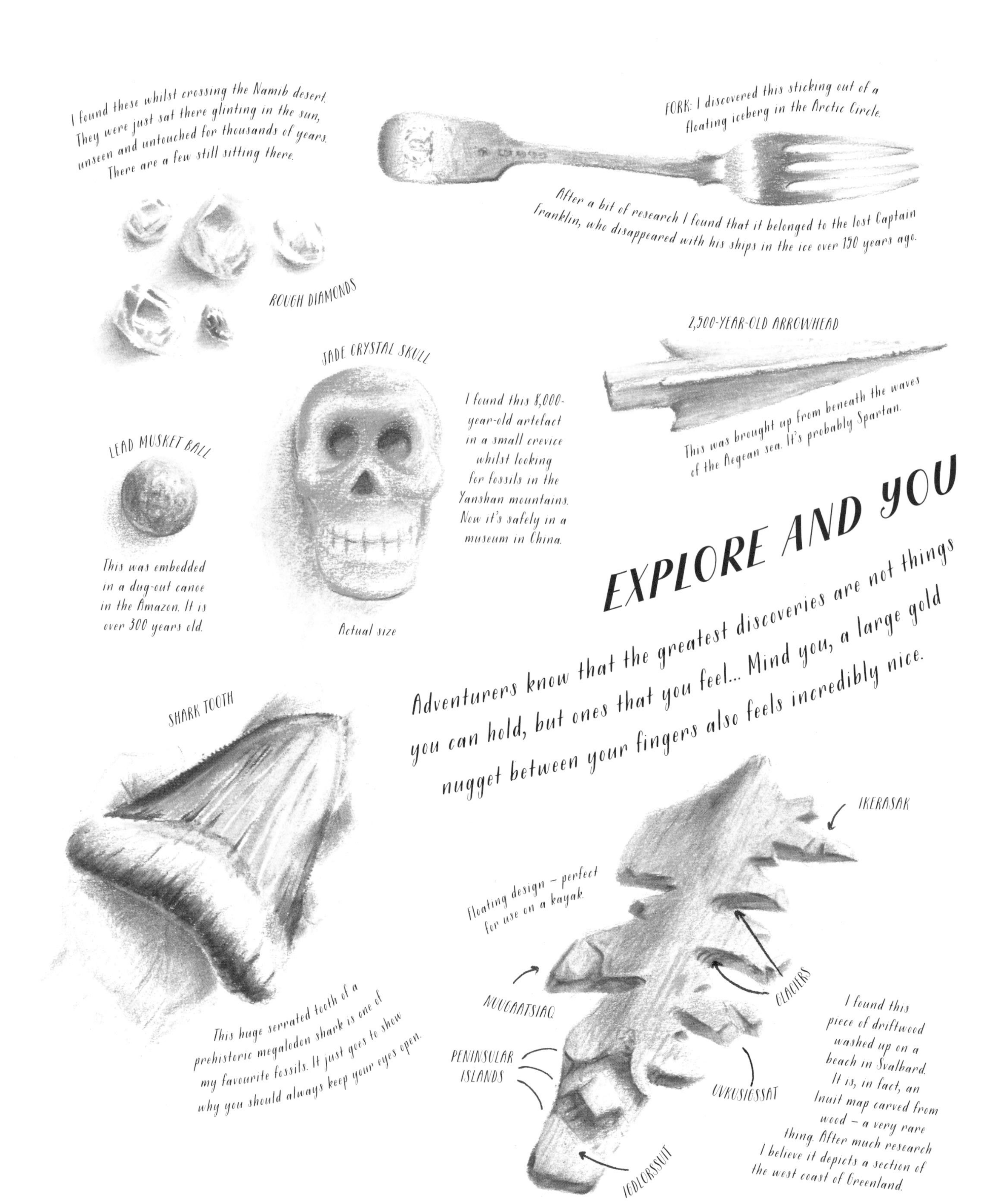

EXPLORE AND YOU

Adventurers know that the greatest discoveries are not things you can hold, but ones that you feel... Mind you, a large gold nugget between your fingers also feels incredibly nice.

THE DART OF A BLOW PIPE: The end had been rolled across the back of a poison dart frog. What made this special was that it was intended for me...

WILL DISCOVER

As you explore you will discover things you wouldn't dream of. Some will be shiny and precious. Some will tell of human stories thousands of years old, whilst prehistoric finds go back millions. They will all be rare. Cherish them. Here are a few of the discoveries that I've made on my little adventures.

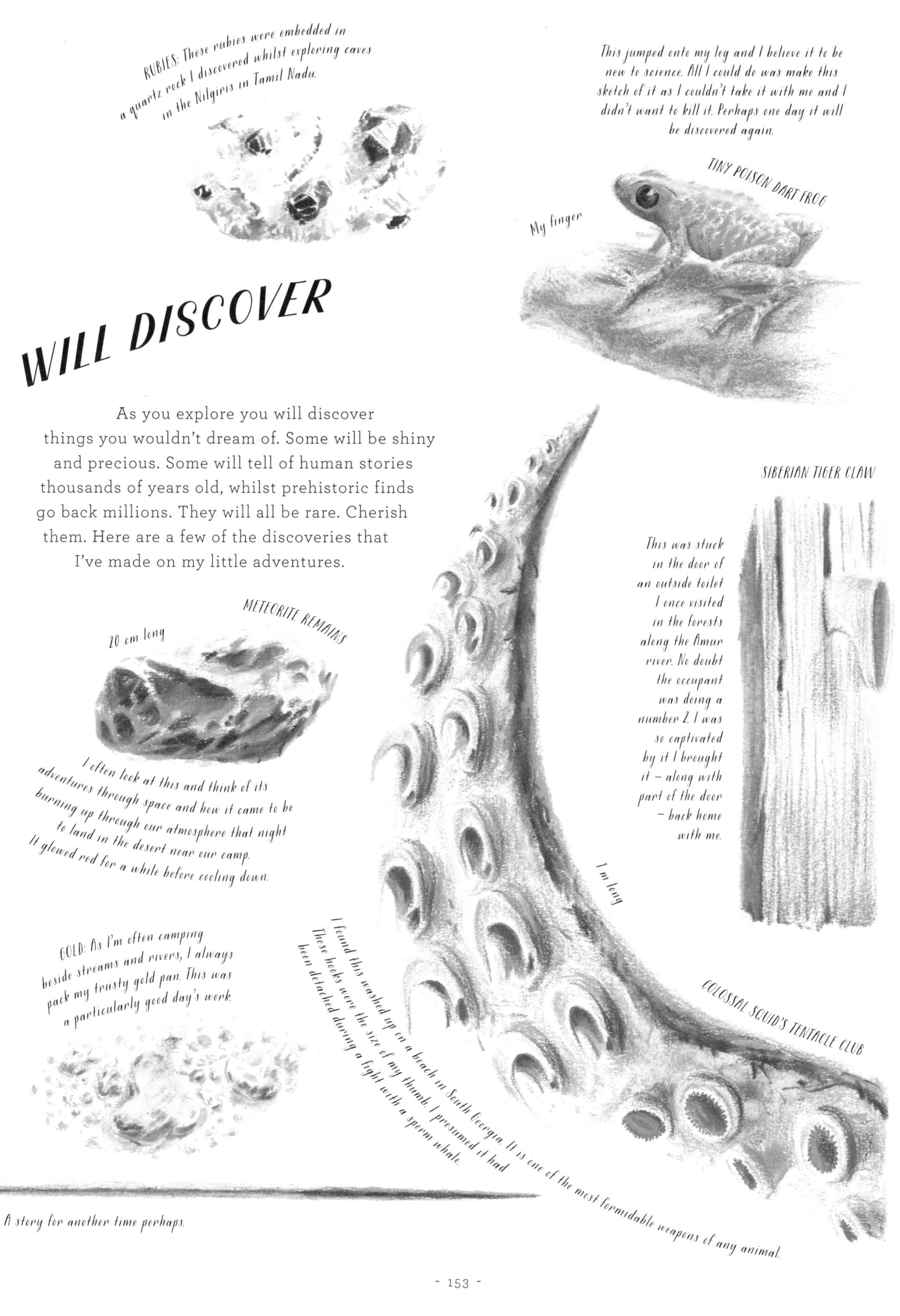

Gold often collects behind a point where shallow water flow over bedrock called a riffle

Just behind this large granite boulder is the perfect spot to find gold.

My well-used pan sits beside a small, remote creek in Australia that was full of gold.

PANNING FOR GOLD

HOW AND WHERE TO FIND IT

You are looking at the secret knowledge of how to find real gold.

You will never forget the moment you discover your first flake of gold. I have found it in streams and rivers all over the world and I'm going to share the secret knowledge of how to find it.

It will take a bit of hard work, a small amount of kit, and patience, but when the hunt starts you won't want to stop.

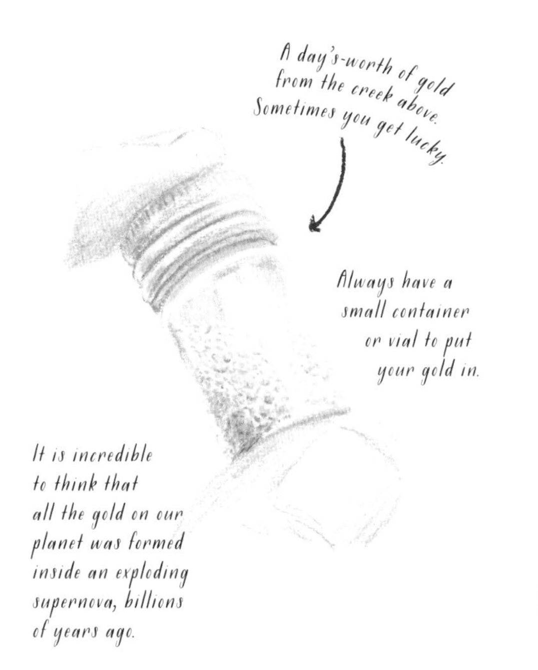

A day's-worth of gold from the creek above. Sometimes you get lucky.

Always have a small container or vial to put your gold in.

It is incredible to think that all the gold on our planet was formed inside an exploding supernova, billions of years ago.

WHICH RIVERS CONTAIN GOLD?

The truth is gold is found in nearly all rivers, but not necessarily in enough quantities to warrant getting your pan out. Look for rivers where gold has been discovered before. Or you can always just try your luck. The best thing is to do some research – then you'll know there's gold to be found.

TIP: Research places where gold has been found before. Try to get hold of a geological map and always check if panning is allowed.

A good gold-bearing stream in the granite hills. Lots of boulders, bends, shallows, pools and little falls.

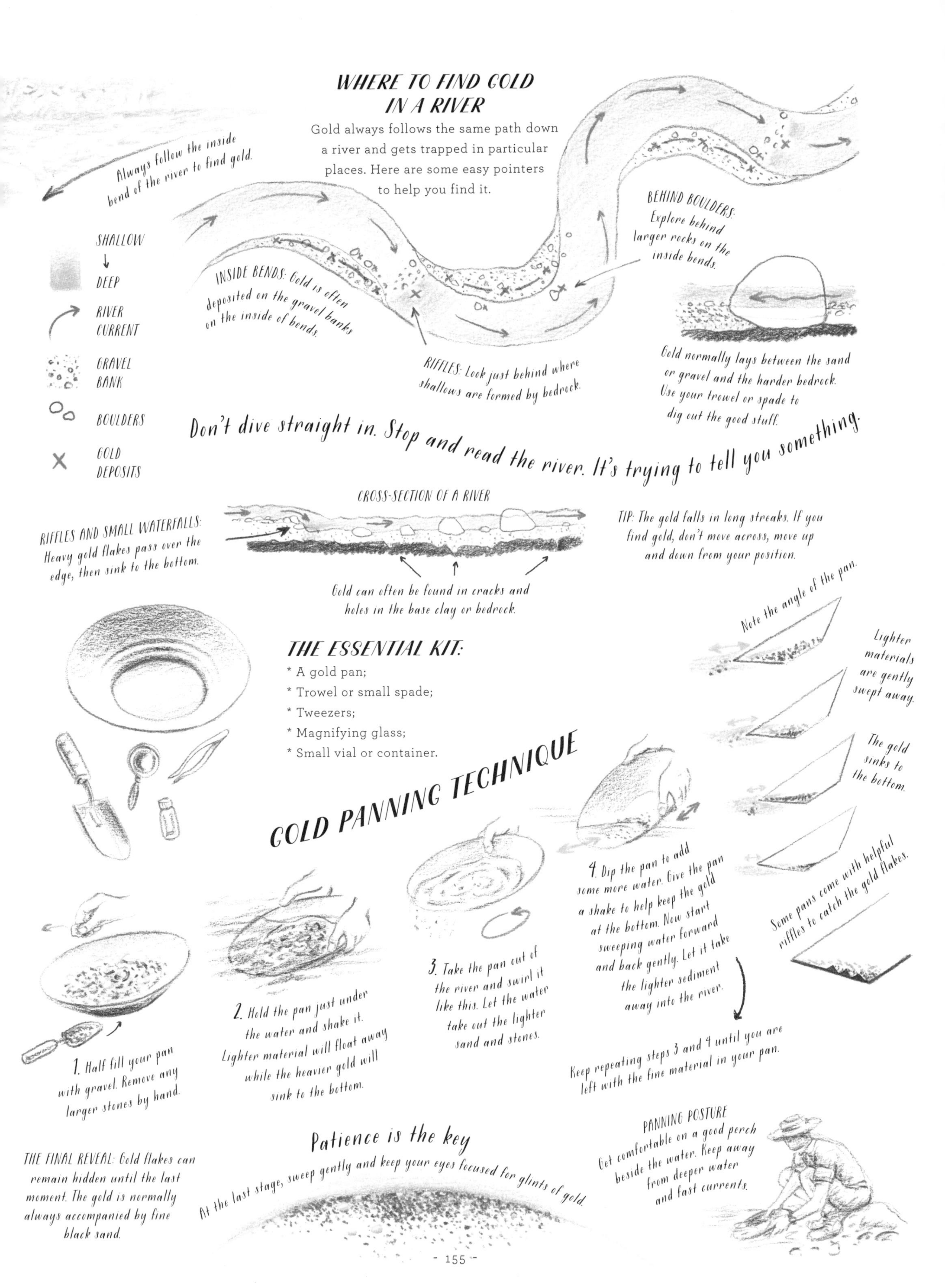
WHERE TO FIND GOLD IN A RIVER
Gold always follows the same path down a river and gets trapped in particular places. Here are some easy pointers to help you find it.
Always follow the inside bend of the river to find gold.
SHALLOW
DEEP
RIVER CURRENT
GRAVEL BANK
BOULDERS
GOLD DEPOSITS
INSIDE BENDS: Gold is often deposited on the gravel banks on the inside of bends.
RIFFLES: Look just behind where shallows are formed by bedrock.
BEHIND BOULDERS: Explore behind larger rocks on the inside bends.
Gold normally lays between the sand or gravel and the harder bedrock. Use your trowel or spade to dig out the good stuff.
Don't dive straight in. Stop and read the river. It's trying to tell you something.
CROSS-SECTION OF A RIVER
RIFFLES AND SMALL WATERFALLS: Heavy gold flakes pass over the edge, then sink to the bottom.
Gold can often be found in cracks and holes in the base clay or bedrock.
TIP: The gold falls in long streaks. If you find gold, don't move across, move up and down from your position.
THE ESSENTIAL KIT:
* A gold pan;
* Trowel or small spade;
* Tweezers;
* Magnifying glass;
* Small vial or container.
Note the angle of the pan.
Lighter materials are gently swept away.
The gold sinks to the bottom.
Some pans come with helpful riffles to catch the gold flakes.
GOLD PANNING TECHNIQUE
1. Half fill your pan with gravel. Remove any larger stones by hand.
2. Hold the pan just under the water and shake it. Lighter material will float away while the heavier gold will sink to the bottom.
3. Take the pan out of the river and swirl it like this. Let the water take out the lighter sand and stones.
4. Dip the pan to add some more water. Give the pan a shake to help keep the gold at the bottom. Now start sweeping water forward and back gently. Let it take the lighter sediment away into the river.
Keep repeating steps 3 and 4 until you are left with the fine material in your pan.
THE FINAL REVEAL: Gold flakes can remain hidden until the last moment. The gold is normally always accompanied by fine black sand.
Patience is the key
At the last stage, sweep gently and keep your eyes focused for glints of gold.
PANNING POSTURE
Get comfortable on a good perch beside the water. Keep away from deeper water and fast currents.

EXPEDITION ON THE RIO JARI

There are still some places out there that have never seen humankind. These places are remote, wild and very hard to reach. When a friend said he had discovered an unexplored river deep in the Amazon jungle, I took a deep breath and said, "What's the worst that can happen?" For the next six months, we paddled deeper and deeper into the unknown, never knowing what we would find, or even whether we would be coming back.

NOT ALONE

A human footprint on the bank of the river, 400 km from civilisation. Had we discovered one of the lost tribes of the Amazon? This was a humbling moment. After that I kept hearing voices in the jungle at night – a figment of my imagination, or something else?

The higher reaches of the river were exciting. The jungle reached in from all sides. We often had to cut our way through as fallen trees had blocked our path.

A jaguar looks up from its drink – we were likely the first humans it had ever seen.

As we paddled through the mist, a million jungle noises came together to make the sweetest music.

When you are catching your dinner, you never know what hideous toothy creature you're pulling up from the depths.

SWIMMING WILD

Floating quietly through the jungle amphitheatre... Sheer bliss. Every morning I would go for a swim. I found the piranhas to be more convivial early in the day.

The payara fish, which is also known the vampire fish for fairly obvious reasons.

MIGHTY RAPIDS

As we approached larger rapids, we would portage (carry) our canoe overland. Here we badly misjudged a section of water. We were lucky to just lose some possessions and not our lives. Always scout ahead and avoid rapids beyond your experience.

A large anaconda swam across the river in front of us after we rudely disturbed it digesting its meal. It made our 5-m canoe look tiddly. What was inside? A caiman? A tapir? It could have easily been one of us.

The canoe – the quiet heroine of adventure, if you let her she will take you on the wildest of adventures.

Further and further we forge, deeper into the unknown. Our paddles quietly dip into the surface in unison – an unthinking rhythm built up between us over months. All around, the jungle's twisting arms reach out across the river, sometimes creating tunnels which we have to hack our way through. The birds and monkeys hush as we pass by, unsure of the strange creatures passing beneath them. It is hard to believe that our eyes are the first to witness this sanctuary. We say nothing, our senses completely in the moment.

Beware – once you're hooked, a canoeing addiction lasts a lifetime.

An Amazon kingfisher with its breakfast.

Look out for the wildlife. Use the stealthiness of the canoe to your advantage.

Fishing is great from a canoe. Unless you hook a huge Pacú. This one dragged us a kilometre up river.

Feel the thrill of small rapids, before building up to the bigger ones.

PLANNING YOUR OWN CANOE ADVENTURE

When renting on a river, they will often organise the transport of you and the canoe back to where you started.

Do you think you're ready for a canoe expedition? Perhaps you think it all sounds a bit hard to arrange.

Fortunately there are many places out there where you can rent out canoes and gear. I've put together some thoughts to help you get started. Now you just need to tempt the adults to join in.

CANOES AND EQUIPMENT

If you have the gear already then you're away. If not, look into canoe hire places. They can provide nearly all the gear you need.

CHOOSING A RIVER OR LAKE

Where you hire the canoe from is often based near the lake or river where your adventure will be. These waters are normally suited to most experience levels, but ask anyway. Start easy, you've plenty of years to take on big rapids. If you already have a canoe, find a river to match your experience.

A monkey-eyed view of us and our canoe

Joined by pink river dolphins in the Amazon. They followed for hours and hours, playing games of hide and seek with us. Delightful company.

Big rapids and weirs can be fun, but also very dangerous with hidden currents. Avoid until you are experienced.

Nothing beats pitching up a tent beside the river or lake after a day on the paddle.

If the adults are too scared, then research canoeing clubs or ask family friends.

CANOE CAMPING

If planning a multi-day trip, check for places along your planned route that could be suitable spots to camp. It could be a campsite or something a little wilder.

TIME PLANNING

For a first canoe adventure, start with a day or weekend trip, or even an hour or two to see how you take to the water. You can cover a surprising distance in that amount of time.

THE TEAM

You'll probably need an adult per canoe, depending on your level. Hiring multiple canoes with other friends and families makes a great adventure.

Just imagine, soon you could be riding the river currents on your own adventure.

CANOE KNOWLEDGE

There are many varieties of adventuring canoe. This is the classic open design based on the original Wabanaki-style birchbark canoes.

PADDLES

CANOE ANATOMY

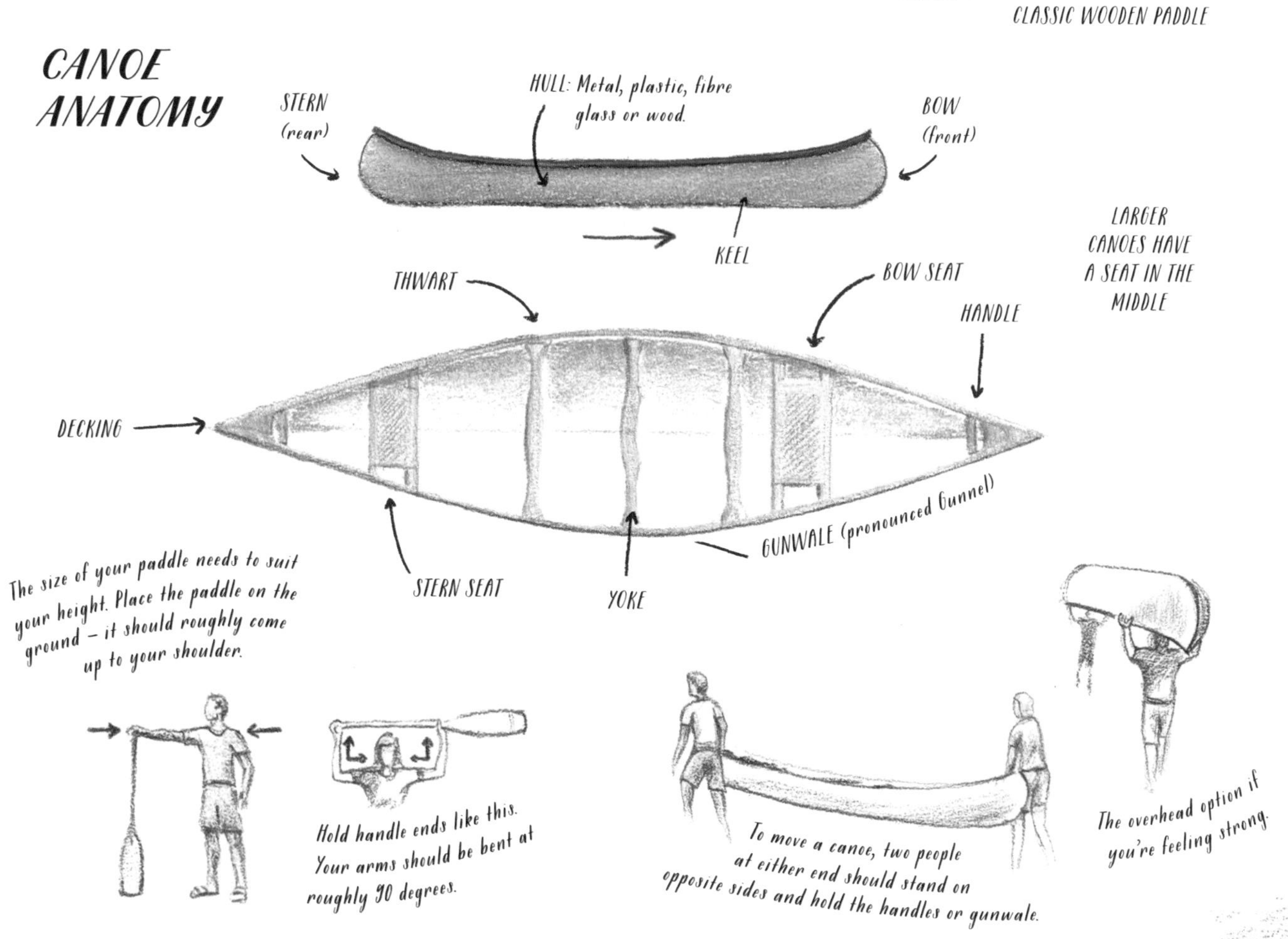

CANOE SIZES

Canoes come in all shapes and sizes. Choose yours based on how big your group is.

A two-seater canoe is my usual choice.

Some canoes will fit a whole family.

In a larger group, split into different canoes and make sure there's an experienced canoeist in each one.

KIT AND SUPPLIES

As with any adventure you'll need to take some essentials. If you are renting out a canoe you will normally be given these items. If in doubt, ask.

CANOE AND PADDLES

A life vest or jacket is almost always essential.

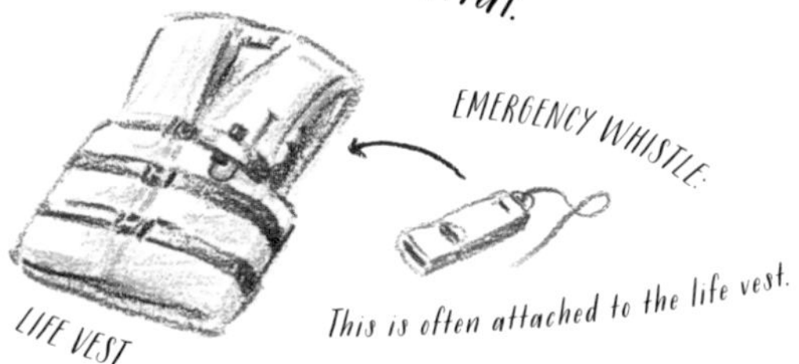

Always pack your gear into watertight containers or dry bags – if you capsize they float quite nicely.

When hot, sun protection is essential. Sports sandals are ideal in the wet.

PACKING LIST:

* The essentials above;
* Suitable clothes that match the weather;
* Coat or anorak;
* Towel;
* Enough food and water;
* Some tasty snacks;
* Footwear that can get wet;
* Sun protection – hat, sunglasses, suncream;
* Insect repellent;
* Camera;
* Binoculars;
* Camping equipment if required;
* Fishing gear.

FISHING HANDLINE

FISHING ROD AND REEL:
Use a small or telescopic rod.

STABLE PACKING
Lightweight
Medium
Heavy

Stopping for lunch and a bit of elephant watching on the banks of the Zambezi River. We also had to keep our eyes open for the crocs – some were longer than our canoes.

Note how the gear has been stowed away in the centre of the canoes. Always tie up your canoe securely or pull well away from the water's edge.

ON THE WATER

The more knowledge and skills you have, the deeper into the wild you can go and the more adventurous you can be. Here are some tips and pointers that will help you master your canoe and begin to understand the water. As always, the best way to learn is on the water with a seasoned canoeist.

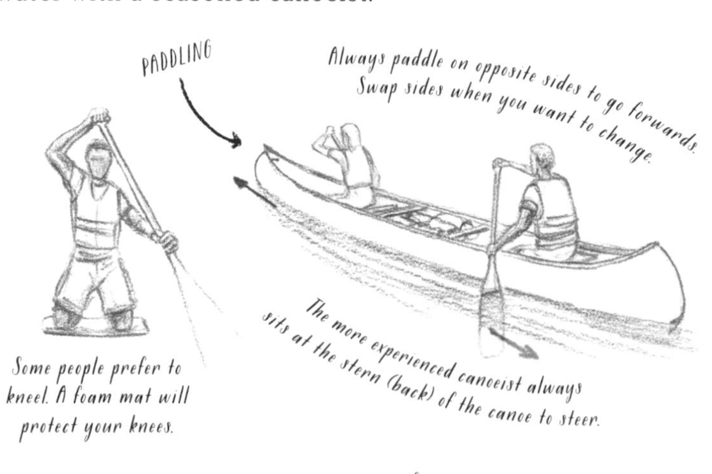

Paddling is about finding a rhythm together. It can take a bit of practice.

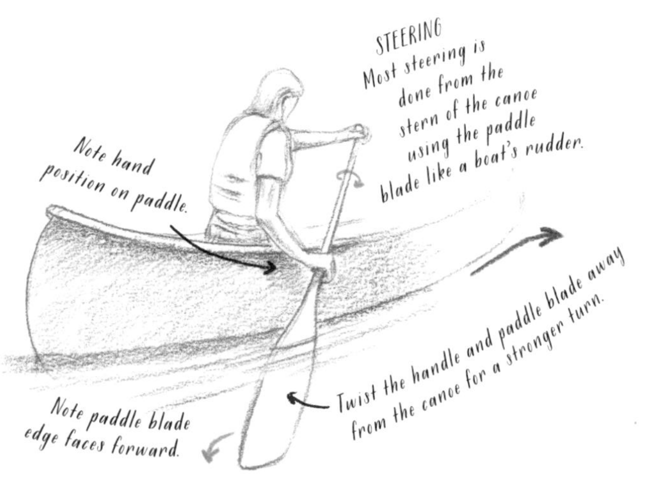

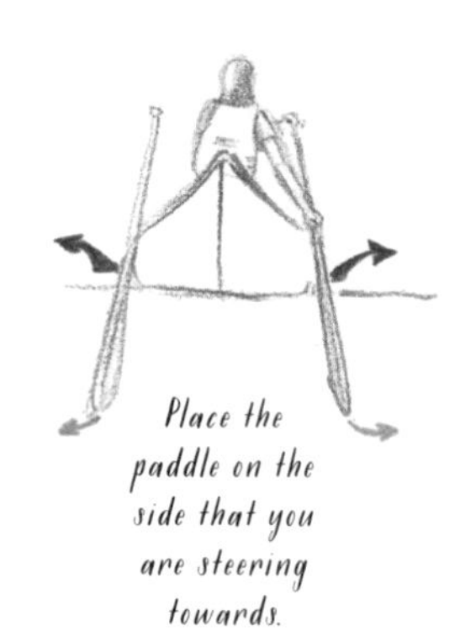

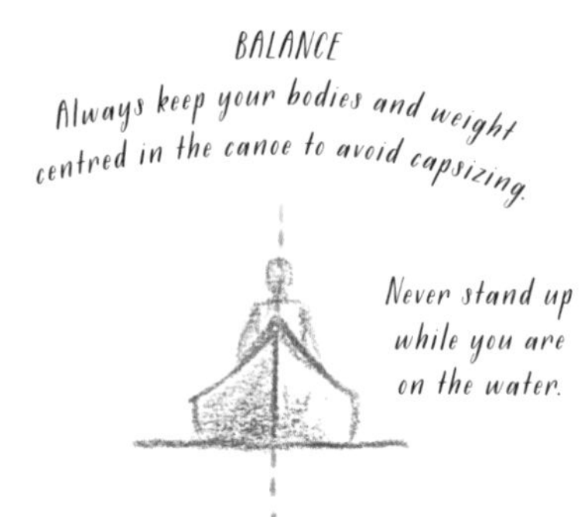

With practice you can steer the canoe as part of your stroke.

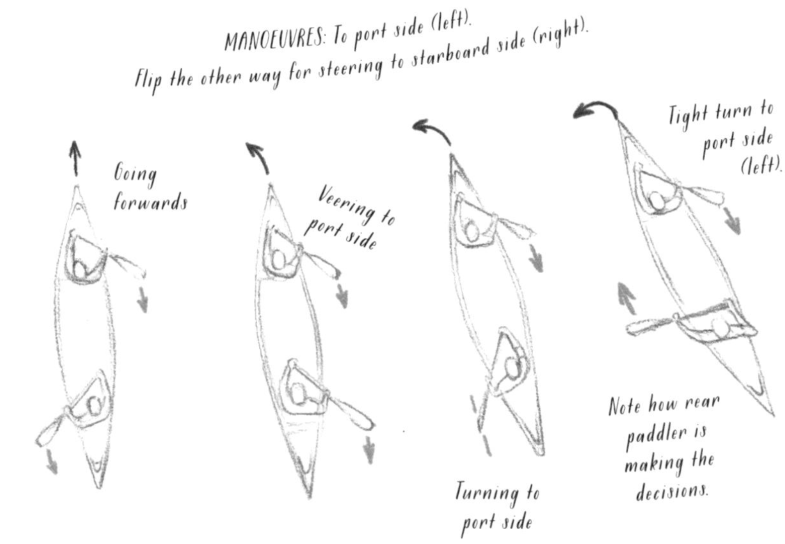

NAVIGATING A RIVER

As it takes you through the wild, being able to read a river as well as the map is important. Always be aware of the potential obstacles on your river route before you embark, either by checking the map, or, even better, asking a canoeist who knows the water.

READING THE RIVER

Always keep your eyes open for obstacles ahead. Here are some tell-tale signs you need to be aware of.

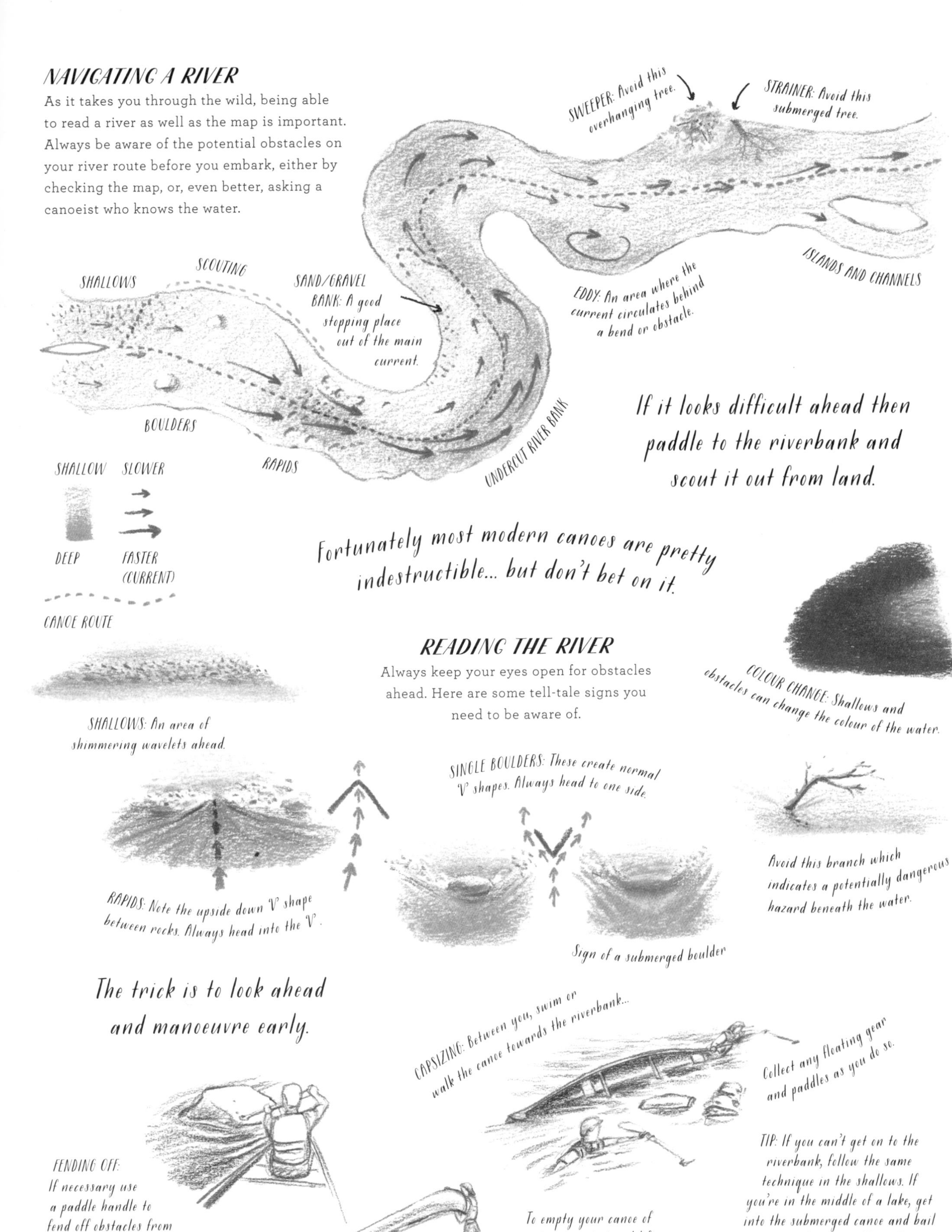

Always check and follow the local rules and regulations when catching fish.

If possible, get an experienced fisherman to show you the ropes and knots... and where the fish are hiding.

HOW TO CATCH A FISH

Fishing line on a stick – basic but highly effective.

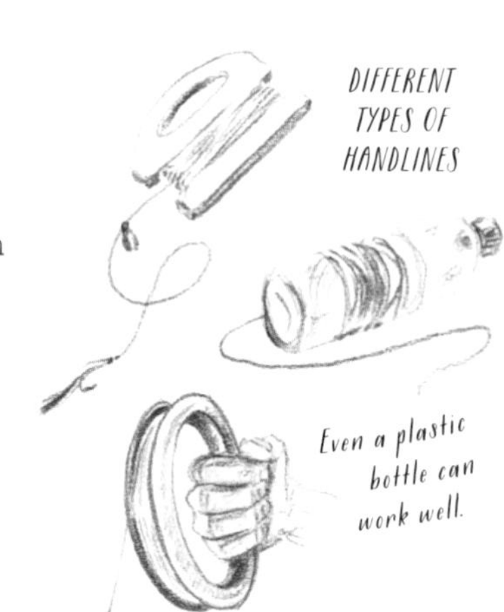

Fishing is not only a handy way of sourcing food in the wild, but it's also immensely exciting.

The ways of catching fish are many, but for me, hand-lining is one of the best. It is simple, convenient when short on space, and incredibly effective in the right hands. It can also be made from scratch in just a few minutes.

TECHNIQUES

TROLLING: A long line and lure (a hook that imitates a small fish) is pulled behind the canoe as you paddle.

GOOD FOR:

* Deep water;
* Fishing whilst paddling;
* Using lures not bait;
* Longer lengths of line of 10 m or more.

GOOD FOR:

* Hands-on fishing;
* Deep to semi-deep water;
* Fishing from the canoe or the shore;
* Shallow waters.

MAKING YOUR OWN HANDLINE

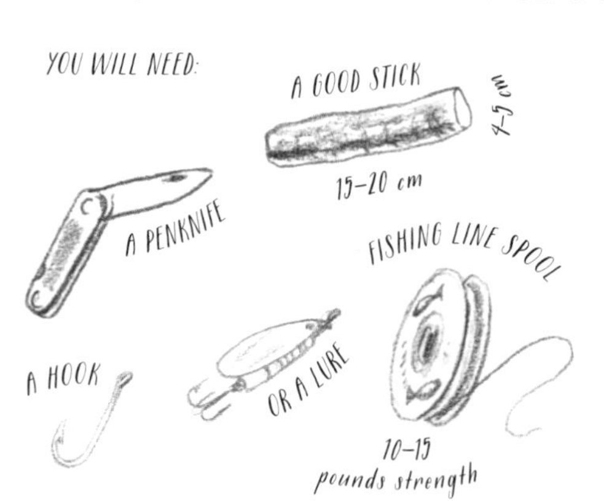

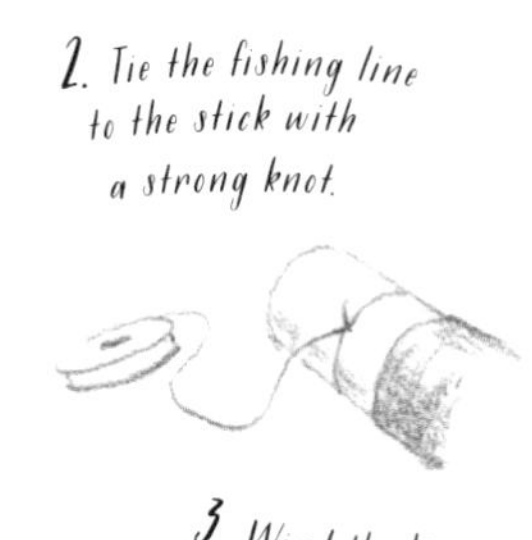

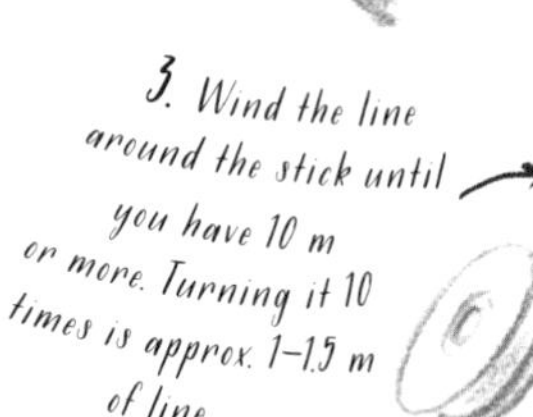

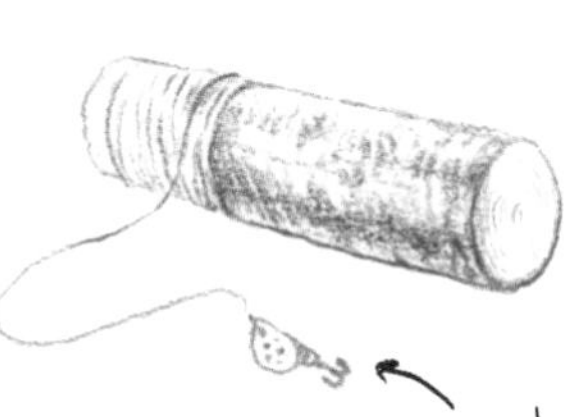

When you feel that first 'thump' as a fish takes the bait, your heart begins to race, your hands shake with excitement – you are now a hunter.

See the knots section for how to tie an easy and strong fishing knot.

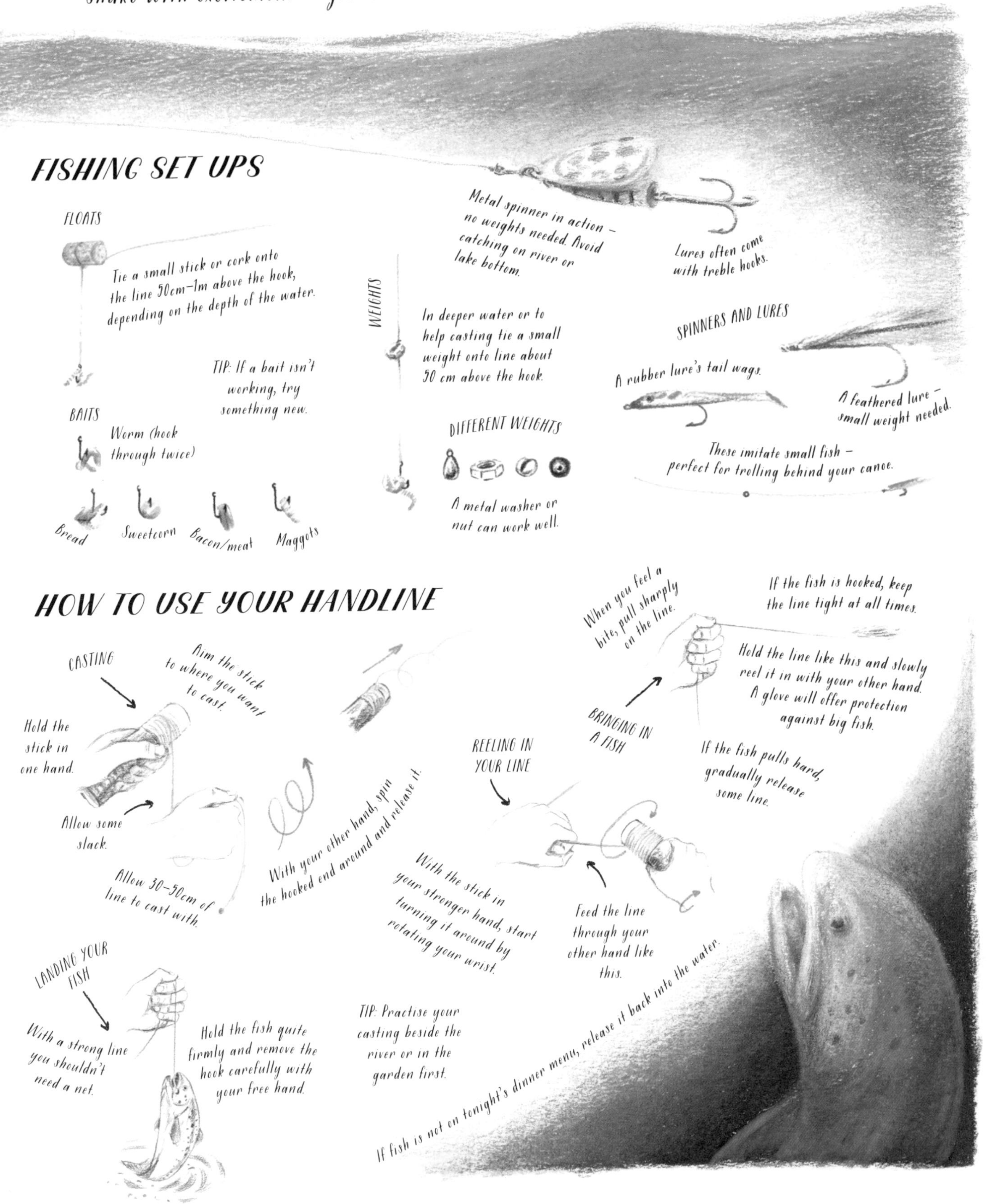

AN EYE FOR AN EYE – A FINGER FOR A FIN

My missing finger — it was like parting company with a dear friend.

The wild has a habit of catching up with those who think they've got it all figured out. Today, it was me that was caught out.

Everything was going well until it came to catching dinner. I took the canoe out onto the river alone – something I'd done a hundred times. After a few casts the rod suddenly arched over as I felt the thump of a fish taking the bait. I wondered what it could be. In these waters the usual suspects were either toothy, electric or had a nasty sting. Whatever it was, it was taking my attention off the river at a bad moment as I heard the distinct sound of rapids behind me. I started reeling in the fish as quickly as I could. Surely I could get it in before we drifted too close. The thrashing fish that emerged from the water wasn't quite what I was hoping for. It was a fearsome black piranha, weighing about two kilos.

I grabbed it behind the head and hoisted it into the canoe. As I did so the fishing line caught on something and the fish slipped from my grip. I reached down quickly to move it away from my toes. Its big red eyes clearly saw my hand coming. There was a brief crunching sound as its jaws snapped shut. I looked down and saw half my little finger had gone, neatly dismembered where the last two bones joined. At that same moment I felt the canoe tipping into the rapids behind me. This couldn't be happening, surely. I grabbed the paddle and started paddling like mad whilst trying hard not to lose a toe to my angry guest.

We finally made it back into the quieter water where I carefully dispatched the fish. My finger tip stared up at me from the hull of the canoe, and as I picked up my dear detached friend a strange thought occurred to me... could I use my lost finger as bait? At least then it wouldn't be wasted.

Fortunately common sense prevailed and I paddled gingerly back to camp.

The black piranha lay dead at the bottom of the canoe, its jaws still mechanically opening and closing. It was clearly laughing at me.

USEFUL KNOWLEDGE

HOW TO MAKE...

Follow these simple instructions on how to make some useful gear that could help you on your adventures.

SNOWSHOES FROM TENNIS RACKETS

YOU WILL NEED:

* Two old tennis rackets;
* Some lengths of rubber inner tube;
* Scissors or a penknife.

TIP: Duct tape or cord can also be used but is less suitable.

TIP: Cut larger tubes into longer, thinner lengths.

1. Start by feeding the rubber between the racket strings and tie the ends to the edge of the frame.

Note how the top length is doubled over.

Tie off ends with a reef knot.

2. Twist the top strap so that it will hold around the toe of your boot tightly.

3. Next, pull the straps apart and place your boot between the straps. It should grip tightly.

4. To tighten the straps place a stick under the rubber and twist to add tension.

Note how boot is centred on the racket.

If needed, lock stick into strings.

When walking, only your heel should lift up.

A heel strap can also be added if extra support is needed.

If it is too loose then pull tighter and re-tie.

A BACKPACK FROM A PAIR OF TROUSERS

YOU WILL NEED:

* A pair of trousers;
* 1 m or more of string or cord.

In a survival situation you won't mind sharing your pants with the wild.

1. Start by tying the two legs of your trousers together.

2. Next, fold the legs over and feed the string through the belt loops.

3. Add your essentials and tie the bag closed with a shoelace knot.

A CANDLE FROM A CRAYON

Simply light a wax crayon – the paper on the side will catch light and continue burning.

Melt bottom to create a base first.

A CANOE SHELTER

YOU WILL NEED:

* A canoe;
* Forked branches;
* Paddles;
* Tarp (with metal eyelets);
* Cord.

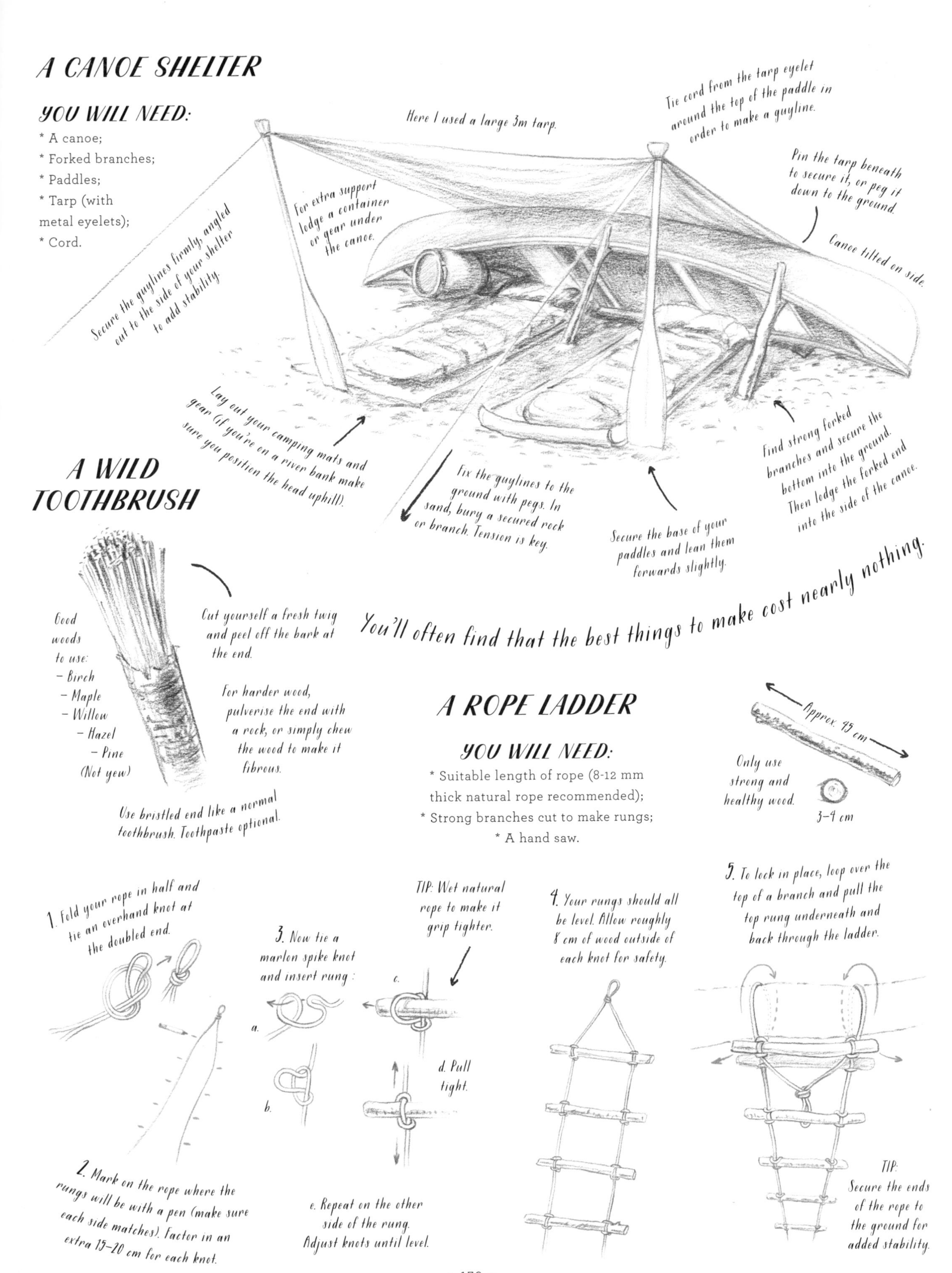

A WILD TOOTHBRUSH

You'll often find that the best things to make cost nearly nothing.

A ROPE LADDER

YOU WILL NEED:

* Suitable length of rope (8-12 mm thick natural rope recommended);
* Strong branches cut to make rungs;
* A hand saw.

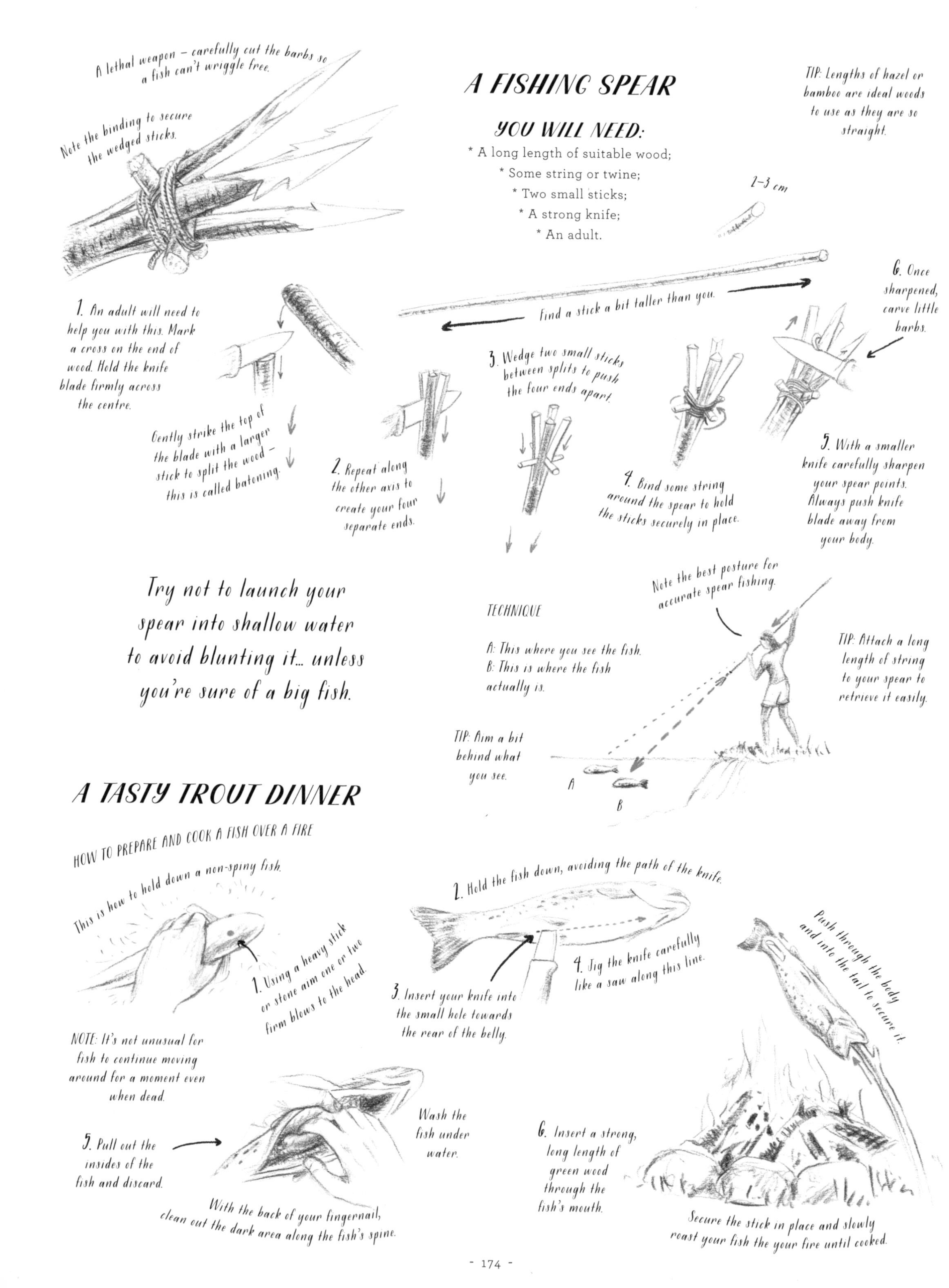

A lethal weapon – carefully cut the barbs so a fish can't wriggle free.

Note the binding to secure the wedged sticks.

A FISHING SPEAR

YOU WILL NEED:

* A long length of suitable wood;
* Some string or twine;
* Two small sticks;
* A strong knife;
* An adult.

TIP: Lengths of hazel or bamboo are ideal woods to use as they are so straight.

2–3 cm

Find a stick a bit taller than you.

1. An adult will need to help you with this. Mark a cross on the end of wood. Hold the knife blade firmly across the centre.

Gently strike the top of the blade with a larger stick to split the wood – this is called batoning.

2. Repeat along the other axis to create your four separate ends.

3. Wedge two small sticks between splits to push the four ends apart.

4. Bind some string around the spear to hold the sticks securely in place.

5. With a smaller knife carefully sharpen your spear points. Always push knife blade away from your body.

6. Once sharpened, carve little barbs.

Try not to launch your spear into shallow water to avoid blunting it... unless you're sure of a big fish.

TECHNIQUE

A: This where you see the fish.
B: This is where the fish actually is.

Note the best posture for accurate spear fishing.

TIP: Attach a long length of string to your spear to retrieve it easily.

TIP: Aim a bit behind what you see.

A

B

A TASTY TROUT DINNER

HOW TO PREPARE AND COOK A FISH OVER A FIRE

This is how to hold down a non-spiny fish.

1. Using a heavy stick or stone aim one or two firm blows to the head.

NOTE: It's not unusual for fish to continue moving around for a moment even when dead.

2. Hold the fish down, avoiding the path of the knife.

3. Insert your knife into the small hole towards the rear of the belly.

4. Jig the knife carefully like a saw along this line.

5. Pull out the insides of the fish and discard.

Wash the fish under water.

With the back of your fingernail, clean out the dark area along the fish's spine.

6. Insert a strong, long length of green wood through the fish's mouth.

Push through the body and into the tail to secure it.

Secure the stick in place and slowly roast your fish the your fire until cooked.

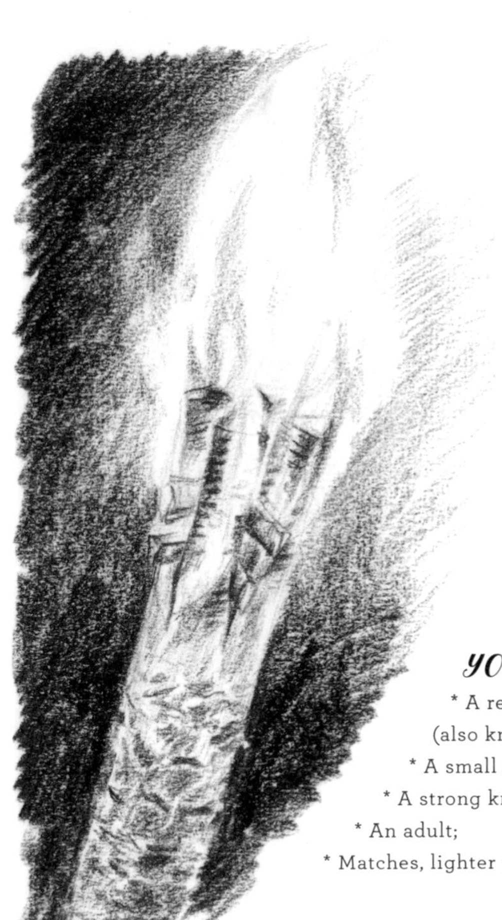

1. Look for lower branches on a fallen pine tree.

Resin often congregates in the wood where the branch meets the tree.

2. With a saw carefully cut off a suitable branch as close to the trunk as possible.

You're looking for richly coloured wood like this, which is saturated in fragrant-smelling resin.

NOTE: You may well need to try another branch or tree.

A PINE TORCH

Pine resin is nature's rocket fuel. By locating the right kind of wood you can create an effective torch that can burn for up to an hour, sometimes more.

YOU WILL NEED:

* A resinous branch (also known as fatwood);
* A small saw or hatchet;
* A strong knife;
* An adult;
* Matches, lighter or fire steel.

3. With the knife, carefully baton the end into four quarters. For a reminder on how to do this look at the fishing spear instructions in my notebooks.

Remove bark from end before batoning.

SAFETY:

* Only an experienced adult should handle a lit torch;
* Keep clear from anything that could catch alight;
* This is not for a dry season – falling resin can start a forest fire.

4. Insert small splints of resinous wood between quartered ends to create airflow. Add shavings to act as tinder when lighting.

5. Secure the torch base into the ground and then light the tinder shavings and wait for the flame to grow.

Red-hot burning resin can fall from the torch so be sure to fix the torch at an angle in a safe area.

Saws, knives and red-hot resin mean a sensible adult is required for this.

10 THINGS OUT OF DUCT TAPE

A SURVIVAL SPEAR WITH YOUR KNIFE

STRETCHER

LASHING

LEAKY SHOES AND BOOTS

TENT

A DRINKING VESSEL

MARKING A ROUTE

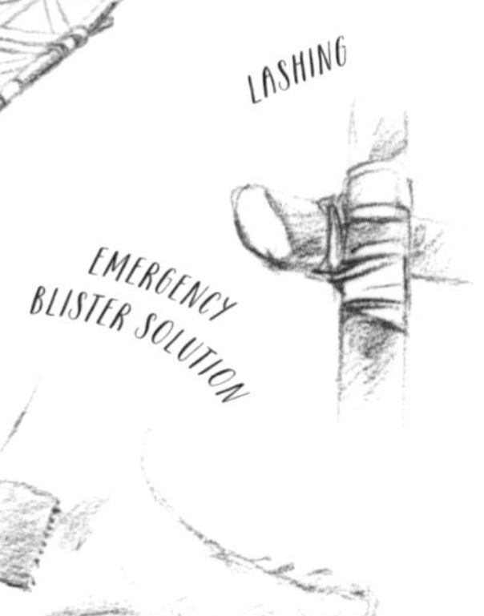

EMERGENCY BLISTER SOLUTION

FIX ALMOST ANYTHING...

BROKEN GLASSES

WATER BOTTLE

ROPES AND KNOTS

It's easy to get lost in the world of ropes and knots so I've laid out the essentials to get you started. Even a small understanding of the subject will unlock real adventures.

A coil or hank of manila rope – a good choice of rope for adventuring. Comes in different sizes.

Natural rope includes manila, sisal, hemp and cotton. Different materials have different strengths, but manila is the best.

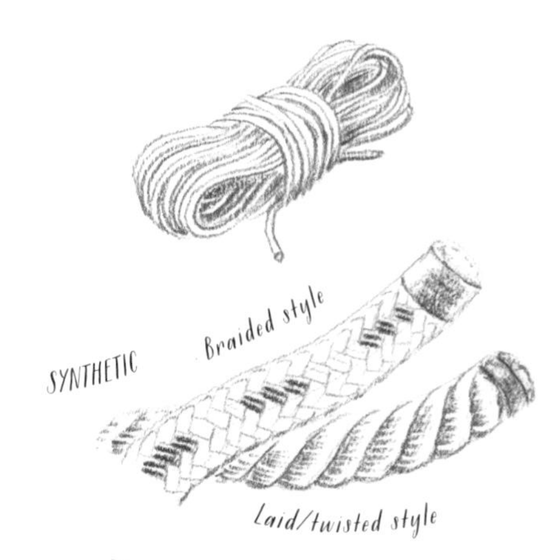

The best man-made ropes are nylon, polyester and polypropylene. They are often associated with sailing and climbing.

MANILA ROPE:

* Good all-round use;
* Good for knots, lashing and heavy duty jobs;
* Doesn't stretch much;
* Heavier/larger than the synthetic equivalent;
* Cut ends need to be spliced or whipped.

MANMADE ROPE:

* Generally stronger than natural rope;
* Lighter and takes up less space;
* Cut ends can be flame sealed;
* Note that nylon has a 20% stretch.

SIZES

THICK ROPE:

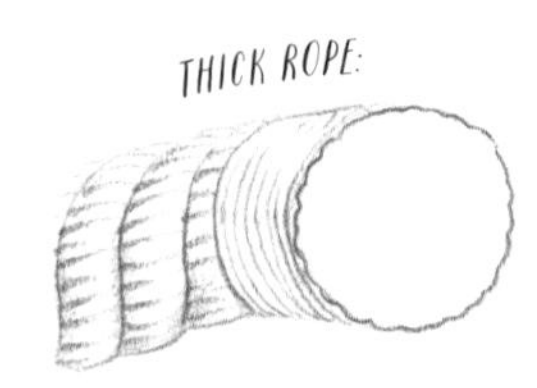

* Good for rope swings and climbing;
* Best for heavy duties;
* Harder to handle and tie knots.

MEDIUM ROPE:

* Good for all-round uses;
* Can often support heavy weight – check first;
*Good for handling, lashing and knot tying.

PARACORD:

* Good for lashing and shelter building;
* Use for guylines for tents and tarps;
* Has many survival uses.

TIMBER HITCH

A simple temporary knot – used to drag logs and start lashings. Effective under strain.

1.

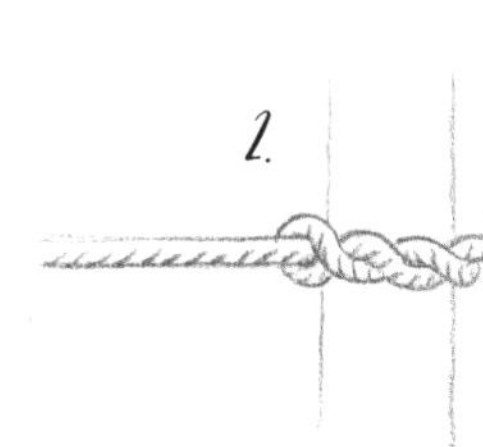

TIP: More twists equals more secure.

CLOVE HITCH

A quick and simple knot – often used to start and end lashing. Not very secure.

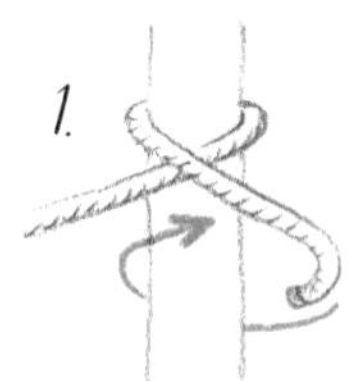
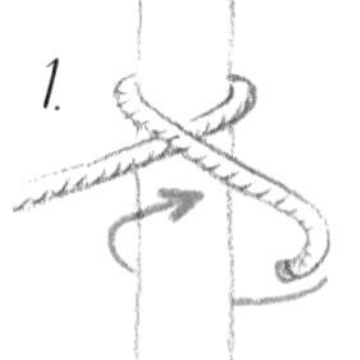

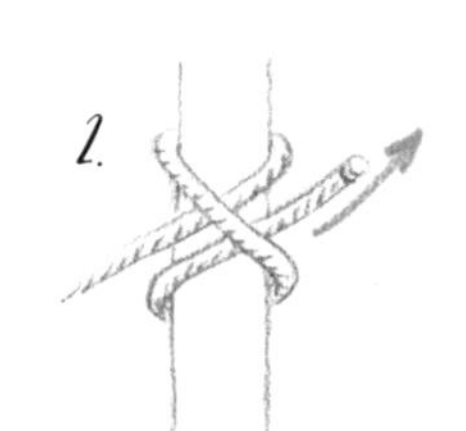

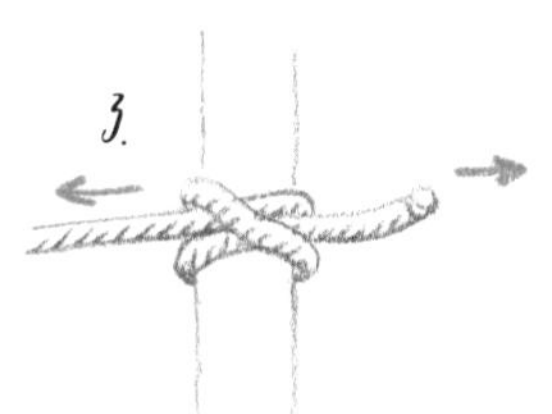

ROUND TURN & TWO HALF HITCHES

A simple and strong knot – good for attaching rope to a pole or tree. Keep tight.

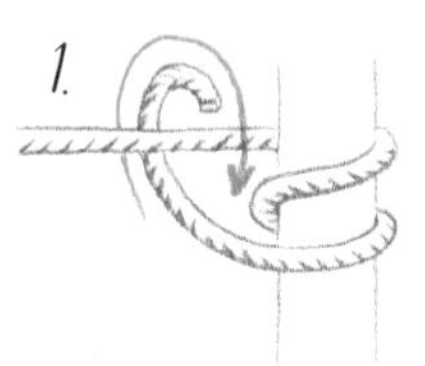

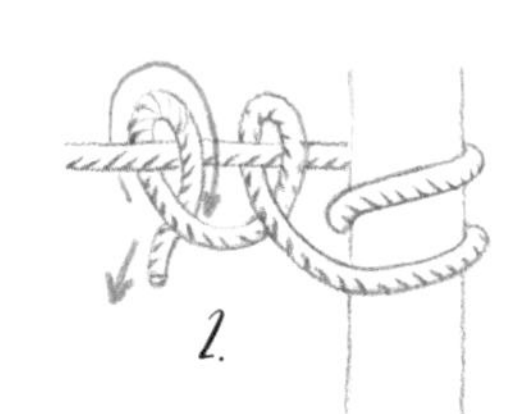

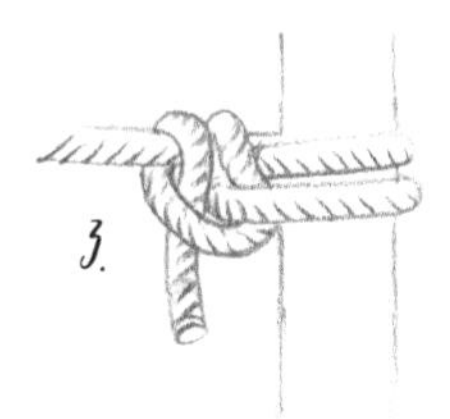

JOINING KNOTS

REEF OR SQUARE KNOT

Simple and effective knot for joining two ends of rope together. Easy to untie.
* Ropes must be the same thickness;
* Not for extending ropes or carrying weight;
* Useful for tying non-rope materials, in first aid for instance.

FISHERMAN'S KNOT

For tying two lengths of rope together or extending vines. Not often used for fishing lines, it can be hard to untie.

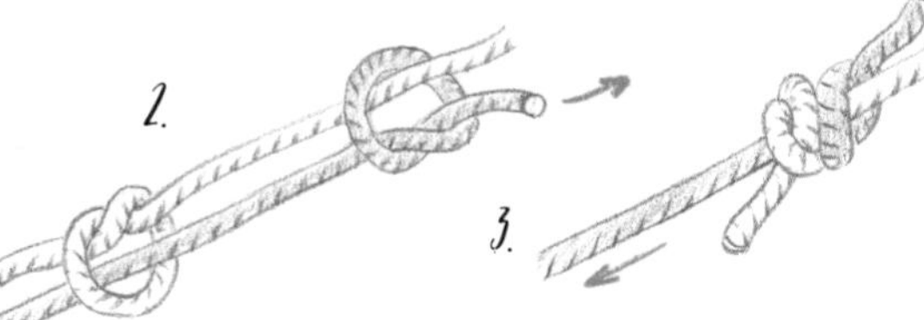

SHEET BEND

Very simple yet strong knot for tying two lengths of different-sized rope together.
* Requires constant strain;
* Note the different roles of the large and small rope.

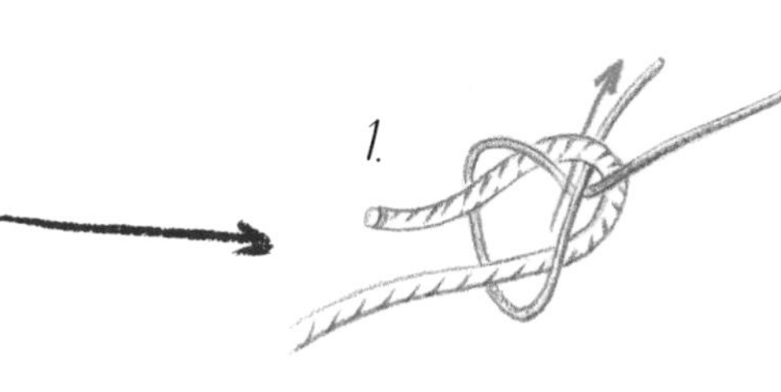

LOOPS

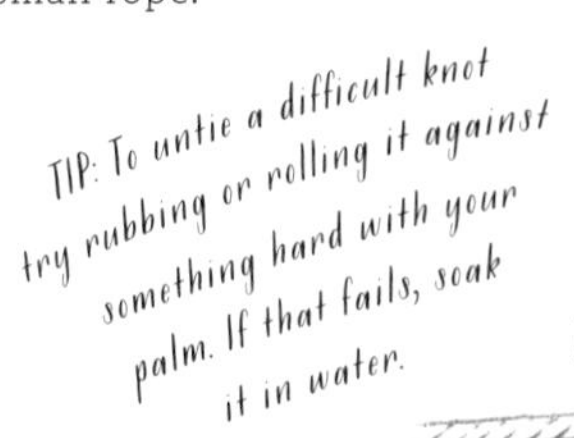

OVERHAND LOOP

A quick and simple knot for fast loop making. Not as strong as a bowline knot.

BOWLINE KNOT

Pronounced 'BO-lin'. A simple and strong knot that won't slip and can be undone easily. All adventurers know this knot.

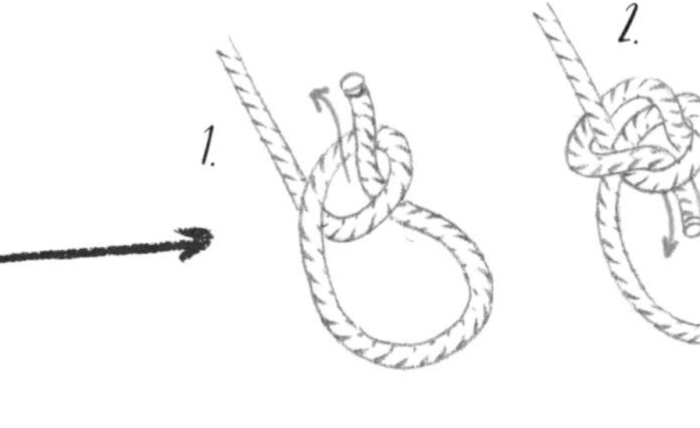

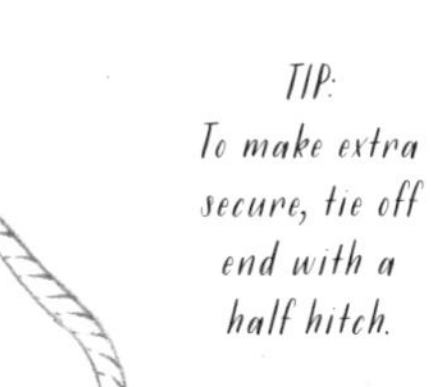

FISHING KNOT

How to attach a hook to your line.

Fiddly is the fishing line. Be patient, the prize will be worth it.

PALOMAR KNOT

A very effective and relatively simple hook knot.

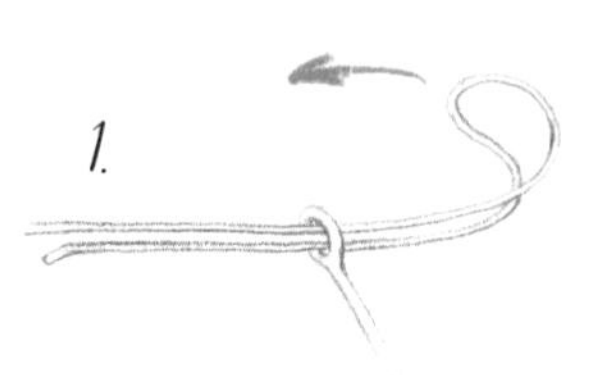

2.

3.

4.

TIP: Wet the loose knot with saliva before tightening to make it stronger. Water will work on rope knots.

HOW TO HOLD A HOOK

Grip the hook behind the barb – if it slips you won't get hooked.

LASHING

With these few simple lashings and a good supply of wood you can create almost any frame. They're particularly handy for shelter and raft building as well as making useful items around camp.

TRIPOD LASHING

For creating a stable standing frame, such as for a wikiup shelter.

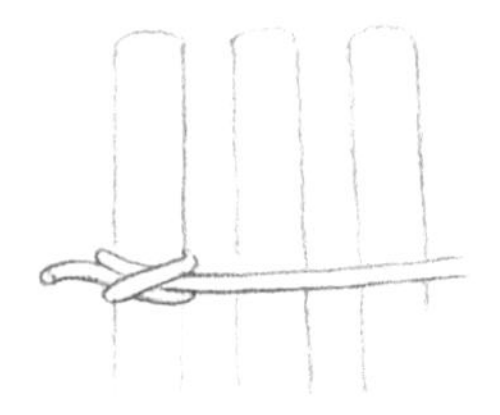

1. Start with a clove hitch on the outside spar (pole).

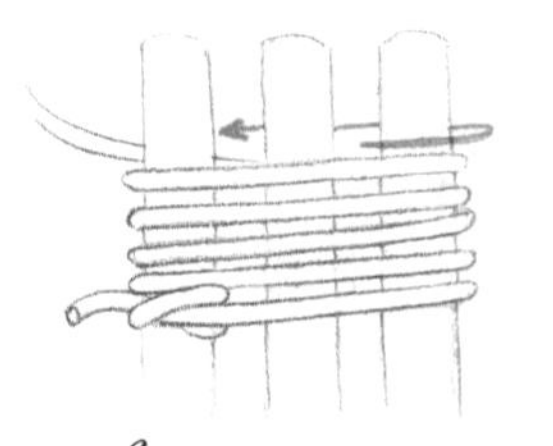

2. Loop around loosely five or six times.

3. In the counter direction (frapping), go around between each spar twice.

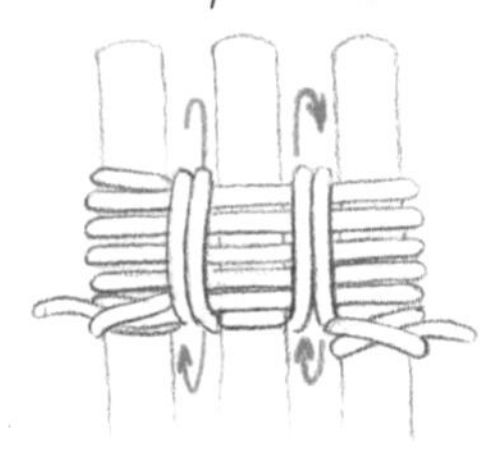

4. Tie off with a clove hitch (add extra hitch if needed).

The trick here is to keep the tripod lashing fairly loose so the poles will be able to move into place.

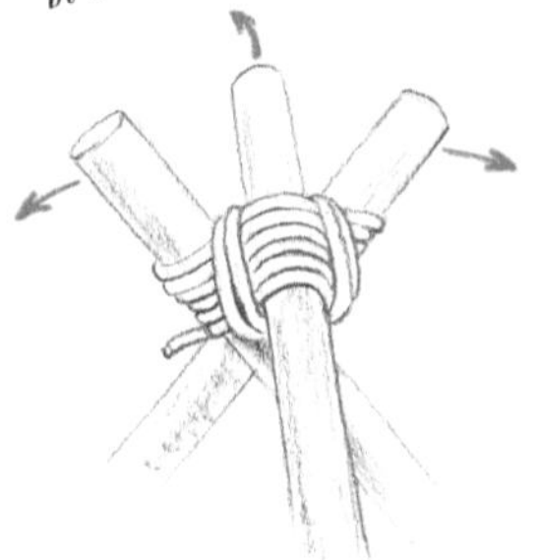

5. Move the outside spars apart. The centre spar should rest between the two. It may take another try to get the tension right.

SQUARE LASHING

For attaching two spars that are at right angles, such as with a lean-to shelter.

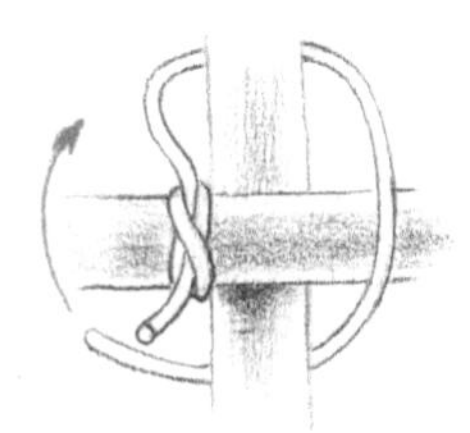

1. Start with a clove hitch. Loop around the back and over the front like this three times.

2. After three turns change direction.

3. Apply a couple of frapping turns between the spars to tighten the lashing.

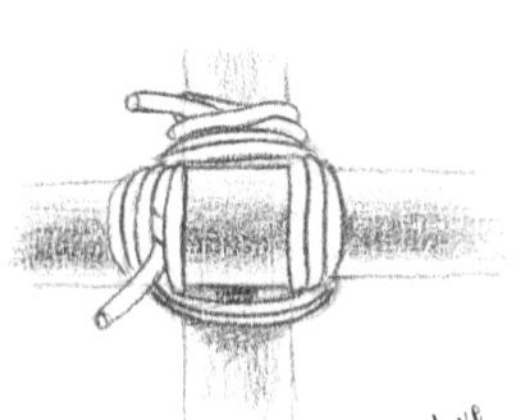

4. Tie off with a clove hitch or two.

DIAGONAL LASHING

For spars which are diagonal to each other – often used when strengthening a frame.

1. Start with a timber hitch holding both spars together. Make three turns in the same direction.

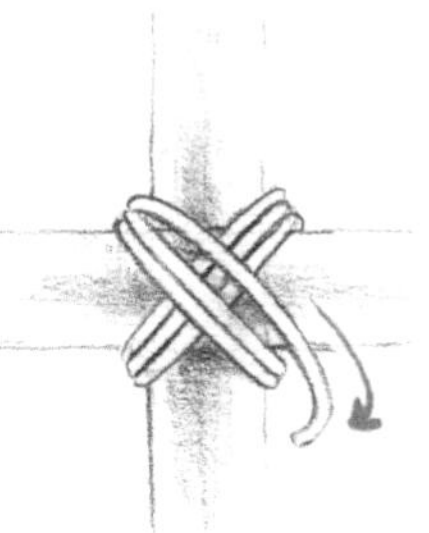

2. Now make three turns on the opposing diagonal.

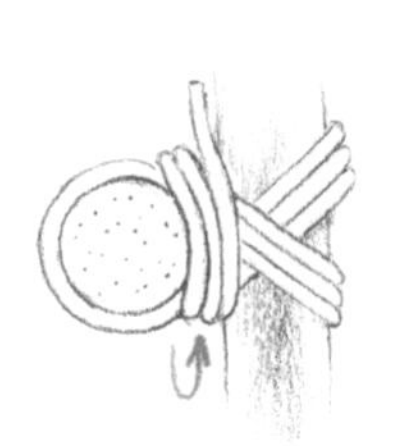

3. Apply a couple of frapping turns between the two spars.

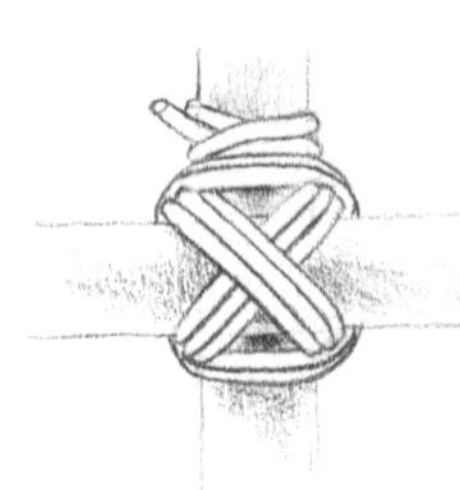

4. Tie off with a clove hitch or two.

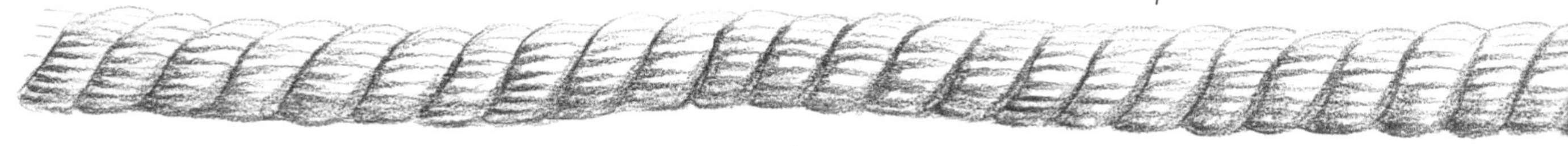

NOW YOU CAN BUILD ALMOST ANYTHING

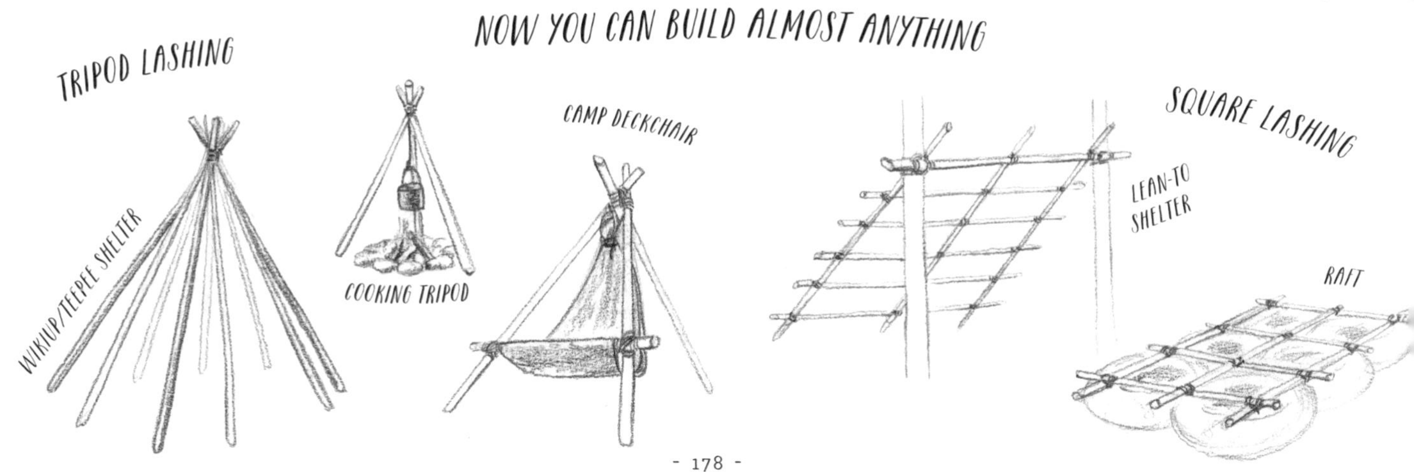

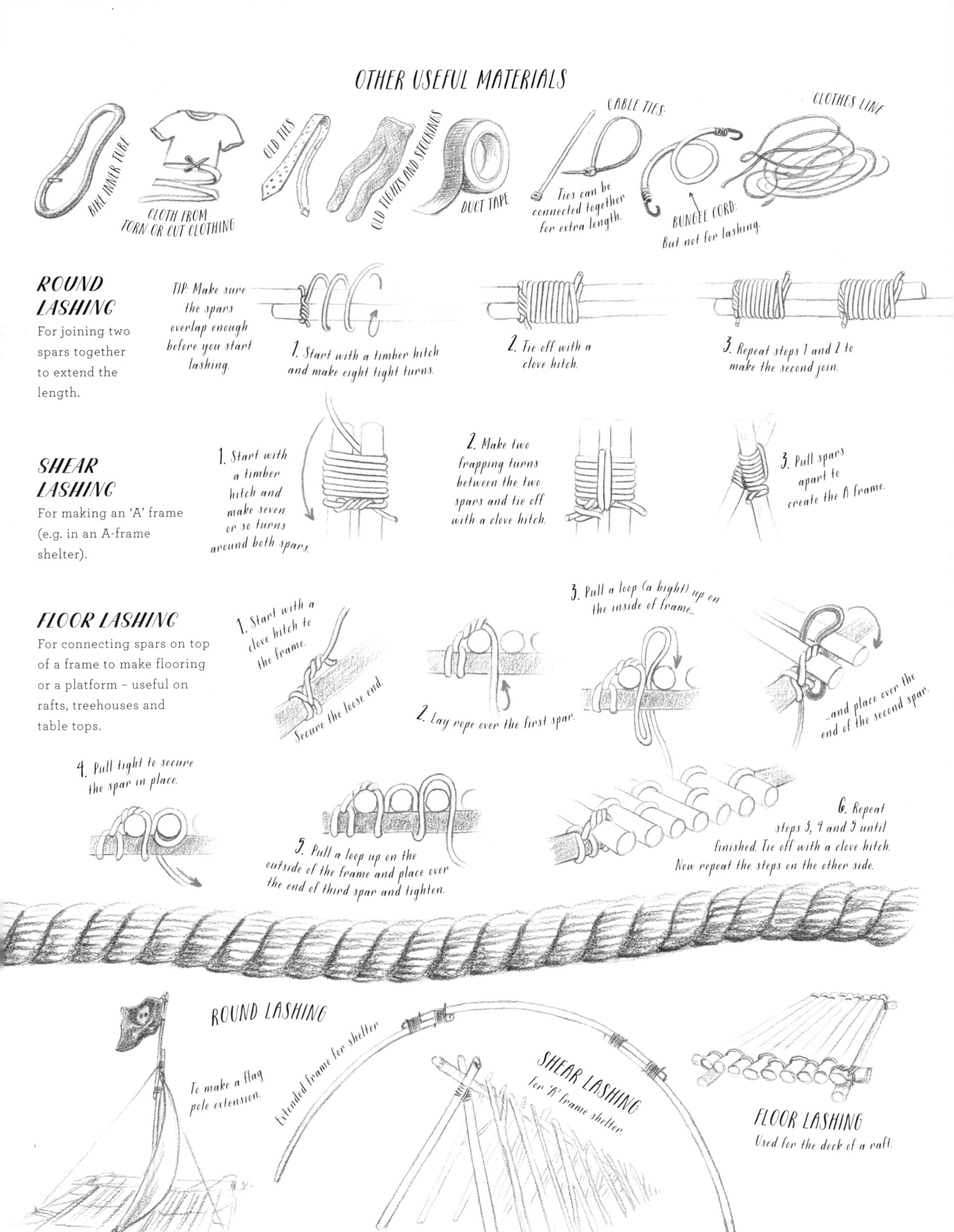
OTHER USEFUL MATERIALS
BIKE INNER TUBE
CLOTH FROM TORN OR CUT CLOTHING
OLD TIES
OLD TIGHTS AND STOCKINGS
DUCT TAPE
CABLE TIES:
Ties can be connected together for extra length.
BUNGEE CORD:
But not for lashing.
CLOTHES LINE
ROUND LASHING
For joining two spars together to extend the length.
TIP: Make sure the spars overlap enough before you start lashing.
1. Start with a timber hitch and make eight tight turns.
2. Tie off with a clove hitch.
3. Repeat steps 1 and 2 to make the second join.
SHEAR LASHING
For making an 'A' frame (e.g. in an A-frame shelter).
1. Start with a timber hitch and make seven or so turns around both spars.
2. Make two frapping turns between the two spars and tie off with a clove hitch.
3. Pull spars apart to create the A frame.
FLOOR LASHING
For connecting spars on top of a frame to make flooring or a platform – useful on rafts, treehouses and table tops.
1. Start with a clove hitch to the frame.
Secure the loose end.
2. Lay rope over the first spar.
3. Pull a loop (a bight) up on the inside of frame...
...and place over the end of the second spar.
4. Pull tight to secure the spar in place.
5. Pull a loop up on the outside of the frame and place over the end of third spar and tighten.
6. Repeat steps 3, 4 and 5 until finished. Tie off with a clove hitch. Now repeat the steps on the other side.
ROUND LASHING
To make a flag pole extension.
Extended frame for shelter
SHEAR LASHING
For 'A' frame shelter
FLOOR LASHING
Used for the deck of a raft.

FIRST AID KIT

There are different kits to choose from but they nearly all share these essential ingredients. On big adventures there should always be a first-aid kit in the group and someone with the experience to use it.

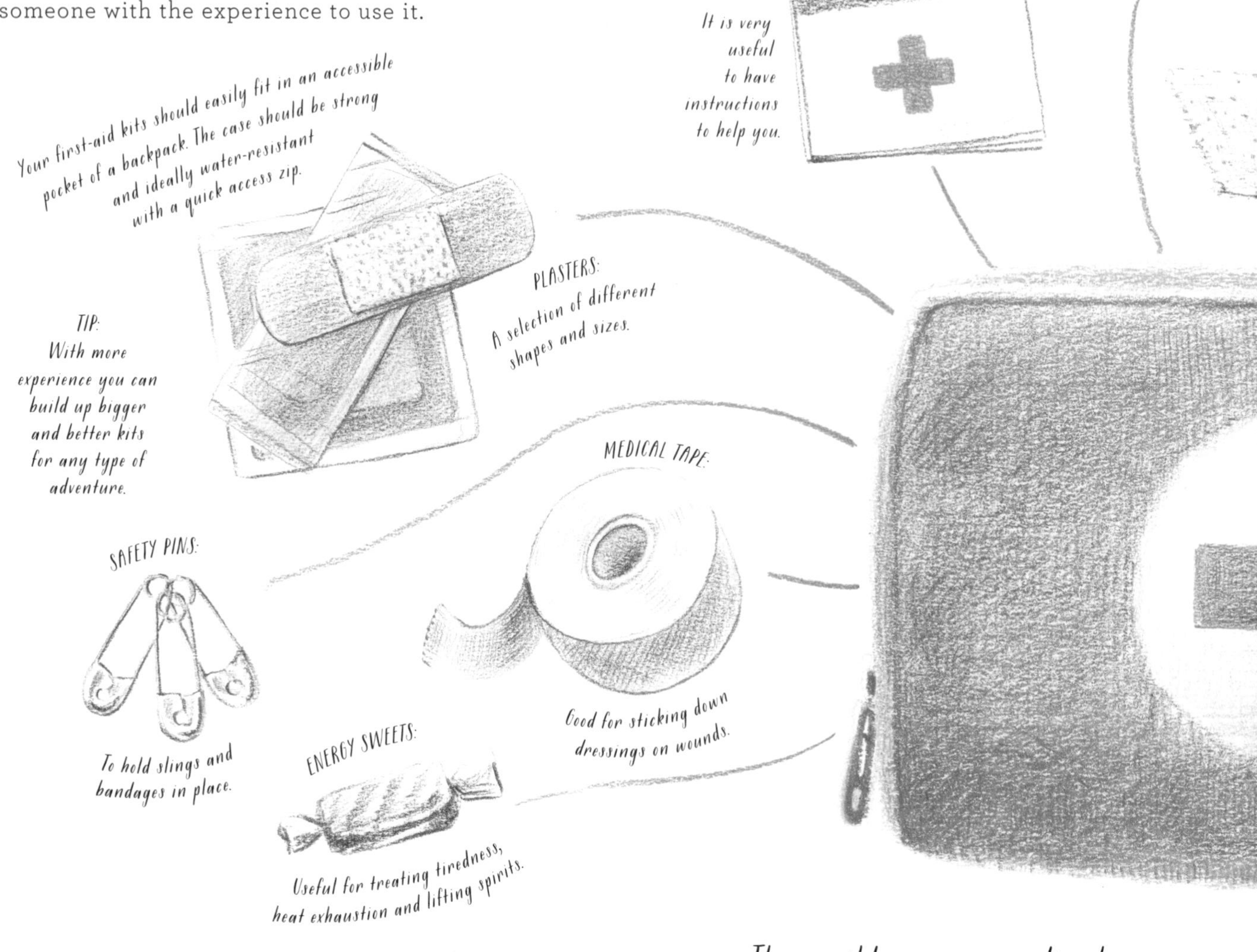

THE WILD FIRST-AID KIT

These wild-grown remedies have been known about and used for thousands of years.

When your first-aid kit isn't handy look around for these natural antiseptic plants.

PLANTAIN LEAVES: Very good for stinging nettles, insect bites and stings as well as dressing wounds.

WILD GARLIC: Apply chewed-up leaf stems to your wound as an antiseptic dressing.

DOCK LEAVES: Good for stinging nettles. Rub leaves onto stings or place onto burns and blisters.

Chew or crush the wild garlic leaves and a mush. Put the mush (poultice) on top of the wound and wrap up with your leaf.

ANTISEPTIC WIPES:
Needed to clean wounds.
TWEEZERS: For removing glass, splinters and ticks.
BANDAGE
For holding dressings in place and supporting sprains and breaks.
Having a good first-aid kit and knowing how to use it is an essential part of becoming a real adventurer.
TOPICAL CREAMS: Such as antiseptic cream or antihistamine – for bites, stings and reactions.
A team leader should know of any medical conditions or allergies within the group and have the required medicines.
PERSONAL MEDICINE
VARIOUS DRESSINGS AND GAUZES: To put on cuts and grazes.
SCISSORS:
Useful for cutting dressings and bandages if needed.
TRIANGULAR BANDAGE: For making an arm sling.
GIANT PUFFBALLS: These large fungi can be cut up and applied to wounds to stem bleeding.
NOTE: Fresh puffballs are completely white throughout.
PINE NEEDLE TEA: Works as an antiseptic, anti-inflammatory, and is good for colds and congestion. Add a few needles to a cup of hot water and let them infuse.
SPAGNUM MOSS: A great, natural antiseptic found in woodlands and damp areas.
Squeeze out any water (dry out if time) then apply to the wound as a dressing.

BITES, BURNS, BLISTERS AND BLOOD

To be able to really help yourself and others you should do a basic first aid course.

Here are a few common first aid scenarios and techniques that every adventurer should know.

SEEK MEDICAL HELP FOR:

* Larger and deeper cuts;
* Continued bleeding;
* Animal bites;
* Puncture wounds;
* Embedded dirt or objects.

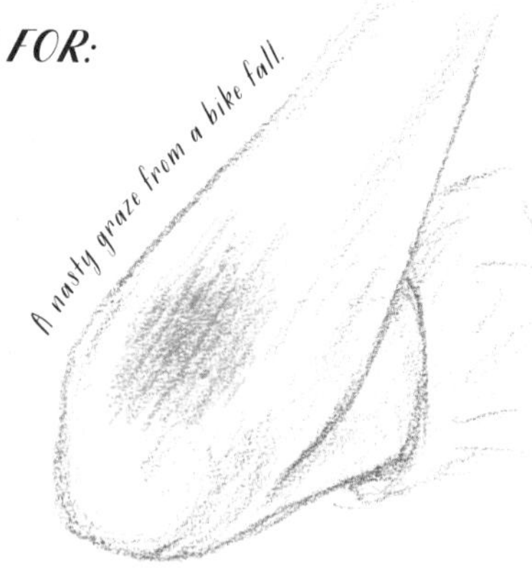

CUTS AND GRAZES

It often stings for a while, but smaller wounds can normally be self-treated.

2. With clean hands wash the wound with clean water. Then, dab area with an antiseptic wipe.

3. Add a sterile dressing. For smaller cuts, use a plaster.

4. Use bandage or medical tape to secure.

USUAL CULPRITS:

* Catching skin on a thorny bush;
* Cutting yourself with a knife;
* Falling from your bike.

1. Stop the bleeding by putting pressure on the wound using a dressing.

CUTS: You may require a tetanus injection if you have not had one in the last five years.

If the bleeding is severe, apply pressure and add a dressing and a bandage. Raise the affected area above the level of the heart and seek medical help immediately.

BURNS

ROPE BURN
Sliding down a rope fast can blister and burn your hands.

WHAT TO DO:

1. Run cool (not cold) running water over the area for 10 minutes.

2. Cover with cling film or dressing. (Not adhesive plasters or cotton wool.)

3. Get medical attention.

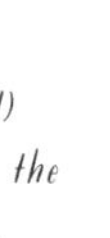

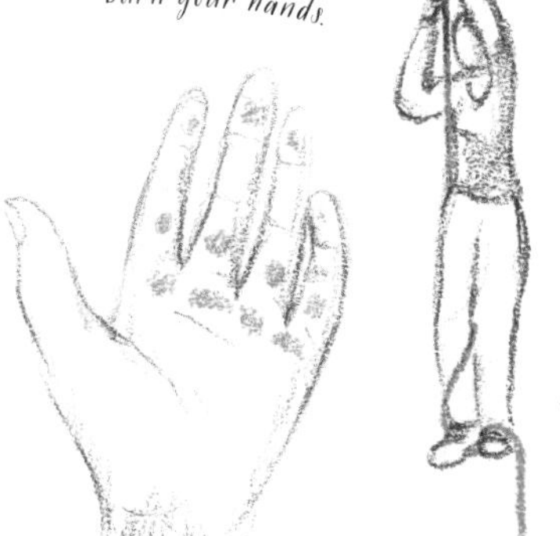

To avoid burns descending a rope, wrap your leg around the rope and lock it with your foot to control your speed. Always wear gloves.

USUAL CULPRITS:

* The campfire;
* Hot pots and pans;
* Hot food and water;
* Gas stoves;
* Matches and lighters;
* Friction burns.

SOLDIER ANT STITCH UP

I've experienced a few 'interesting' ways to treat wounds but when my guide suggested I use the local soldier ants to suture a nasty gash on my arm I thought he was making an amusing joke. He wasn't. I watched through squinted eyes as he proceeded to hold giant Eciton army ants to my wound. Their large mandibles clamped into my skin - I think I nearly fainted. He then broke off the body leaving the locked jaws in place. It was a fine stitch up in many ways.

I named my new friends after the Monty Python members: Graham, Terry, Eric, Michael, John and Terry

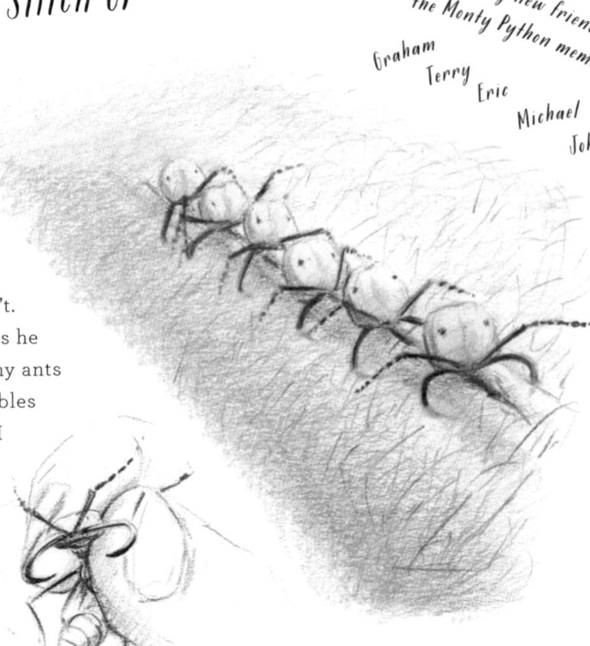

Do not try this at home.

TIP: As soon as you feel skin discomfort on your feet, put on a plaster or blister pad.

BLISTERS

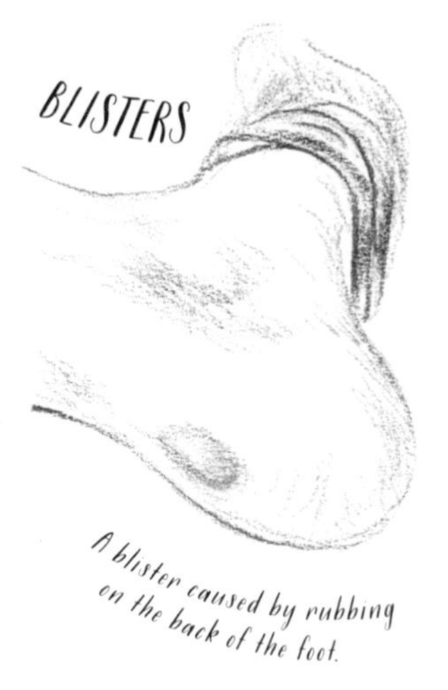

A blister caused by rubbing on the back of the foot.

Ticks can transfer infections like Lyme disease. If you get a growing red rash around a bite or flu-like symptoms then seek medical advice.

BITES AND STINGS

You are entering their habitat. Be courteous and be prepared.

MOSQUITOS

Wear insect repellent and cover up your skin. Try not to scratch bites, it only makes them itchier.

TIP: Mosquitos steer clear of smoke and wind.

BEES, WASPS AND HORNETS

If the pain or swelling continues to get worse, seek medical advice.

Stings can be painful and cause swelling. Scrape away the stinger if in the skin. Treat the area with bag of ice or a cool cloth.

TICKS

Removing a tick with tweezers.

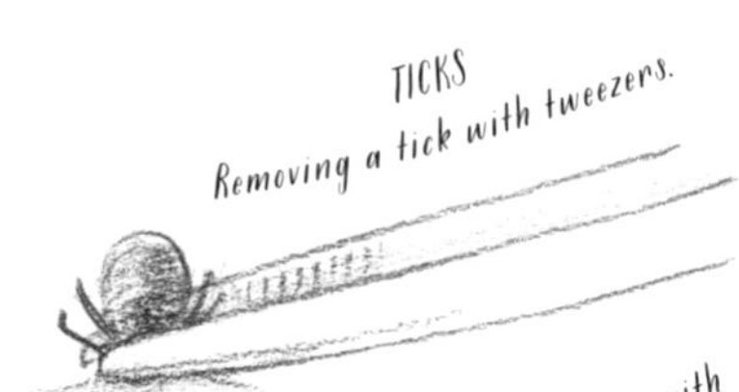

1. Place the tweezers close to the skin and the head of the tick and pull away smoothly.
2. Rub the bite with an antiseptic wipe.

TIP: Tuck your trousers into your socks.

Actual sizes

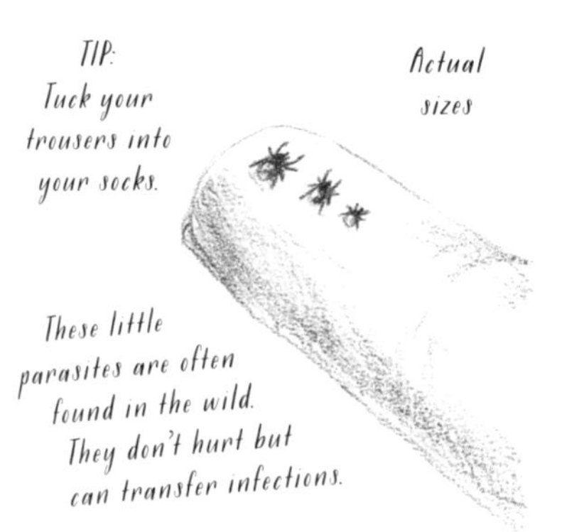

These little parasites are often found in the wild. They don't hurt but can transfer infections.

SNAKES

If you get bitten by a snake, treat and secure the wound like you would a cut. Remember most snakes aren't poisonous and 50% of snake bites are dry bites – no venom. Seek medical attention straight away to be safe and sure.

TIP: In snake habitats don't walk or poke where you can't see. Make some noise and use a stick to sweep your path ahead.

Try to remember what the snake looks like, take a photo for identification, but don't try and catch it. You might end up bitten twice.

In the wild I do at least one tick check daily and remove any visitors I find.

SPRAINS AND STRAINS

These feel like very bad bruises, normally affecting the movement of arms, legs and ankles.

SPRAINED ANKLE

Note the swollen area around the ankle. Cover with something cold.

The bandage is wrapped around the ankle in a figure of eight. The bandage should be tight enough to create effective support but not restrict blood flow to the toes.

LIKELY CAUSES:

* Twisting an ankle;
* Jumping from a height;
* Sudden strained movements;
* Falling off a bike.

It's often hard to tell if something might be fractured. Always seek medical attention if in doubt.

Here two people are used as supports for a sprained ankle. In the wild you may have to help the injured person to get to help.

To treat both strains and sprains remember the word RICE:

R – Rest injured area;

I – Apply something cold to the area like ice or a cold cloth;

C – Comfortably support and compress the injury;

E – Elevate the injured area.

HOW TO MAKE A SLING FROM A JUMPER OR COAT

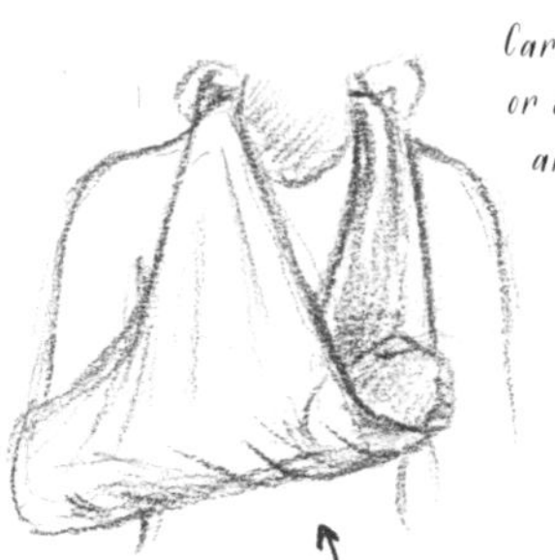

Carefully place a jumper or coat under the injured arm.

Tie the arms of the jumper in a square knot behind the neck.

Make sure the arm is held comfortably into the chest at this angle.

If alone you can pull up the bottom of your t-shirt to create a sling if it isn't too baggy.

BREAKS

A break: symptoms can include – pain & shock, as well as swelling, bruising, deformity and loss of movement.

If the break is on the arm, apply a sling and walk to safety only if the injured person feels ready.

1. Sit the injured person down and make them feel comfortable.
2. Support the injured area and cushion it with clothes to limit movement.
3. Wrap the injured person up so they are warm, sheltered and off the cold ground.
4. Get help or call for help. Do not leave the injured person alone.

Here a sleeping mat is placed beneath to add insulation.

USUAL CAUSES:

* A heavy fall onto a hard surface;
* A bang or knock on a rock;
* A severe twisted ankle.

One of your greatest assets as an adventurer is calmness. Being calm is effective. It is also contagious.

SERIOUS STUFF – GET MEDICAL HELP

HYPOTHERMIA (TOO COLD)

Symptoms:
* Shivering;
* Cold pale skin;
* Mumbled talking;
* Weak breathing;
* Losing consciousness;
* Dizziness and confusion.

What to do:
* Call for medical support and warm up the person until help arrives;
* Give them warm fluids and energy bars (if they can swallow);
* Keep talking to them and giving them encouragement.

HEAT EXHAUSTION (TOO HOT)

Symptoms:
* Thirst;
* Feeling weak and faint;
* Dizziness;
* Headache;
* Feeling sick.

What to do:
* Cool down. Get out of the sun and remove any excess clothes.
* Hydrate with sugary drinks – or water if that is the only option.
* Seek medical help.
* If not treated, heat exhaustion can lead to sun or heat stroke which is life threatening.

DEHYDRATION

Symptoms:
* Thirst;
* Dry or sticky mouth;
* Darker coloured urine;
* Inability to urinate;
* Feeling tired, angry, or sick;
* Feeling dizzy and confused;
* Headaches;
* Muscle cramps.

What to do:
* Find somewhere sheltered, sit down and drink fluids slowly. Rest until feeling recovered.

SHOCK

There are two types of shock after an accident. One is emotional, the other is serious and affects your pulse, breathing and makes skin cold, pale and sweaty. Warm up and comfort the person and seek help immediately.

Early symptoms:
* A rapid pulse;
* Shallow/fast breathing;
* Cold, pale and sweaty skin.

Developing symptoms:
* Yawning/tiredness;
* Agitation and confusion;
* Severe thirst.

What to do:
* Lay person down on a warm blanket;
* Comfort and encourage them;
* Raise and support legs above heart;
* Call/seek help immediately

ALLERGIC REACTIONS

If you suspect any of the following symptoms it could be an allergic reaction. Seek help immediately.

Symptoms may include:
* Red and itchy skin reaction;
* Swollen eyes;
* Swelling in throat area;
* Feeling sick;
* Feeling faint.

What to do:
* Sit person down and make them comfortable;
* Call or get medical help;
* If the person knows of an allergy and has medication, help them administer it.

HEAD KNOCKS

After a bad bang to the head get checked out even if you feel fine.

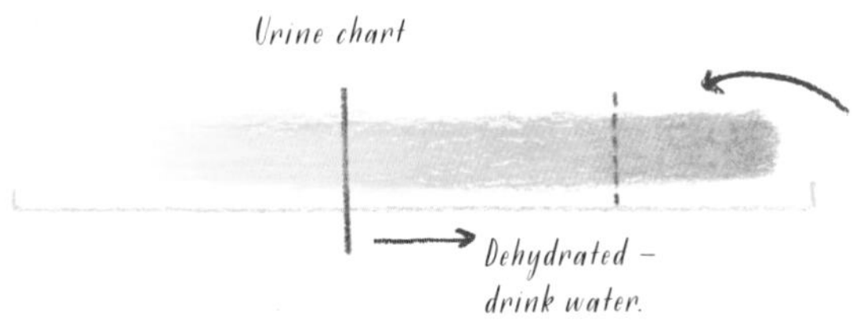

LIFE SAVING SCENARIOS

Here are some serious situations you should know how to avoid and survive. Feel free to pass this knowledge on to your friends.

With this knowledge you should never have to put it into practice.

FALLING THROUGH ICE

This normally happens where thin patches of ice take people by surprise. Cold is the greatest danger. You need to get yourself out or call for help.

* Never go out on ice without experienced adults;
* Always know the thickness of the ice;
* Never try and pull someone out. Use a rope or call for help;
* Always look out for changes in the ice colour or shade.

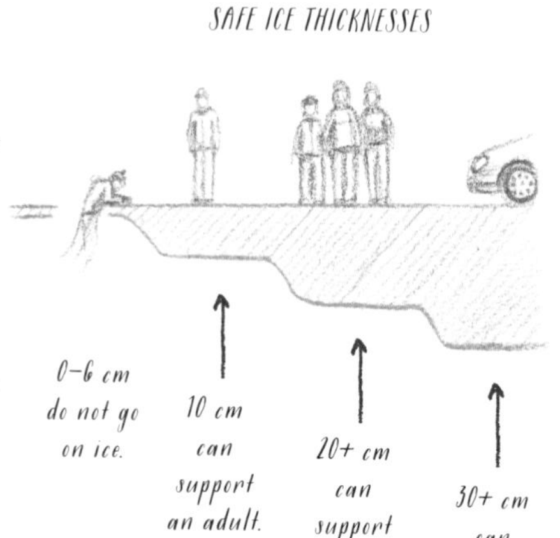

2. When you are ready kick hard with your feet so you get horizontal.

Try a butterfly kick (feet together) for more power.

Keep kicking whilst hauling yourself out using your elbows and arms.

3. Once on the ice roll towards safety. This technique distributes your weight best.

A shade of darker ice often means it's thinner.

Note the colour of the water – the rip channel is often visible as lighter or darker than the surrounding sea.

Rip current

CAUGHT IN A RIP CURRENT

A rip is a hidden current of water that moves out to sea. It occurs on some beaches often when incoming waves move over sandbars channeling the water in a particular way. They are dangerous, especially if you try and swim directly to shore.

Look for channels where waves aren't forming for signs of a rip.

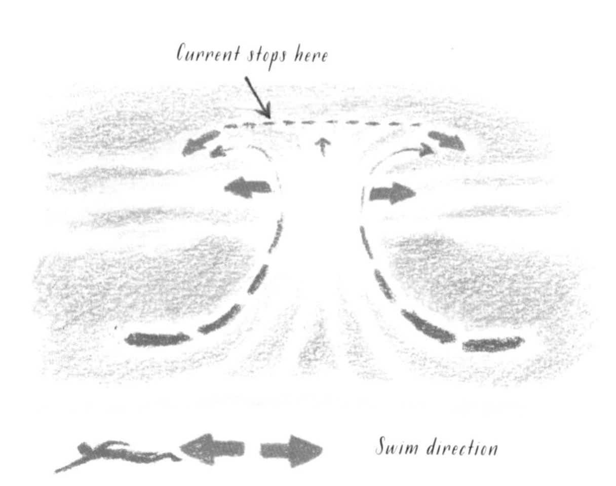

WHAT TO DO:

* First don't panic or try to swim directly to shore – you'll get exhausted;
* Tread water and wave or call to get attention and help;
* To swim to shore, swim parallel to the beach until you feel the current diminish. Use the waves to help you get back to shore.

Rips don't go far out to sea, if you've been spotted you can tread water to save energy.

LIGHTNING

Thunderstorms and lightning can pose a serious risk but can normally be avoided. If you get caught in one here's what you need to know.

An unwelcome sight – you need to be off the mountain before a storm appears.

To calculate how far away the lightning is, count the time between seeing the flash and hearing the thunder. Three seconds = 1 km away. Six seconds = 2 kms... and so on.

Keep a wary eye on these Cumulonimbus clouds. They can can turn into storms.

WHAT TO DO

* If possible get inside a building or car when the thunder is close;
* If this isn't possible, find low ground, like a gulley;
* If in the woods, avoid larger trees;
* Avoid flat open ground or being near tall objects or knolls that might attract lightning;
* If lightning is close, get into a crouch position – see the diagram to the right;
*Swap your tent for the car if it's nearby or crouch on your sleeping mat.

✕ THE SAFETY POSITION: Touch the heels of your shoes together.

This crouching position is the best posture. Stand on a mat or backpack if available.

Cars are safe places to be, even if struck, but keep your hands on your lap.

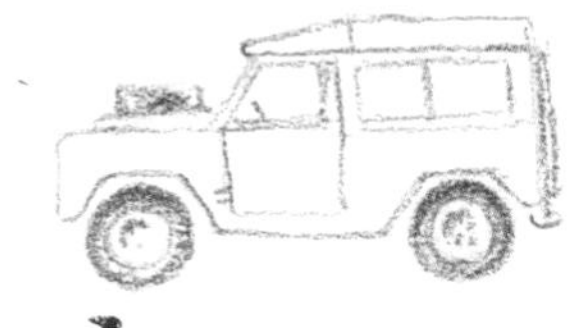

If caught in the mountains there's a safer zone created by pinnacles and cliffs, but beware of falling rocks.

Safer zone

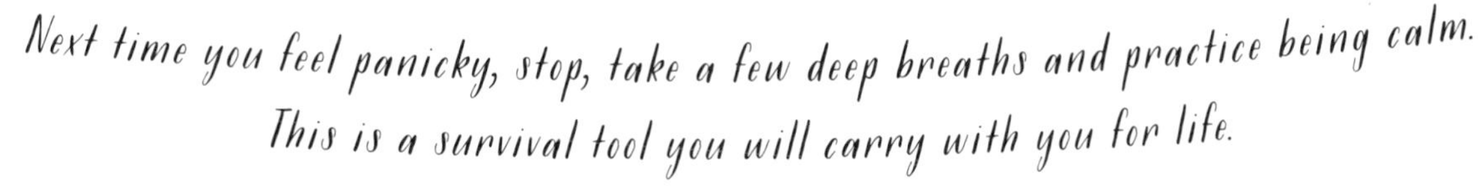

ESCAPING SINKING MUD AND QUICKSAND

Although rare, sinking mud or sand can be hard to spot. Luckily we are lighter than mud or sand so we can float on it if you follow these steps.

You won't go deeper than your waist, but it's the grip that poses the problem.

Actual depth

1. As soon as you feel yourself sinking prepare to sit back and spread your weight. Call and wave if help is nearby.

2. Lying back will stop you from sinking any deeper. It may feel uncomfortable, but it's only water and mud or sand.

3. Gradually wriggle your legs out one at a time. Using your arms in a backstroke motion start pulling yourself free.

4. When near firmer ground, roll onto your front and crawl like a muddy lizard to safety.

Harder ground

Don't wait to see how far you'll sink, spread your weight as soon as you realise you're sinking.

WILD TRACKS AND TRACKING

Wild animals can be hard to see. Their senses often pick us up long before we come near, but all animals leave clues, and their footprints are the easiest to identify and study. Here are a few that I've come across on my travels.

TRACK SPOTTING TIPS:

* In dry weather look on sandy/gravelly ground;
* Mud makes good prints – head out after the rain;
* After a snowfall you can uncover all sorts of goings on;
* Animals often leave prints on the banks of streams and rivers where they come to drink at night.

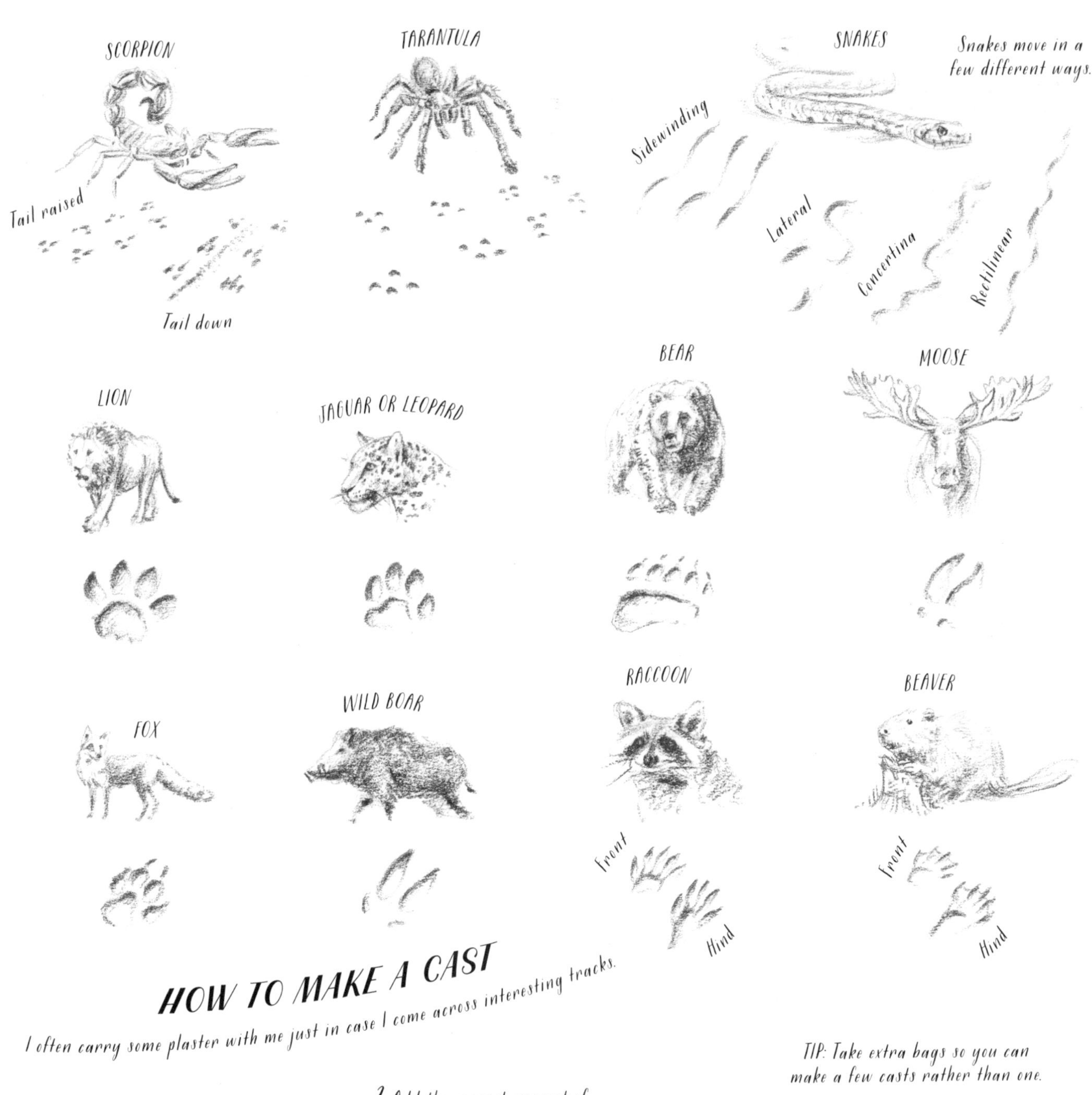

HOW TO MAKE A CAST

I often carry some plaster with me just in case I come across interesting tracks.

YOU WILL NEED:

* Casting plaster in a sealed plastic bag (or two);
* Some water;
* A small spade or trowel;
* Cardboard;
* A stirring stick.

a.

b.

1. When you've chosen your wild footprint create a mould around it by pushing your cardboard into the ground (a.) or make a small wall around it with the earth (b.).

2. Add the correct amount of water to your bag – two parts water to one part powder – and stir with a stick.

3. Gently pour the plaster into your print mould and wait for about 20 minutes.

4. When the plaster is hard, dig underneath and lift up your cast. Remove the earth to reveal your wild print. Clean off remaining earth with a brush or stick.

TIP: Take extra bags so you can make a few casts rather than one.

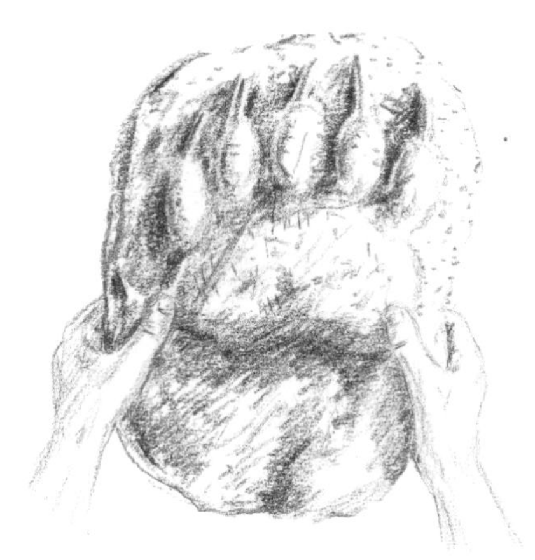

A grizzly bear paw print I found on a beach in the Aleutian islands near Alaska. The print measured 23 cm wide by 32 cm long – the largest I'd ever seen.

WILD NAVIGATION

In the wild we are surrounded by clues to help us navigate. Plants, animals, rivers and winds can help us find our way, but the greatest clue giver when it comes to navigation is the sun. Here are a few handy ways to find your bearings if you forget to pack your compass.

USING A WATCH

S

12

If you have an analogue watch simply point the hour hand towards the sun. Now imagine a line halfway between the hour hand and 12 o'clock. That is approximately where south is.

USING THE MOON

S

When the moon is in its crescent shape simply imagine a line running between its two end points, down to the ground. In the northern hemisphere this line will point you close to south. In the southern hemisphere it will be directing you to the north.

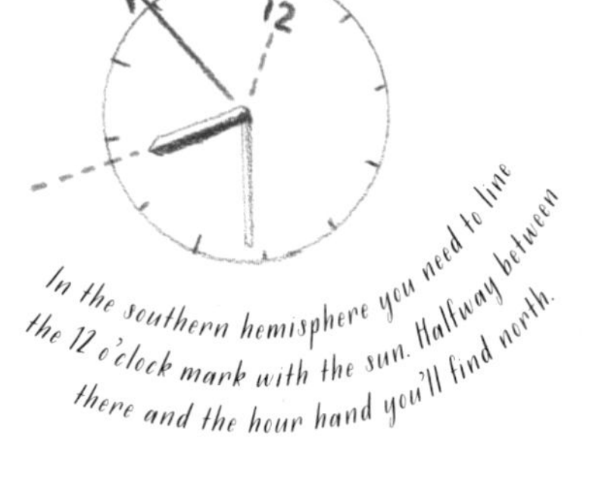

In the southern hemisphere you need to line the 12 o'clock mark with the sun. Halfway between there and the hour hand you'll find north.

Once you've found one direction you can quickly figure out where the other points of the compass are.

EAST: *The sun always rises in the east.*

SOUTH: *At midday the sun is in the south.*

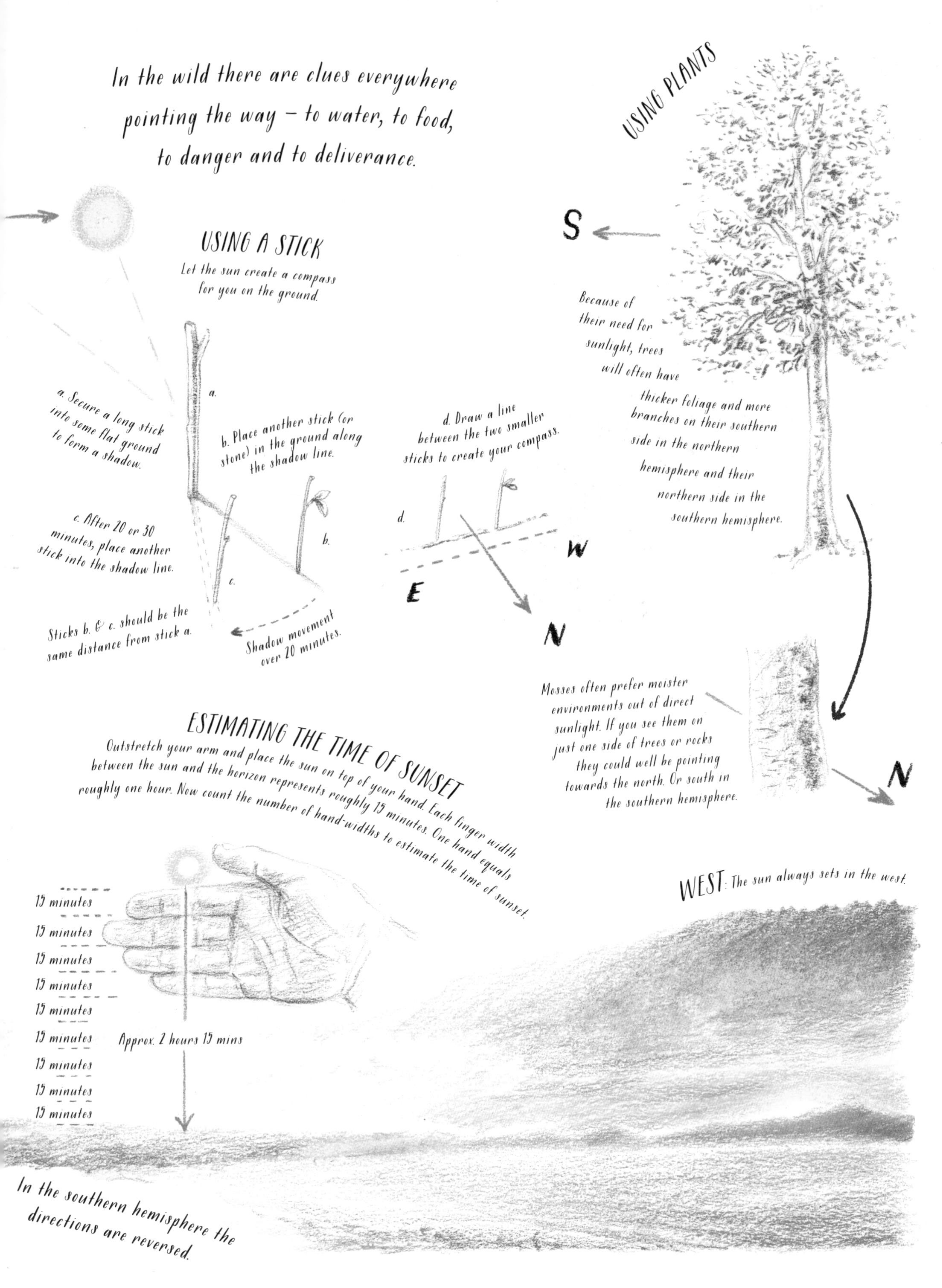

In the wild there are clues everywhere pointing the way – to water, to food, to danger and to deliverance.
USING A STICK
Let the sun create a compass for you on the ground.
a. Secure a long stick into some flat ground to form a shadow.
a.
b. Place another stick (or stone) in the ground along the shadow line.
b.
c. After 20 or 30 minutes, place another stick into the shadow line.
c.
Sticks b. & c. should be the same distance from stick a.
Shadow movement over 20 minutes.
d. Draw a line between the two smaller sticks to create your compass.
d.
E
W
N
USING PLANTS
S
Because of their need for sunlight, trees will often have thicker foliage and more branches on their southern side in the northern hemisphere and their northern side in the southern hemisphere.
Mosses often prefer moister environments out of direct sunlight. If you see them on just one side of trees or rocks they could well be pointing towards the north. Or south in the southern hemisphere.
N
ESTIMATING THE TIME OF SUNSET
Outstretch your arm and place the sun on top of your hand. Each finger width between the sun and the horizon represents roughly 15 minutes. One hand equals roughly one hour. Now count the number of hand-widths to estimate the time of sunset.
15 minutes
15 minutes
15 minutes
15 minutes
15 minutes
15 minutes
15 minutes
15 minutes
15 minutes
Approx. 2 hours 15 mins
WEST: The sun always sets in the west.
In the southern hemisphere the directions are reversed.

The best adventures are always shared.
On my walking stick are carved the initials of those
I've been lucky enough to journey with.

Brimming with creative inspiration, how-to projects, and useful information to enrich your everyday life, Quarto Knows is a favourite destination for those pursuing their interests and passions. Visit our site and dig deeper with our books into your area of interest: Quarto Creates, Quarto Cooks, Quarto Homes, Quarto Lives, Quarto Drives, Quarto Explores, Quarto Gifts, or Quarto Kids.

First Published in 2019 by Frances Lincoln Children's Books,
an imprint of The Quarto Group.
The Old Brewery, 6 Blundell Street, London N7 9BH, United Kingdom.
T (0)20 7700 6700 F (0)20 7700 8066 **www.QuartoKnows.com**

A catalogue record for this book is available from the British Library.

ISBN 978-1-78603-296-6

The illustrations were created with pencil
Set in Archer Pro, Frosted and Raindrop

Published and edited by Rachel Williams and Jenny Broom
Designed and art directed by Nicola Price
Design assitance from Sasha Moxon
Production by Nicolas Zeifman

Manufactured in Shenzen, China HH112018

9 8 7 6 5 4 3 2 1